GLENN HUGHES

THE AUTOBIOGRAPHY

In New York City, September 2010,
photographed by Julian Lennon.
All you need is love ...

GLENN HUGHES

THE AUTOBIOGRAPHY

HUGHES

From Deep Purple To Black Country Communion

by **GLENN HUGHES**

with JOEL McIVER

This book is dedicated to the three women in my life: my
grandmother Nell (RIP), my mother Sheila, and my wife Gabi.
You have all shown me unconditional love. And to my father William:
thanks for telling me the truth.

GLENN HUGHES: THE AUTOBIOGRAPHY
FROM DEEP PURPLE TO BLACK COUNTRY COMMUNION

Glenn Hughes with Joel McIver

A Jawbone book
First edition 2011
Published in the UK and the USA by Jawbone Press
2a Union Court,
20–22 Union Road,
London SW4 6JP,
England
www.jawbonepress.com

This edition published by permission of Foruli Ltd, London, England
www.foruli.co.uk

ISBN 978-1-906002-92-3

EDITOR John Morrish
DESIGN Paul Cooper Design

Printed by Everbest Printing Co Ltd, China

1 2 3 4 5 15 14 13 12 11

CONTENTS

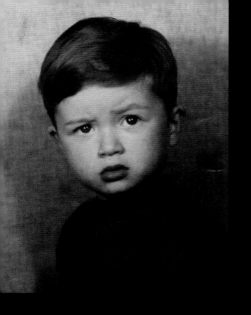

TOP LEFT: **Me, aged four or thereabouts. This is a great picture – I look as if I'm questioning something.**
ABOVE LEFT: **My parents, to whom I owe my life.**
FAR LEFT: **Trapeze, photographed in New York City. Mel was homesick for his wife and child and always wanted to finish the tours early. I always wanted to tour more – that's one reason why I left the band.**
ABOVE: **Rockin' the Roundhouse, Camden Town, London 1971.**
LEFT: **Clearwell Castle, *Stormbringer* sessions, 1974.**

LEFT: **In Memphis at the Overton Park Shell, 1973. Up on the high wire, without a net …**
ABOVE: **Deep Purple and the Starship. Do not fuck with us.**
BELOW: **The glory days: every young man's dream, encapsulated in a single picture. This is the Cal-Jam tour of 1974 and there I am, with my bag that held all the blow.**

The Cal-Jam tour, 1974.
See the look on my face?
This is my stage!

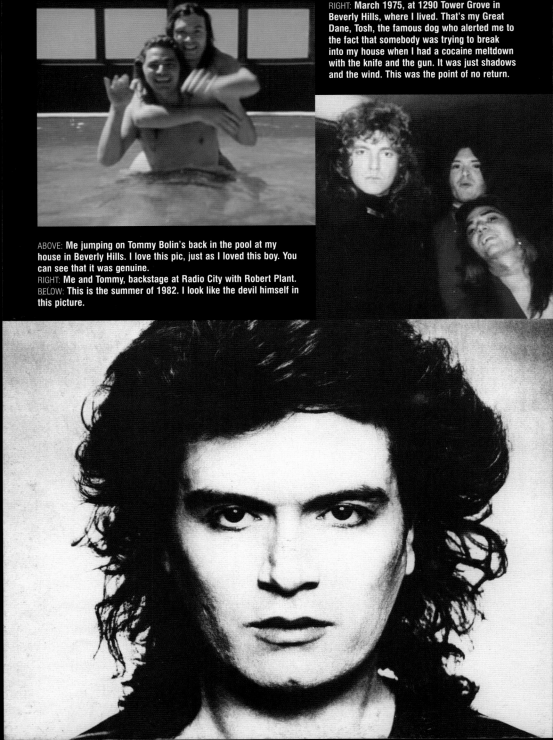

ABOVE: **Me jumping on Tommy Bolin's back in the pool at my house in Beverly Hills. I love this pic, just as I loved this boy. You can see that it was genuine.**
RIGHT: **Me and Tommy, backstage at Radio City with Robert Plant.**
BELOW: **This is the summer of 1982. I look like the devil himself in this picture.**

LEFT: **Gabi Hughes: my wife, life partner, and protector of all things Hughes. The funniest girl on the planet.**
BELOW: **I'm going back – to the Black Country.**
RIGHT: **Full circle: I've lived to tell the tale. With Black Country Communion at Wolverhampton Civic Hall, 2010.**
BELOW RIGHT: **With Alice Cooper and my dear friend and fashion icon, John Varvatos.**

Me, Glenn Hughes. Mr Hyde is long gone, and he ain't never – *ever* – coming back.

FOREWORD
by LARS ULRICH of METALLICA

Deep Purple has played a huge role in my life. I saw Purple twice with Glenn Hughes. When I saw Glenn up on stage in that white satin suit, with that Fender Precision bass, and the mane of hair, he looked like a rock god! He had that aura. I was just, "Oh my God … this guy is so cool!"

I went to the first show they played in Copenhagen, Denmark, in December 1973: I was nine years old. I'd seen Purple a few months earlier with Gillan and Glover – this was the first time with the Mark III line-up. They played quite a few songs from *Burn*, which hadn't been released yet, so there was a fair amount of checking-it-out vibe for the new songs, but then they played 'Smoke On The Water' and 'Space Truckin'', I believe, and it was pretty awesome. When they came back again in March 1975, and played a bigger place called the Brondbyhalle, with Elf opening – in their last two weeks with Ritchie Blackmore – I went and saw them and met a couple of them at the Plaza hotel. I saw them twice … not bad at that age!

Obviously things got a little more versatile with the Mark III line-up, and they expanded. The biggest news was that they were harmonising together, so when you got to the chorus of 'Burn', all of a sudden there was something that you'd never got on a Deep Purple record before – harmony vocals. That added another level – I thought it was great. *Burn* was a very hard record, and had a lot of traditional Blackmore-type signature things, but then by the time they moved on to *Stormbringer*, things got a little more versatile, and everyone knows the story about Blackmore being pissed off.

By the time *Stormbringer* came out I was what, 11? I wasn't versed in American R&B, ha ha! So I couldn't sit there and go, "Oh my God, there's the Stevie Wonder influence," or anything like that. I liked *Stormbringer*, I thought it was more of a versatile record, but I wasn't schooled enough to draw comparisons with it. At that point, pretty much anything Purple did was godlike.

I thought that *Come Taste The Band* had better songs on it than *Stormbringer*. There are songs on that third album that are a little more non-signature Purple – like 'Drifter' – although the opening track, 'Comin' Home', was a little more rock, and 'You Keep On Moving' was a beautiful, beautiful song. That was a great record, and you could feel that Glenn had become a major, major player in what was going on. Some of the songs that seemed to come from his different background to the rest of them resonated well on that band. No disrespect to Roger Glover at all, but it felt as if the rhythm section had definitely livened up a bit – it felt as if Ian had started playing with a bit more funk. Glenn and Ian had brought it to someplace interesting.

I first met Glenn in 1996 when Metallica were playing at the NEC in Birmingham. Tony Iommi and Glenn were working on a record together, and they came down to the show and hung out and swapped old stories. Obviously Glenn had been through a lot in the years since Purple, but he looked great: he was super-personable and easy-going and unaffected. It was really cool to have him and Tony there at the same time. It was exciting. I got my picture taken with them!

It's always an honour when the people who were plastered on my walls when I was a kid show up at a Metallica gig, and show some form of appreciation for what we do. It was great, absolutely great – Glenn was a true gentleman. I really look forward to meeting him again.

Lars Ulrich

CO-WRITER'S NOTE

This book contains explicit information about various drug dealers, Mafiosi, and gangsters. Some of these lovely people are currently incarcerated, but many are still at large and doing business in a town near you. Accordingly, names have been changed or omitted so that Glenn and I don't get 'whacked'.

Joel McIver

INTRODUCTION

I t was 7:30pm on Christmas Day 1991, but it could have been any day. The guests were leaving the house. As their car made its way down the driveway, once again I felt a wave of euphoria surge over me. Yeah, better lock the house up and put on the alarm: I didn't want to see anyone. I'd gone over to meet my dealer on Christmas Eve, knowing that this would be the last time. "Better get an ounce!" said a voice somewhere in my brain.

Only a week before, I had been diagnosed as an alcoholic and drug addict by the good people at the Betty Ford Center, but they were full over the Christmas period. I guess their clientele were hoping to get a head start on sobriety for 1992 – but not me, not yet. I had one more journey to take, into my own hell. A hell called cocaine psychosis. "Relax! It'll be different this time," said the voice inside my head.

I'd done a few rails of coke after dinner. An hour later I was in the master bathroom, standing in front of a giant mirror, looking down at my coke paraphernalia. The centrepieces were two brand-new crack pipes, bought for the occasion.

I began to cook the cocaine. My method was to mix two parts coke with one part baking soda, put it into a large vial, add water and then heat it with a lighter held underneath. When the powder became a rock, it made a cracking sound as it hit the inside of the vial. To every crack user, this sound is magic time.

I was pretty high from the lines I'd done an hour before, and I was anxious. I put the spoon into the bag and scooped out a couple of grams. My whole body was shivering, going from hot to cold. My obsession was complete, it was my everything, my purpose, my God. Nothing else mattered. Babies were being born, people were dying, so what? Time stood still.

I lit the cotton ball, soaked in 151 per cent rum, and placed a big hit, a headbanger, into the bowl of the pipe – and began to ingest my curse, my demon. As a child I'd read *The Strange Case Of Dr Jekyll And Mr Hyde*, and now I'd become Hyde in all his glory, with his mannerisms and gait.

In a few seconds I felt the universe shift. Every sound and smell was magnified. What was real seconds ago was now unreal. This was what I craved.

My body shook and I fell to my knees, I could hear what freebasers call 'Hell's Bells' – the deafening sound of something so hideous and yet so beautiful, coming from somewhere inside me. This hit was beyond belief.

My girlfriend asked nervously if I was OK. I mumbled some gibberish and found my way to the bed.

I was in a state of shock. This was the perfect hit. I tried to speak, but no words came and I was overcome by a wave of euphoria.

I lay on the bed. My euphoria was about to be replaced by a gigantic case of paranoia. I was frozen to the bed. I could hear sirens going off and the sound of doors closing. There were footsteps coming from the basement – and was that music coming from upstairs? Were they here in my house? Better go and get that carving knife …

I somehow peeled myself off the bed and stumbled back into the bathroom, loading the pipe with another rock and babbling something about the music I heard coming from upstairs. Fuck it.

I took my hit and made my way back to the bed to lie down. In all my years on this twisted, satanic merry-go-round, I had never felt so unsettled.

As the evening became morning and the sun was rising, I played out my dance of death – and found myself alone, one more time, cornered by my own shadow and my reflection in that demonic mirror. As I stood, eyes fixed on my reflection, I found myself asking the stranger who I was facing, "Who are you and what do you want?" I didn't recognise the shell that was me.

I took another hit. It buckled my knees and I crawled to the bed like a wounded animal. My girlfriend asked me what was wrong, and my words came out in slow motion. "Something's wrong," I said.

She drove me to the hospital. I said to a nurse, "I've taken too much cocaine." Then I blacked out. When I came to, a doctor stood over me and said, "Mr Hughes, you've had a heart attack."

I WAS THE MUSIC

MY YOUTH AND EARLY BANDS

Despite what you've just read, there are no skeletons in the closet in my family. I had an extremely happy childhood. I was born on August 21 1951 into a home on St John's Road in Cannock in Staffordshire, next to a pub called the Crystal Fountain. My parents loved music and named me after Glenn Miller. I lived in a two-bedroom house with my mom, Sheila; my dad, William; my grandmother on my mother's side, Nelly Ball; and my great-grandmother, Sally Rogers. My great-grandmother lived in the living room. It was difficult: Dad used to work for the National Coal Board, and Mom stayed at home for a while before she went out to work later on. I was given a lot of love: my mom was a very touchy-feely person, and so was my grandma. The word 'love' was used a lot, which was important for me, although I always wanted a brother or sister. Dad would say, "You're enough for us."

Sheila Hughes *We never stuck at one child in our minds. It was just one of those things. I'm sorry for Glenn that it didn't happen – very sorry. He would have loved a brother or sister, I know.*

I went to Sunday school and I was deep into religious studies at school. Now, most Catholics have a fear of God, right? I'm not in fear of God, I never was. I knew from a very, very early age that there was something bigger than us. Some people laughed: some kids didn't want to talk about God. I never really thought about it: he was just living inside me. I remember when I was 12 or 13 and I found out about the devil: it scared the living shit out of me. Later on I found out about ouija boards, and they're nothing to be fucked around with, I can tell you.

I was surrounded by religion. Mom went to Catholic school. Dad didn't believe in a God for most of his life, until I got sober. Now he does, because of my survival: he realises that there's got to be a God.

Sheila Hughes *Glenn was lovely as a child. There was always a great bond between him and me. He loved his grandmother, too. He was a quiet boy at school: he wasn't very interested in anything but music.*

Bill Hughes *Football was his big thing: he played for the school and was a very good footballer. Whenever I could, I'd go to his matches.*

Now, understand this: I was a very happy kid. Very early on, I was sports-minded. Playing football, throwing the discus and the javelin, playing netball. I went to John Wood Infants' School, then Walhouse Primary School, and then Blake Secondary Modern School after I failed the 11-plus exam.

My first pet was a dog that I got when I was about five – a mongrel called Kim. I loved him. We moved in 1957 to Clarion Way in Chadsmoor, a town near Cannock, and I remember that we lived about 400 yards from the main road. When I was about eight, I was out shopping with my gran, and Kim ran into the road in front of the number nine bus. I saw it happen right in front of me. There was blood and guts everywhere – it was devastating for me.

Dad buried him in the garden on Cup Final day in 1959. The next day we got a little kitten, who became my new pal: we named her Sugar, after an American cowboy show in the 1950s called *Sugarfoot*. She fitted in really well. Sugar lived to be about 19 years old.

Still, I always look back at Kim as my brother or sister. Everybody I knew – my neighbours, or the kids at school – had a brother, or a sister, or two brothers, and so on. I was the only one who was an only child. That's why Kim's death affected me so badly. But the rest of my childhood was great: I had everything I asked for, and my gran spoiled me rotten. Only children are often spoiled.

I suppose it was a working-class childhood, but it wasn't like Ozzy Osbourne's or Tony Iommi's childhoods, where you had to go to the toilet outside. We were a good family: we went to Blackpool or Rhyl on holiday every year, and Dad was always in work, every day of his life. Every Christmas, my stocking was full: I had all the clothes I needed and all the suits I needed when I was growing up. Sometimes, though, I used to have nightmares about being chased by Harvey, the giant rabbit out of the James Stewart film. That scared the living shit out of me. In my dream, the bunny-headed person would chase me around the house: I remember very vividly having nightmares about it.

I started going to see Wolverhampton Wanderers in 1961, after they won the FA Cup in 1960. I remember creeping down to listen to the results at 10pm when I was five or six years old, and if they'd lost I'd cry. That's what it's like to be an English kid in a house full of football fans.

In 1962 I was at Blake Secondary Modern and I remember one of the teachers talking about the Bay Of Pigs crisis. I was a little too young to understand what was going on, but I got the impression that the Russians were evil and our enemies: it was all dark and immoral. I was very pro-American as a lad. Everything was surfing music and *Bonanza*: Frank Sinatra ruled our house.

The following year, I remember I was on my way to a friend's house and it was getting dark. His mother came out and said that President Kennedy had been killed. I went back to my parents' house and everybody was quite upset. It was so sad, and of course those vivid images of the car and the hole in his head were shown on the TV over and over again. It was like a movie to us, but a sad one. It's still an awful thing. Any shooting like that makes us realise how vulnerable we are. There must be a curse on that family.

My first instrument was the trombone: they were recruiting for the school orchestra and picked me for the trombone because my lips were right for an embouchure. I didn't really enjoy playing it, though: it was hard work and I had to read music, which was tough. Then Mom bought me a plastic Elvis Presley guitar, and I played the crap out of it – so she went and bought me a cheap acoustic.

I feel enormous gratitude to my parents for their complete backing of my wanting to be a musician. Mom never thought twice about buying guitars for me – a Futurama in 1964, a Burns in '65, a Rickenbacker in '66, and finally a Fender Telecaster in '67.

Sheila Hughes *We were very interested in Glenn: we wanted him to do whatever he wanted to do. He would go and sit on his bed and play the guitar, because he always had music going through his mind – which we probably didn't appreciate at the time.*

We just wanted him to be happy, but in those days it was hard. We hadn't got any money. I bought his first guitar and amplifier on the knock [in installments], but every week it was paid and that was that. Things got better, but at that time it wasn't marvellous.

There was always something drawing me toward everything I've done in my life. An inner voice. I saw The Beatles on TV around the time of *Twist And Shout* in early 1963, and I noticed that the chicks were screaming at them. I was only 12, but I liked that.

Before The Beatles, my concept of popular music was The Shadows. I wanted to be a guitar player, so who was the best guitar player in the world at that time? Hank Marvin, with his cherry-red Fender Stratocaster. When I heard 'Apache', that was it for me. I wasn't really a big fan of Elvis or Cliff Richard: funnily enough, I used to like high-pitched crooners like Frankie Valli. Doo-wop stood out for me.

I listened to music on the radio, and I had this wind-up Dansette record player like everybody did. At Woolworth's you could get cheaper 45s on the Embassy label, that were not the real band – they were some fake version – so you wouldn't buy the Cliff Richard version of 'The Young Ones', you'd buy a bad version by somebody else.

Sheila Hughes *He was popular with the girls, of course – we had them coming to the door, ha ha! They were generally nice girls: he didn't seem to attract the common type, if you see what I mean.*

Margaret Colley [née Williams] *Glenn was my first love. We actually met at school in Cannock when we were 15 or 16 – we were in the same year. He didn't have the confidence to ask me on a date, so he sent his friend over – but of course I said yes, because he was absolutely gorgeous: very good-looking and charming. Just the business. I was very happy to have him on my arm.*

Sheila Hughes *I remember Margaret Williams, very well – I loved Margaret. She's beautiful, and always was, but I think their romance was too big for them at the time. That's how I see it.*

Margaret Colley [née Williams] *It just fizzled out in the end. He didn't arrive one time, and it broke my heart. It wasn't a big deal, though, because it was all so innocent. We used to go to youth clubs where he was playing in bands, and we used to walk home from school and have something to eat. We were together over a year: I was besotted with him and I was the envy of the school. I loved his parents, too: they're such lovely people.*

If you look at Glenn Hughes the musician, it makes sense that I was never convinced by Elvis Presley and Cliff Richard, and that I was much more blown away melodically by Hank Marvin. Bill Haley didn't do anything for me when I was a lad of 10 or 11 years old. I'd hear Mom and Dad playing Johnny Mathis and Nat 'King' Cole and I'd think, that's nice but I'm too young for that. When I was first becoming a singer, I was transfixed by soul. Always soul. It could be a white guy, a black guy, or a yellow guy, it didn't matter.

Paul Reaney *I was with a mate playing a game of putting on Cannock park. Midway though our game, Glenn and a chum arrived and began playing. I was a little surprised to see him there because he had, some time earlier, told me that he was due to start work in the record department of [department store] D.W. Clarke's. I asked why he wasn't at work. "I decided not to go," he said. "I'm gonna be a rock star instead." We all laughed and continued our game.*

By now, I'd begun to play in a series of school bands. One of my closest friends was Andy Attwood.

Andy Attwood *Glenn is one of the best artists you can ever see live. The first time I saw him play I didn't actually meet him: Mel Galley [later of Trapeze] and I watched two numbers, then Mel said, "He's good, I want him in the band." I guess I first met him in about 1966 or '67. Mel was in a band called Finders Keepers, and I was their roadie. I used to get the gear in and set everything up: it wasn't as complicated as it is these days. All the gear and the band would fit in a Transit. Glenn heard that the bass player, who used to sing the high parts, was leaving, so he joined the band.*

Around 1968 or '69, before the drugs and booze, there was a real innocence. When I was in Finders Keepers and the early Trapeze, this period was about The Beatles and the other great music that changed my life. Music was becoming really important to me, and American music in particular. It was *incredibly* important. I remember meeting Robert Plant in about 1969 and him telling me about Arthur Lee and Love, and their album *Forever Changes*. It was life-changing for me, even though the music I went on to make sounded nothing like it: that album smelled and felt like Los Angeles to me. It felt like something that I wasn't used to, and I wanted these flavours in my life. I felt the music as profoundly as *Sgt Pepper* and the first Crosby Stills & Nash album. All these albums influenced me.

Mel Galley was the funniest guy I ever met, along with David Coverdale. Mel was always the go-to guy if you wanted to feel good. I used to go to pubs with him when I was 18: he would drink a few pints of beer and not slur his words, and he never got fat. He even taught me how to shag. I was at a friend's party in Cannock when I was 14 or 15, and Mel was with this girl in a bedroom and he said, "Hughesy, come in here!" and he was shagging this bird. I was like, "Ah, that's how you do it!" I used to sit in front of him when I was still in short pants, watching him play his blonde Gibson 335, and I thought, "I want to be this guy." My heroes on the guitar were Hendrix, Clapton, and Mel. I adored him and he took me under his wing: when I joined Finders Keepers I played bass, but I didn't care, I would have played the tuba if he'd asked me to.

Andy Attwood *Glenn and I have always been in touch: I've always been his best friend and he's always been mine. One thing about Glenn is that he's very hard to work for at times, because he's so demanding – but I've told him I don't mind that, because he's demanding on himself as well. If somebody wants the best, and they believe in it themselves, you don't mind orders. We'd have our arguments, like you do, but the next morning he'd call me up and say, "See you in the restaurant in ten minutes."*

We've always got on well: me and Glenn went out every night when the band weren't playing. We'd go back to his house at night and he'd say, "Come round in the morning" and I'd be there all day. We were together even when we didn't have to be. Obviously when someone moves to the States you do drift apart, but I'm always the first person he rings when he gets here. We speak or text nearly every day anyway, and he's a superb friend. He'd give anybody anything. If there's one person who should have been a parent, it's him. He'd have made a great parent, although the only problem is, when he'd have made a great parent he wasn't in a fit state to do it …

CHAPTER 2

FIRST STEPS TO STARDOM

TRAPEZE

By 1969 I was playing in a great band called Trapeze, managed by Tony Perry, who became a great friend. That was when I really found out who I was meant to be.

Tony Perry *I was a director of an entertainment agency based in Wolverhampton, called Astra. One of my responsibilities at that time was to look after a band called Finders Keepers, which led to my meeting up with Glenn. He was the bass player with the line-up, which also included Mel Galley on lead guitar and Dave Holland on drums. This was around 1968 and even then it was obvious that Glenn was an outstanding vocal talent. These three musicians eventually teamed up with Johnny Jones and Terry Rowley from a group called The Montanas, who were also with Astra, and a new band calling themselves Trapeze was formed. I was appointed as their manager. The five-piece Trapeze was an exceptionally talented band, with Johnny on lead vocals and with Mel, Terry, and Glenn in support. Their harmonies were outstanding. Mel was on lead guitar with Dave on drums, Glenn on bass, and the multi-talented Terry on keyboards and guitar. The group was as solid as a rock.*

Andy Attwood *Glenn always used to come over to me at the side of the stage and say, "We've got them now", but once he broke a string and so did Mel.*

The audience had to wait, and started clapping because they were bored. He came over and I said to him, "You haven't got them now, have you?" He still reminds me of that story. Another thing about Glenn is he never criticises anyone. If I was a musician I'd say, "Listen to this shit." But Glenn never knocks anything, and I really admire him for that. He also knows that half his problems are of his own making, and he's the first to say that. So I admire that in him.

I was in Trapeze for four years, during which time the band switched from a quintet to a trio – which was me, Mel Galley, and drummer Dave Holland, later of Judas Priest – and released three albums.

Tony Perry *While I managed Trapeze on both a personal and business basis, I did so on behalf of Astra, to whom they were signed contractually. Astra was based in offices above the Lafayette, a live music club in Wolverhampton that we owned and operated from. We promoted bands there seven nights a week. In addition to local groups, we booked national attractions that included Led Zeppelin, Fleetwood Mac, the Sex Pistols, Status Quo, and so on. Glenn spent many hours at the Laff as it became known, both as a musician and socially, as the club became a focal point for all live music fans. Among the audience you would often find people like Robert Plant, John Bonham, Keith Moon, and even Stevie Wonder, who paid us a visit following his appearance at the Gaumont Theatre in Wolverhampton. In fact this was typical of the environment in which Glenn spent his latter teenage years – live bands, musicians, rock clubs …*

The first major exercise following the formation of Trapeze was to secure a record deal. We put together a tape with numbers that the group had written themselves, and went from there. One of my partners, Alan Clayton, used to go to the same college as John Lodge from The Moody Blues. They had just formed a new label called Threshold Records, so I made contact there. We also had interest from CBS.

However, enquiries for the band really took off after their appearance on a BBC2 television show called Colour Me Pop. *I had invited the producer of the show, Steve Turner, to come and visit the Lafayette to see three bands that we managed: each performed a 20-minute set. After seeing all three bands he eventually chose Trapeze as the act most suited to the show. The programme was aired on a Saturday evening, and on the following Monday morning someone contacted our office on behalf of George Martin. We arranged a meeting at George Martin's office, where he explained that he had spoken with the "boys" (meaning The Beatles) and invited us to join the Apple label. However, as he explained his ideas for Trapeze, it would have resulted in the band going in a musical direction that they were in fact trying to get away from.*

Several meetings ensued and despite being approached by other record companies, the band finally signed with Threshold. The first album, simply called Trapeze, *was produced by John Lodge and was launched on BBC Radio 1 with [DJ] Dave Symonds playing the complete album track by track. At the time that was quite extraordinary: it was only ever done on the release of a new Beatles album.*

The release was accompanied by a national tour of the UK supporting the Moodies. This was a sell-out tour that included two shows at the Albert Hall, and which gave Glenn his first experience of performing in bigger venues. A single was taken from the album, called 'Send Me No More Letters', written by Terry Rowley. But despite extensive airplay on both Radio 1 and Radio Luxembourg, it just failed to make the charts. While both the band and the album were critically acclaimed, Trapeze as a five-piece didn't make the progress that we were looking for. This led to a complete musical rethink, resulting in Mel, Dave, and Glenn breaking away and retaining the name Trapeze. As a three-piece, they were a lot heavier, and a complete contrast to the five-piece harmony band that had been originally signed to the Threshold label a couple of years earlier. John Lodge was still fully supportive of the new Trapeze and produced the band's next album, Medusa. *Obviously, as a three-piece, this album featured Mel's guitar work much more prominently than on the previous LP, but it also gave Glenn a greater opportunity to display his vocal abilities.*

We could have gone a long way; I think the band never got the success they deserved in the UK.

Tony Perry *Once again, the release of this album was backed up by a sell-out tour supporting the Moodies, this time across the USA. It included two shows at the Carnegie Hall in New York. A single, 'Black Cloud', was taken from the album. Glenn took to the States like a duck to water: he enjoyed and appreciated the total environment that accompanied the North American music scene. The whole business of performing and recording was treated, at least in those days, with much more respect in America than it was back home in the UK. In the States, to be a musician was largely recognised as a career, whereas in the land of his birth Glenn would be more likely cast as someone who needed to get a "proper job".*

America loved us. Get this snapshot from my early career. Trapeze played three nights at the famous Whisky A Go Go in Los Angeles in December 1970, and we did great. We did 15 more shows in 15 days and ended up back in LA. We didn't have enough money to get home, though, so we phoned our agency and they said, "Well, you can't play in New York again, because you've just played there." So we said, "How about somewhere in between?" because we didn't have any money. They came back to us the next day and said, "There's a club in Houston that really wants you to play," so we went to Houston and they sold out the first night, with 600 or 700 people. Then they asked for a second night. That one gig broke Trapeze in America.

Tony Perry *Trapeze spent the best part of three years travelling the length and breadth of the USA in an attempt to make a name for themselves. This resulted in a second album for the three-piece called* You Are The Music ... We're Just The Band. *It was their third album on Threshold, but this time with a new producer, Neil Slaven. There was a distinct change of feel about this album. While the three-piece English rock style was retained, there was a leaning towards funk in some of the numbers. This was a direct result of the band listening for hour upon hour to dozens of radio stations across the Southern states while they travelled from gig to gig. One American critic, Chris Knab, described their music as "the first successful merging of black soul and white power-rock".*

This was long before any drugs: we were drinking Cold Duck, which is a cheap American beverage. We'd opened for The Moody Blues and we'd been working hard: the strength of our show in Houston, Austin, and Dallas supporting the Moodies had made us big in Texas, which has always loved rock trios. That was the turning-point for me, when I knew that we'd achieved something big.

The whole of 1971 for me was about touring the USA and having encounters with girls. It was an age of innocence: I remember going to Tony Perry and asking him for five dollars. We'd have parties in our hotel, and people would be smoking opium and PCP and snorting coke, and I'd look at them and think, "These people are insane." We'd go to the houses of the record company executives and they'd be smoking dope and swimming naked in the pool. It was like the film *Almost Famous*, but I'd be a shrinking violet in the corner, standing there with Tony Perry and Mel and Dave, saying, "Look at those fucking drugs!" I had a very normal life and I was very frightened of drugs. Even when I took a Tylenol or an Advil I'd be like, "I don't want to do this."

Here's another story from the summer of 1971. Trapeze were back in the UK, where we didn't spend too much time as we were constantly touring the USA. We were playing at a venue called Mothers in Birmingham. The show was going great. We were about halfway through the set and I could see the unmistakable John Bonham walking briskly to the stage. Without missing a beat, he hoisted himself up onto the deck with the help of his assistant Matthew. He walked up to Dave Holland in mid-song, took the drumsticks and proceeded to rock. We were playing the song 'Medusa'. It was John's first encounter with the Trapeze trio. The crazy thing is that John didn't want to stop playing the song, so we extended it and it became the '15-minute Bonzo version'.

I was a huge Bonzo fan. Being a bass player, I was very much influenced by whoever my rhythm section partner was, and now it was the man himself, John Henry Bonham. It was a massive moment for our band and myself. Afterwards John took me to his home in West Hagley: he wanted to play me some new Zep. What happened next was a life-changer. It was 3am: he pulled out an acetate LP and dropped the needle onto track one on his stereo system – and played me *Led Zeppelin IV*, a good four months before its global release. We must have heard the album five times. By the time the sun came up, 'When The Levee Breaks' was tattooed into my brain.

We both crashed, and I was woken by Robert Plant a few hours later as I lay on a couch in John's music room. Zeppelin were off to Europe that morning. Bonzo was up like a shot, and he and Robert got in the limo. John was asking me when the next UK Trapeze show was … I was rubbing my eyes and scratching my head. "The Black Swan in Kent next Sunday," I eventually said. "Great," he said, "I'll drive you down there with Matthew." He was a man of his word.

Andy Attwood *I was with Trapeze from the start, but I didn't go on the first American tour where they were supporting The Moody Blues, because The Moody Blues paid for all that. I don't think the band got paid, though. Trapeze's second US tour was mainly clubs, but a lot of those clubs would hold 3,000 people. Nobody we knew had ever been that far south. We played in Houston for two nights, supporting The James Gang: Trapeze blew them off the stage. Tony went and got a newspaper the next day, which described The James Gang as a poor man's Led Zeppelin, and that was all it said about them. Trapeze got so big in Texas that they had Joe Cocker and Ike & Tina Turner supporting them. The USA is big enough that you can be massive in one state and not in another, whereas over here if you sell 20,000 tickets in Plymouth you're known nationwide.*

David Coverdale *My first impressions of Glenn were taken from the Trapeze album,* You Are The Music … We're Just The Band. *To say the least, I was most intimidated. Extraordinarily gifted singer – sweet Jesus! – and, of course, a bass player to die for.*

Kid Jensen [Planet Rock DJ] *It was when I heard* You Are The Music … We're Just The Band *that I met Glenn. He came over to [Radio] Luxembourg to promote the album and we hit it off immediately. He had a great personality and he really looked the part of a rock star. His attitude was so 'up': he was one of the most positive people I can ever remember meeting. What I remember about him is his enthusiasm: he was living the dream and* *he loved it all. The music was unusual: it wasn't hard rock – although Trapeze did rock hard – but it had that funk touch to it, which was what I found appealing. Some bands just get under your skin after a few plays, and you wonder why you didn't get into it the first time round, but it was just instant with Trapeze. There was nothing that you had to work on: it was instantly likeable music, and one of the bands that I would pick up an air guitar and play along to if I was off-air and there was no-one else around.*

A lot of bands were around at the time who weren't that great, if I'm honest, and they were benefiting from a lot of marketing hype and being darlings of the music press, but in Trapeze's case there was none of that. I just thought they were good. Thin Lizzy were similar, in that they were slow burners – at least initially – and I wanted to champion them too. I just felt that Trapeze weren't getting the sort of attention that they so richly deserved in the UK, even though I was living 400 miles away from London at the time. Glenn had a fantastic voice and he's developed into an amazing musician over the years. Later I moved to Radio 1, which segregated rock from other kinds of music: the rock shows were marginalised.

As for Deep Purple, Glenn was good for them and Purple were good for Glenn: both got better when they were playing as a single unit. I last saw him in the mid 70s, when he came back over to Luxembourg and we did a fair bit of drinking and reminiscing. I'm sure he regrets the time in his life when he was less than 100 per cent artistically, because more people should know who he is. He's a survivor, and the fact that he's come back from drug addiction is commendable.

My first American girlfriend was called Yvonne Dupree – and God, she was beautiful. She was the sexiest dancer: an absolutely drop-dead gorgeous French-American gal. I was so hot for that chick. She became my second love after Margaret Williams. She was living in LA, so with my money from the Trapeze tours I bought a four-bedroom house in a village called Penkridge, not far from Cannock, with the help of my great-aunt Clara, who helped me with the down payment. Yvonne was into pot. Once she blew some of a joint into my mouth, and it was fucking horrible. Now I never liked pot: I tried it in 1969 and I hated it. I didn't like anything to do with smoke, and it burned my throat, which wasn't good. I also didn't like the effect of not being in control. Things were distorted: people were bigger than they were, and their voices changed. I didn't even like drinking back then.

Tony Perry *At this stage in his career, Glenn seemed reasonably happy. The band was slowly progressing but always needed more gigs. He certainly didn't have any problems with either drink or drugs. However, on reflection, it was probably a few months after the release of* You Are The Music ... *that Glenn started to question his own future.*

I had never seen a girl as beautiful as Yvonne: she was stunning, a hippie from California who smelled great and kissed like a goddess. The sex was amazing. All the boxes were ticked, so we moved to the UK where Trapeze were touring. We weren't as big over here as we were in the States, but she didn't complain. After a while, though, she started to miss the dope. She didn't ask for any, but she did start to miss it and she got cranky – and we began to drift apart. In the end she simply got on a train, waved goodbye, and went to stay with Mick Taylor of The Rolling Stones. When she left, I was like, "Thank God she's gone," and she probably thought, "Thank God I'm out of that fuckin' place!" Penkridge wasn't California anymore, baby, it was village living!

Andy Attwood *Glenn always cared about how he looked. When we used to go out, if he had any change he'd throw it away, because his trousers were so* *tight he didn't like the shape of a coin showing through. We went to the Lafayette one night and he says, "We'll go and check those two girls out." He had a Mini at the time: this was about 1971. We went to a block of flats and he says, "I'll pick you up." So I went upstairs with this girl, and I didn't know at the time but her husband was in jail. I'd been in the room literally 10 seconds and there was a knock on the door: the girl answered the door and this guy comes in. He asked where so-and-so was, which is obviously the girl that Glenn was with – and she says, "I don't know, she went home a couple of hours ago." He said "OK" and went out. Two minutes later he was back: he walked in and just hit me. My eye was right out, bleeding. He wasn't daft: he knew that if I was with this girl, someone else would be with her friend, who was his wife. So we're on the balcony looking for Glenn, and we see Glenn arrive and drop the girl off – and then he fucks off home! So I have to walk eight miles home with my eye hanging out. No taxis or buses or anything. He said to me the other day, "Sorry about that." Anyway, we were in the Lafayette again a few days later and he says to me, "Those two girls are in again." I said, "Fuck off Glenn – you can go with them, but I'm not."*

Tony Perry *Trapeze had started to create a reputation for themselves, and as a consequence began to attract some well known musicians to their gigs. At the Whisky in LA, Jon Lord and [renowned session drummer] Joe Lala climbed on stage: in the UK John Bonham would play drums during the encore. So now Glenn was in the company of some of the best-known musicians in the business. This camaraderie also came at a time when our relationship with Threshold was not all that it should have been. This was in no way due to any of the Moodies, as they were constantly either touring or recording. As a band, we never had the same relationship with the guy who was appointed to manage the label as we'd had with either John Lodge or Justin Hayward. We had signed to the label as a five-piece harmony band, but we had finished up as a* *three-piece heavy funk group, and therefore the original enthusiasm shown from Threshold was – maybe understandably – no longer at the same level. However, this overall environment caused Glenn to become unsettled. It was during this period that we received an offer from [label executive] Phil Carson to join Atlantic Records, with John Bonham involved on the production side. Unfortunately this collaboration never materialised.*

It was now early March in 1973 and, to my surprise, I kept seeing members of Deep Purple showing up at Trapeze's gigs. They'd recently lost their singer Ian Gillan and their bassist Roger Glover, and were looking for replacements, but I didn't know they were actually courting me.

Pete Makowski [journalist] *I was a massive fan of Trapeze and saw them several times at the Marquee. I love rock with a soulful element, and they had it to the hilt. They were an amazing live band and performed like they were in a stadium. Glenn was an overpowering front-man, but all three of them were phenomenal players. People might find this surprising, but Ritchie Blackmore loved disco music in the 70s and it's easy to see why he was impressed with Glenn.*

I had been seeing Vicky Gibbs, whom I had met in Trapeze. She had a twin sister, Jacky, whom I later introduced to Ian Paice: they became our girlfriends. They were models and practically stars in their own right. Their parents owned a country club called Oakley House in a nearby town called Brewood. I would go down there with Johnny Jones, the original lead singer in Trapeze, who was my mentor: he was the first rock star I'd ever met, because The News and The Montanas were minor bands in comparison. I wanted to be this guy so much: I'd sit at his feet and listen to him speak.

When Vicky and Jacky weren't modelling or travelling, I'd go down there and pray that the twins were there. I'd go, and mostly they were around: I'd have a drink with Johnny and watch out for them, and about two in the morning they'd come down, and then it would be three in the morning and I'd go upstairs with them and sit and listen to Crosby Stills & Nash. Just sit there! I'd sit until seven o'clock in the morning, chatting and getting to know each other.

Nothing happened between us for months, until it became obvious that Vicky and I were pairing off. I kid you not: for the next six months we were very fond of each other, but it was just holding hands and smooching here and there – but no more than that. This went on for about a year. I'm serious. It was so mind-blowingly innocent. I want to stress how devastating it was later when we broke up, because we had only held hands for a year in the early days in 1969 to '70. The relationship went on for four years: I was away in America a lot of the time, but I'd see her when I was back at my parents' house.

Music was the backdrop to all this: not so much R&B but hippie music – the velvet pants and so on. I was meticulously dressed and never fucked up, ever. It went completely the other way in four years, but back then I was like a little boy: it was a real age of innocence. I was always around people who were older than me – maybe only three or four years, but that's a lot when you're 18 or 19. I would always look up to anyone who was older than me. I never wanted to drink, but I did it because I wanted to look older. When you're young, you stay in the bar until it closes and then you go and have a curry at three o'clock in the morning, because you can. It was all about the candles; the incense burning; listening to Neil Young's *Harvest*; holding a girl's hand for three years, man. It was young love: a real love affair. We were cultivating something, without knowing where we were going.

I was in Jersey in the Channel Isles when they landed on the moon in 1969, on vacation with my friend Andy Archer. This is a funny story. Back in the 60s I didn't know any gay people apart from Andy, but I didn't realise it. We even shared a bed in all innocence, although he never made a pass at me. He was a very successful DJ on the pirate station Radio Caroline and he was very camp: I was 17, and Terry Rowley from Trapeze and his wife were also with us, and we were staying with some friends of ours who had a guest house. We were all standing around in the street and watching the moon landing in shop windows. It was incredible.

Now, I'd seen Deep Purple when they played at the Wolverhampton Civic, and I thought they were pretty good and that the guitar player, Ritchie Blackmore, was a bit eccentric. They were all good musicians, but it wasn't soulful. To be honest with you, if it wasn't soulful and funky, it didn't interest me. In 1970, when I went into the three-piece version of Trapeze, my experience of funk was Sly & The Family Stone, so when I heard 'Highway Star' or whatever, I thought it was OK, but it didn't really do it for me. I was speechless when Purple asked me to join them.

Tony Perry *When any band has problems, it becomes more apparent when they are on the road, and this was the case with Trapeze when they commenced their US tour, on April 7 1973. Rumours that Glenn was leaving the band were now constant, and this gave rise to a very uncomfortable atmosphere for everyone involved. I have to say, however, that this did not affect any of their stage performances, with a distinctly professional attitude being adopted by all concerned. Neither Dave, Mel, nor I wanted Glenn to leave, and many discussions and meetings were held in an attempt to keep the band together. At the same time, I was getting messages from back home that Glenn was all primed to join Deep Purple.*

CHAPTER 3

MAN ON FIRE
JOINING DEEP PURPLE AND RECORDING *BURN*

Sheila Hughes *Before Deep Purple, Glenn was asked to join ELO – and he was so upset, because he couldn't make a decision. Roy Wood was ringing up saying, "Please come!" but in the end I said to Woody, "Please leave him alone, because he'll have a breakdown."*

In retrospect, I had no choice. I knew that if I was going to join this group that I would make my mark on the international stage immediately. I realised that I had to leave my babies, my Trapeze, to go and find the world with another thing. But Trapeze's music was my heart and soul. Our third album, *You Are The Music … We're Just The Band*, was coming out and it was brilliant. I knew that I would have to go backward, musically. Way back – to play what I called traditional rock. The saddest part for me was leaving Mel and Dave. Those guys had been my companions since my childhood.

Tony Perry *Trapeze had a few days off between June 10 and 14 1973, and Glenn flew to New York with our agent Morris Price. After a couple of days had passed, we learnt that Glenn had made social contact with some of the members of Deep Purple; this left Mel, Dave, and myself feeling very frustrated and annoyed. Our next gig was in Indianapolis, where we met up with Glenn and our agent, who were flying directly to the venue. If my memory* *is correct, the gig was at a university, and the backstage area where the band were supposed to get changed was in a gym: any instrument played in this area would be affected by a huge natural echo. On our arrival, we were guided to our dressing room area, and as we approached we could hear Glenn playing his bass. He had obviously arrived at the gig well before us. However, he wasn't simply tuning up as normal; he was blasting out the bassline to 'Smoke On The Water', a world-renowned riff, at full volume with loads of echo. Mel and I stopped and looked at each other, knowing full well what the other was thinking.*

Glenn's final gig with Trapeze before joining Deep Purple was an outdoor festival held at Chuck Berry's farm, just outside St Louis, on Sunday June 17 1973. Enveloped by frustration and disappointment, Trapeze returned to the UK, where I held meetings with the management of Deep Purple. These obviously resulted in Glenn being confirmed as Deep Purple's new bassist and vocalist. It was a difficult situation for everyone concerned. Glenn wanted success, which was understandable – and it was being offered to him on a plate, so to speak. We, Trapeze, also wanted success but were prepared to achieve it on our own terms, which in our estimation would have taken at least another 12 to 18 months.

Dave, Mel, and I were shell-shocked when Glenn left, but I shook his hand and wished him all the best for his future. Despite his commitment to Purple, Glenn still found time to visit the Lafayette in Wolverhampton, and kept in touch with most of his old friends. In fact the relationship between all of us became more cordial as the months passed. Glenn invited me to a Purple concert in LA when I was visiting Warner Bros, and he actually guested on a couple of tracks on Trapeze's second album for Warners.

It was always a mom-and-pop operation with Trapeze – your schoolfriends were your roadies and your manager was your mate, and it was all that Midlands-based thing. Breaking out of Cannock, Staffordshire, and going on to sell out arenas in America was unheard-of – but here I was now with the big boys. I'm glad I had my apprenticeship in Trapeze. If I'd had a choice – and this is no disrespect to any band on the planet – I would like to have had the momentum to go all the way with Trapeze. Who wouldn't? You ask any member of Purple, or anyone who had a teen band, and they'll tell you that they would have loved to see that band go completely all the way. But it wasn't to be.

Andy Attwood *At 21, joining Deep Purple was an offer Glenn couldn't refuse. He was a millionaire overnight: his dad was using his Rolls-Royce to drive to work. I'd see him every time he came home.*

I felt better about the offer to join Purple when I heard that they'd asked a hero of mine, Paul Rodgers of Free, to join too. It was also attractive to me to join the world's top band, who were bigger than Led Zeppelin at the time. That on its own was pretty persuasive, but it wasn't so much the money or the fame as the chance to have a bigger stage to play on and more people to sing for. And make no mistake: in 1973 Deep Purple were the biggest band on the planet.

And so I went off with Deep Purple, who were the number one band in 1973, and I knew the job I had to do was going be different and I knew that everybody had a say. I came into the band full of confidence – not arrogance. I was in great shape and it was before the drugs. I wasn't drinking alcoholically and I was in a relationship with a girl that was normal. It was all pie-in-the-sky stuff. There was a real innocence.

The last gig I did with Trapeze was in June 1973, and I joined

Purple in July. So now I'm living with Deep Purple's drummer, Ian Paice, down in Fulham in London on Harbledown Road. I went to Germany for a weekend with Ritchie Blackmore, because he always likes to go to Hamburg when he has the time. We sat in a few after-hours bars and talked about what my role was going to be in the band. Now, *You Are The Music ...* had established me as a lead singer. The voice I went on to use with Deep Purple had been there for a while, and at 22 years old I felt that my calling was to be a singer. Ritchie thought my role would be the glue between the band-members, bringing the harmonies into it. He looked at me as a kind of Paul McCartney-style player and singer, working alongside a guy – who hadn't yet been found at this point – who would be more like Paul Rodgers, with that kind of bluesy voice. I understood completely.

Ritchie and I had a great weekend of bonding in Germany: he was one of the three guitar gods in the world at the time, and it was a great honour to play with him. We got on really well. I was fresh new blood coming into the band, and the vibe was great. We hadn't auditioned any singers, but the office had had about 200 cassettes sent in.

One of them was from David Coverdale, who sang 'You've Lost That Lovin' Feelin''. The other guys loved the tone of his voice. It matched mine really well. In the end, he was the only guy who auditioned for us, even though other guys were on the list to audition later. He was slightly pissed when he got there, because he had a half-bottle of whisky with him.

David had charisma, he was funny, and he was intelligent.

David Coverdale *My audition for the Purps took place during the summer of 1973, at Scorpio Sound Studios on London's Marylebone Road, in the* *high-rise building that housed the original Capital Radio. I'd arrived early, and slowly but surely the members of Purple drifted in.*

Glenn was the last to arrive. He basically fell into the studio, with his huge mane of hair all over his face and Polaroid sunglasses hanging off his nose as he struggled through the door with his bass case and shoulder bag falling off. Very, very funny. His arrival helped lift some of my nerves – he was definitely human. When they started to play, he – as well as the rest of the band – just blew me away. He was incredibly confident and secure. I definitely needed a pretty good shot of Bell's whisky to loosen me up to jam with those guys.

We jammed some blues stuff and at one point David and I sat down at the piano and sang together. At that point I knew we were going to work really well together.

David Coverdale *The blend was amazing from the start. Our mutual love and experience of American soul music resonated immediately. Vibrato happened effortlessly. I remember sitting at the piano when everyone was taking a break, and I started playing a song I'd written just to keep myself busy. It was full of major and minor sevenths, totally inspired by Stevie Wonder, and Glenn wandered over and started harmonising with me. It was a hairs-on-the-back-of-your-neck, chilling moment, and our vocal relationship grew from that moment.*

David had to wait a week until we told him that he'd got the job. We got him in the band in early August, and by then we were down at Clearwell Castle in Gloucestershire for the next Deep Purple album, *Burn*, which we wrote in the castle dungeon. Ritchie got there first. I arrived second and got a good choice of bedroom, unaware that he had wired my room up and put speakers in the closet, and of course at three o'clock in the morning there were these ghostly wails. Blackmore had waited up to do it. When you're in a 700-year-old castle and you hear that, it's pretty spooky. I knew what was going on as soon as I woke up, though. They warned me that he was a famous prankster. Yeah, it was funny: I bet he's still carrying a water pistol now, at 65 years old.

The organ player, Jon Lord, was mentoring me. He was very sociable and a great dinner companion, funny, bright and very big-brotherish to me. We hit it off really well. I liked all of them, but I had a kinship with Jon that was passionate and a good thing.

It didn't take long for David and me to feel comfortable in the band. He adapted to it pretty quickly, and I'd already toured extensively in big venues, so I was used to playing for a lot of people. They were all pretty important players in that band, and I always felt that I was coasting a little bit. It was an easy gig for me in the sense that it was a band of musicians that flowed. The scales that Ritchie was writing in were that kind of traditional, Bach-influenced approach, which is a different animal to me. I enjoyed being in the moment on stage: Paicey was playing incredibly back then and we were really an in-your-face, dangerous band. We were really volatile and really pumped up. It was very aggressive.

How did I feel about being in Purple? This is the truth, and I don't give a fuck if it sounds arrogant: I was born to be on stage with a band like this. I had that gift. I knew I was a talented musician when I wrote the first Trapeze songs, so the moment I put my bass on and played 'Mistreated' with Blackmore at his house in Surrey, I wasn't at all nervous.

In fact, the only song which had been partly written before the *Burn* sessions was 'Mistreated' – the bare bones of it had set the tone of the bluesier aspect of the song. The way David and I took the singing parts on the album was pretty simple: we were both writing lyrics and sort of eyeing each other and saying, "Shall I sing here?"

The bridges in the songs were mine, mostly, although there was no-one pressuring me to sing at all. The parameters were pretty much set before I joined the band: I'd told them that I wasn't going to be happy just being a bass player. It would be like George Best playing at right back: what would be the point? When we wrote the song 'Burn' it was obvious to me that I was going to sing at certain points, so we arranged the vocals appropriately.

When you compare *Burn* with Purple's previous album, *Who Do We Think We Are*, it's apparent that we new guys were throwing down the gauntlet a bit – and also that we were firing on all cylinders. We all looked at each other as a brand-new band, as if we were five new guys together, even Jon, Ian, and Ritchie. Half the rhythm section and all the singers had changed: it was a breath of fresh air.

David Coverdale *Glenn was, and still is, a significantly superior singer in many ways than my good self. I am in awe when he extrapolates. Ooh, that sounds rude! But we are both natural singers and our angels were smiling upon us. It just worked – that simple. No effort required. His bass playing was astonishingly muscular and powerful. He was much more of a groove player than they'd had before, from what I've heard. He created an immensely strong foundation, along with Ian Paice, for us to build on. Glenn is a totally natural musician. I never saw him practise. He would take his bass out of the case, strap it on, plug in, and play amazing stuff – beautiful counter-melodies and a huge bass sound.*

An ex-girlfriend sent me a scented letter while we were recording *Burn*. In it there was a bundle of white powder. I'd tried a couple of lines of cocaine once or twice, so after dinner one night I went into my room and did a line of what I thought was cocaine – but it wasn't, it was fucking PCP. Elephant tranquilliser.

PCP is a psychedelic drug, so when I went out of my room and saw Ian Paice, his head was about 20 feet in circumference. Huge. It frightened me. Then I saw Ritchie smile, and his smile was like eight feet wide. You see, Purple weren't a big drugs band. Let's be very clear: before I joined them, none of them had ever tried cocaine. Ian Paice can't do drugs because he only has one kidney and asthma, so he was just a drinker. Ritchie used to like his scotch and Cokes, and Jon was an avid wine and brandy drinker. Remy Martin was his drug of choice. I wasn't a drinker, personally: I maybe had a sip of brandy sometimes. And nobody smoked any weed, ever. So they were all laughing at me, because they'd never seen me loaded before. Apparently Ritchie walked me out into the garden, and I was talking to him in what I thought was fluent German. Then I tried to take a piss, and I couldn't find my cock. It was all very funny.

I found out later that it was trendy in LA to lace joints with PCP. I hated it and never did it again, it was horrible. The rest of the guys saw how remorseful I was about it the next day. God, I was bright-eyed and bushy-tailed back then. Shit soon got different, as you'll see.

We had a huge press event in the castle, with servants dressed in mediaeval clothes: Blackmore loved it, he was in his element. The album was recorded in Montreux, Switzerland, with Martin Birch, whom I got on with really well. We recorded all the tracks live: if someone made a mistake we just started again. It was very live and very raw, and I was up on my bass chops because I'd been on tour with Trapeze in America not long before. We used The Rolling Stones' mobile studio there, which Purple had also used on *Machine Head*.

David and I stood side by side and sang on the same mic most of the time. I wanted him to feel supported by me, because he'd never really performed on a large stage like this before. It was important to us to bond as singers as well as people.

We mixed the album at Olympic Studios in London and we were all there. The bass wasn't loud enough: it was ridiculous. I always had a problem with people mixing me: every band I've been in has been bass-heavy. My bass is groovy: it hangs with the bass drum and makes people move. That's why I want it to be high in the mix.

We knew that we were going to set the world on fire with this album.

BURN

'Burn' One of the last songs we wrote. Me and David came up with the title and Ritchie came up with the riff. I came up with the unison introduction and the chords in the "You know we have no time ..." part. I thought the song needed a really good middle-eight.

'Might Just Save Your Life' This song started out with a riff by Jon Lord: a big organ riff!

'Lay Down, Stay Down' A Blackmore riff, but the main significance of that song is to do with the amazing vocals.

'Sail Away' This has a very bass-driven riff, with a very Glenn Hughes groove in the bass part. One of my favourites to this day.

'You Fool No One' Paicey came up with this drum pattern, which we all loved, and then Ritchie added the main riff and I added the bridge. I got to show another side of my voice on that song, which was really interesting. It came in the moment and I carried that style forward to *Stormbringer*.

'What's Goin' On Here' A cool song. Very of its time.

'Mistreated' I wasn't involved in the writing of this song, but I was definitely involved in the groove of it.

"A' 200' A thrown-together song and the sore point of the album, for me. It's a bit of a filler. I guess we were short of a song, so we jammed this one.

Let's talk about the credits on *Burn*. I had signed to a different publishing company with Trapeze, and I was still signed to them when I joined Purple, and so the management said they would give me a higher percentage on the album if I was a silent writer on it. That's why you didn't see my name on *Burn*, although you do nowadays. I should have had a lawyer look at all this stuff, but I was young. We all got 20 percent of tour income and that seemed like a good deal to me.

Next, we're off on tour. The first gig was in Copenhagen and it was amazing. Lars Ulrich, later of Metallica, was there with his dad and he was a massive Purple fan. He told me that I was the only one who signed an autograph. I remember when I was a kid, I once asked Gordon Waller of Peter & Gordon to sign my book and he told me to fuck off: I swore that if I ever got to be in that position and be a star, I would never do that. I never have done, and I sign everybody's autographs to this day.

The opening band on the *Burn* US tour were Elf, fronted by a man named Ronnie Dio, who I befriended. We spent a lot of time together after the shows, and we hung out on the Starship, the aircraft we'd chartered for the tour. Ronnie's voice was massive, with great midrange – we had a lot of respect for one another. We became even closer while Ronnie was in Rainbow. When he left the band, he and his wife Wendy called my then-wife Karen and me, and told us they were moving to LA, and that they wanted to find a house similar to ours. They bought a home in Studio City, and from that point the Dio and Hughes families were inseparable. We went everywhere together, there was so much love and laughter – we adored them.

I was so happy for Ronnie when he teamed up with Tony Iommi, Geezer Butler, and Bill Ward in Black Sabbath in 1980: it wasn't easy replacing Ozzy, but Ronnie was the perfect fit. Karen made all of Ronnie's stage clothes in Sabbath. We had quite a few parties at my house in Northridge, where Bill would normally get a grape stuck up one of his nostrils.

I never felt comfortable doing coke around Ronnie, so I restricted my use as much as possible, plus Wendy's parents Reg and Ivy spent a lot of time in our company – making it practically impossible for me to turn into Mr Hyde without being noticed. I have wonderful memories of Ronnie, who sadly died of cancer in May 2010.

A German guy, Ossie Hoppe, was Purple's amazing tour manager: he protected me. I was a social butterfly in that band, and I attracted a lot of attention. By all accounts I was a handsome, strapping young lad back then, so I guess a lot of women were interested. They were everywhere, although I was very much in love with Vicky. I was definitely a taken man, so I used to have to fight the birds off with a stick. From time to time one would slip under the radar, though: after all, rock stars will be rock stars. Two or three girls would want to hang out with me and some shenanigans would occur. It was impossible to avoid. I wasn't a monk, and I was 22 years old. Coverdale was having a fucking blast, as you can imagine.

David Coverdale *We were the new boys, and thank God we got on well from the start. Both of us are from families where we were the only child – spoiled rotten by our mams, of course – and we both adored soul music and the* *musicians and singers who played it. That was an immense connection for us. We could talk music and musicians all day and night.*

So here we are now, on the front pages of the *Melody Maker* and the *NME*. Purple were introducing me to the world, so there was a picture of me and Ritchie, a picture of me and Lordy and another picture of me and Ian. There I am – the new guy in Deep Purple.

Pete Makowski [journalist] *My abiding memory of Glenn is those ludicrous furry boots he wore, which made him look like a fluffy Norse god. He looked very rock'n'roll with his fur coat, shades, and long flowing locks. Strangely enough he reminded me of Bob Hope – they had similar chins and noses.*

Now I'm touring the world, making a record and playing in one of the biggest groups on the planet. I never thought about money, let's make that clear: I never thought, "I want to be a millionaire now." I never thought, "I want to have the chicks." I certainly didn't think about drugs.

The tour was a major, major production. There were 40 people in the crew and I've always made it a point to become friendly with everyone, from the carpenter to the production manager. Those shows were groundbreaking for us: the *Burn* album came out in early 1974 and a gig was cancelled because Jon Lord had to have his appendix out.

This is where cocaine starts to come into the picture a little more. I'd buy a bit of coke and it would last me for weeks, but when Ian and Jacky and Vicky and I went on holiday to Miami Beach, I met a coke dealer. That was the first time I bought coke in America, and we stayed up all night. I thought it was normal. A bit of Johnny Walker and a few lines of coke, surely that was normal for everyone? Well, no it isn't. Coke makes you want to make plans and change the world.

You want to make friends with bellboys and barmaids in hotels. It lies to you. It makes you want to give things away and it makes you cry uncontrollably.

In 1974, when anyone became successful in the public eye, you'd get women thrown at you, with free booze and free this and that. Everything was always free – although in reality, nothing is free. You have to pay the price, and the price has always been spiritual for me. It was becoming apparent by this tour in 1974 that I wasn't going off the rails – it was still working for me – but it almost felt normal to be stuck in a room with lockjaw. I used to have a line with Lordy or David, although I must emphasise that those two guys were not addicted like I was. Jon would come alive at about six or seven in the morning, when everyone else was winding down. I never wound down.

So the tour was off and running. We did our first shows in the States and we were now on the infamous Starship, a Boeing airliner which had been used by Elvis, Elton John, and Led Zeppelin before us. It had our name on the side and its own library, bar, and shower. I remember feeling very settled into my job. It was fantastic.

Some nights we were a revelation. Ritchie Blackmore was incredible when he wanted to be, but not when he was in a bad mood. I was pretty much at my best every night on this run; it wasn't until late '75 that the wheels started to fall off. I would play a solo with wah-wah bass and vocals, and it was different every night. I like to push myself and always have. I was playing a Rickenbacker bass at this point, for that trademark Purple sound, before I switched to a '62 Fender Precision later on.

Girls were everywhere, waiting for me at the hotels – even though I checked into hotels under an assumed name – and it was a smorgasbord for me. The girls who were around us were beautiful. I think Zeppelin and Purple had the same chicks, sometimes; I'd meet girls who had been with Robert Plant or John Bonham, as well as some who'd been with Trapeze. I remember playing in Buffalo and getting up for breakfast and seeing a girl leaving Jon's room. It was freezing and she was wearing hot-pants. I couldn't believe it.

In 1974, coke was the hip, slick drug that people would go into bathrooms and do. It wasn't out of control. Get a visual of this: Ossie and I were with Purple's security men, Jim Callahan and Patsy Collins, and a dealer comes in and puts a quarter-ounce of coke on the mirror. Someone sneezes, just like in the Woody Allen movies, and the whole lot goes into the shagpile carpet. I wasn't in my disease yet, so I just laughed and thought we'd better buy another quarter-ounce.

A high point of 1974, of course, was the California Jam on April 6 at the Ontario Motor Speedway in California. I met up with my dear friends Tony Iommi and Ozzy Osbourne of Black Sabbath, and we got some coke and stayed up all night on the 5th, the night before the Cal-Jam. So what you see on the Cal-Jam footage on the 6th is a Glenn Hughes who's been up all night, and it was still a monumental show. It was working for me then: when you're 22 you can stay up all night and hang out, and it's fine.

Ozzy Osbourne *Glenn is a great guy. He is a dear friend of mine and I'm glad he's doing some fucking good work. He's a great singer, man. I remember back in the days of what was it called, the Cal-Jam? We all had loads of white powder and everybody was fucked up on the plane. I was just laying there thinking, "I'm gonna die when I get off this plane." And Glenn said, "You may need a bit of this ..." Glenn and I go back for ever, and he's a great, great friend of mine. I love him.*

Purple headlined the Cal-Jam: we were taking most of the gate receipts and the film rights. These events always ran late, but we had a clause in our contract which said that we would hit the stage after the sun had set. But for the first time in rock history, this show was running 45 minutes early! So the promoter came into one of our trailers and told us that we had to go on stage 45 minutes before we'd planned to go on, in other words while it was still daylight. Of course we said no, and Ritchie locked his trailer and barricaded himself in. The marshals came and broke the door down: there were 250,000 tickets sold, but over 400,000 people were there. I remember being railroaded onto the stage by security.

The famous white suit that you see me wearing in the Cal-Jam footage was bought by Russ Shaw, the head of the promo department at Warner Bros. He told me he'd brought it for me to counteract the black suit that Blackmore was wearing. I didn't know it was going to become a famous thing. I didn't wear a shirt with it because I was so hot: coke makes your body temperature rise.

Ritchie wasn't himself. When he's in a bad mood, all bets are off, and we were warned that something was going to happen. We didn't know what it was but we were told to be on our guard. We were into 'Burn' and we were rocking away, and there was a certain amount of aggression coming from me: you can see that I was in full rock mode. Be as grandiose as you like: I was born to headline that stage. I owned that fucking stage, and I felt comfortable. It was back in the days when David wasn't really speaking on stage, so I did most of the introductions. Again, nobody put a gun to my head.

I remember doing a massive fucking line of coke at the side of the stage and running back on stage and taking the jacket off and going mental. If you're a cocaine addict, that's what you do – and the coke was still working for me at this point, especially in front of 400,000 people. It was all about to go to hell in a handbasket, though.

There was a huge pyrotechnic explosion, of course, which you can see in the film footage. The gunpowder knocked Paicey's glasses off. Obviously the security and the pyro team knew that there was going to be a massive explosion, but I didn't. It was just Blackmore wanting to create a stir. Also, he didn't like anyone being on his peripheral left: not roadies, not anybody – and there was a film camera on a crane there. Blackmore told the cameraman to back off, and ended up shoving the neck of his guitar into the lens. He broke the whole front of the camera and we ended up paying for it. He wasn't apologetic: the cameraman was on his turf and he took him out. We were dangerous at this point: I used to throw my shit around as well. The Deep Purple stage was a dangerous place to be. I'd get in the zone by the end of the set where I was completely exhausted and it was all fire and brimstone.

On the way out I was ushered into a helicopter on my own. I was pretty high because I'd done a couple of bumps of coke in my trailer: I still had the white suit on. There was a girl dressed as a cop in there, who said she was there to arrest me … and when we got up in the air she took her hat off, letting her hair fall down, unzipped my white satin pants, and proceeded to give me a blowjob. I was completely freaked out, because I'd always had this slight fear of authority figures.

You know, I thought all this stuff was never going to end. I thought I'd be doing it for ever. Time stands still when you're doing this. We used to go to bed – kind of – and come to: never wake up, just come to. Sometimes in my clothes, sometimes not: sometimes alone, sometimes not. Sometimes I'd wake up and go "Where am I? What city is this?" It really was like that. We were on a massive tour and the Cal-Jam had been a huge success. All the US dates were a great success: the Americans loved Coverdale, and we conquered the country.

I became a whirling tornado, people: mood swings were happening and coke was everywhere. When you're on tour with a major rock band, it has to be, because dealers – who are fucking scum – attach themselves to road crews across the world and we're off to the races. You could always find coke. I was never worried about my next hit.

On a trip back to the UK, I played with Trapeze a couple of times. It was great to play with them again: they'd recorded the *Hot Wire* album. I would have been really comfortable singing on that album. The songs were so funky, it made me laugh how funky they were without me in the band. I was glowing with pride for them: I was as proud of them as I was of me in Purple. I was so excited for them. They'd replaced me with Pete Wright and added Rob Kendrick on guitar.

Trapeze never had huge acclaim in the UK, so it was great to come to Scotland and England with Purple and play massive shows. Looking at the gig schedule, I remember Mom and Dad coming down to the Birmingham show in the limo with me, and we were handed a gold disc for *Burn*. All the press were flown up from London. Ian Broad was Ritchie's assistant: Ritchie asked him to go and moon my parents. They laughed it off.

The madness continued. I remember playing a gig in Belgrade on March 16 1975 very clearly. All of us, including Blackmore, went to a nightclub after the show, and I remember that the men in the club were mortified that we were coming onto their patch to steal their women: there was some real posturing going on. I felt really weird about it, even though we had a great security team.

CHAPTER 4

CLOUDS GATHERING
STORMBRINGER

Although we recorded our second album, *Stormbringer*, in August 1974, there was barely any communication between the band and Ritchie by the end of the year. There'd never been much anyway. If he wasn't happy about something, he'd send a roadie to us with a note. But I knew what kind of guy he was before I got in the band. When Jon had a couple of drinks he became the David Niven of rock, doing card tricks and telling stories and being great company. Ian was more isolated, and Ritchie was out on his own most of the time, so apart from Coverdale and me it wasn't really a band of pals – which was unusual because I'd come from Trapeze, who were all close friends.

We'd already been to Clearwell Castle for *Burn*, and it was very clear in my memory because David and I had been there and the press had come down – *Sounds* and the *NME* and Chris Welch, the old school. They were all down there and it was amazing. This time we weren't the new boys any more: we had our own minds and our own thoughts. Mind you, when we went back down there we had hardly any songs completed: the only one that Ritchie had come close to finishing was 'Stormbringer'. The rest of it was pretty much written around David, myself, and Jon. 'Holy Man' was written around the piano, for sure.

When we got to record that song at Musicland Studios in Munich, it came to the guitar solo, and Ritchie didn't want anyone in the room. I was actually in the room, though: just me and him. I think he liked my humour, you know. I suggested to him – not told him, just suggested to him – that he should play with a slide. About four feet from him was his bottleneck slide on the console, but six inches away was a screwdriver – and rather than get out of his chair and get the bottleneck, he picked up the screwdriver and did the solo with that. He looked at me as if he was thinking "OK then, I'll fuckin' play it like this," but not in a mean way. It was done in one take. That's Ritchie Blackmore.

We were having fun: we would go to the pub and behave like any ordinary young guys. David and I decided between ourselves which of us would sing which parts, so I sang my song 'Holy Man' and he sang his song 'Soldier Of Fortune'. David and I were always very generous with each other in the studio, even when I was fucked up on coke on *Come Taste The Band*. I like to do my vocals first or second take, but he likes to take his time a bit more. I think *Burn* is the vibrant sound of a brand-new band, but *Stormbringer* was made by a band that has found its feet. By now we were writing great songs: we were in the zone.

Now, here's a story. When we were in Musicland in Germany in 1974, making *Stormbringer*, we had to get out of there because The Rolling Stones were coming in to use the studio, so most of the vocals were done at the Record Plant in Los Angeles. We were also two songs short – hence 'High Ball Shooter' and 'The Gypsy'. But we hadn't sung 'Hold On' and we hadn't sung 'You Can't Do It Right'. So, Blackmore was gone and it was basically just me and David. We're doing vocals and I've gone in the toilet for a pee. There I am, alone, and in walks Stevie Wonder and his cousin. Stevie stands next to me and takes a pee. I look over at him.

Now, you know my story with Stevie Wonder: he was my hero. He finished up and while he was washing his hands I walked up to him and I introduced myself and I told him who I was. I tell him that I'd just recorded a song and ripped him off: I said, "Stevie, I'm in this rock band and I've got to tell you, there's a song that I've recorded called 'You Can't Do It Right' where I stole some of your style." He said, "I gotta hear it!" and so I got a copy and brought him into a small editing suite with his cousin.

I played him the song, which contained one of his melodies but with a different lyric. It was just for fun. I wanted to see if he was OK with it. He was so freaked. First he touched my face, and then he touched my hair, and he said, "You've been listening to my records!" and called me "Leo" because my hair was so long. We gave each other a big hug. He was sweet, tender, and kind. We sat there for an hour, talking about rock music and my love for his albums. I told him that we were recording at the time and asked him to come and say hi to David Coverdale.

So I walk in, and Martin Birch is there and an engineer, and David was there with big thick glasses on. I walk Stevie in, and he's on my arm, and Coverdale is singing his part in 'Hold On'. And he can see me with somebody in the control room, so he shouts, "G! I've told you before, I don't want nobody in here while I'm fuckin' recording! Get out, go on!" And I said, "But it's ..." and he shouted, "Go on!' and I said, "But it's Stevie Wonder!" It was a moment to treasure. Coverdale was a huge soul fanatic and came out and of course he was very sweet. It was all jokes. I stayed with Stevie for most of the night and I watched him play keyboards and sing.

Oh, and how about this? While I was staying at the Beverly Wilshire, having met David Bowie, I invited him to come down to the Record Plant where we were recording those extra tracks for *Stormbringer*. It was my vocal day and I was going to sing the song 'Hold On'. At this time in his career, the Thin White Duke was having his R&B *Soul Train* moment. While I was singing at the mic, Bowie was dancing away next to me ... I must say it spurred me on. 'Hold On' has a relentless groove. There was a real vibe in the studio that day.

STORMBRINGER

'Stormbringer' One of the few songs that Blackmore came up with for this album was this one. It's a very straightforward, Deep Purple-sounding song. David says, "Your mother sucks cocks in hell" on it, the line from *The Exorcist*. We'd been to a private showing of the movie.

'Love Don't Mean A Thing' One of my favourites. Ritchie found a busker in Chicago on the street, got him on the Starship [Purple's chartered aircraft] and flew him down, and on the way he sang a song about money. Ritchie called me and David into the library on the Starship and said, "We should do something with this song," and I think we paid the guy some money. David and I were singing at our best on this album.

'Holy Man' I just love this song. It was agreed that I would do a song on my own, and David and I came up with the chords one night in the studio.

'Hold On' Bowie was with me in the studio when I was singing this song.

'Lady Double Dealer' A straightforward Blackmore song. It was just straight rock. It was OK.

'You Can't Do It Right (With The One You Love)' Love this song. This is the song I played Stevie Wonder when I met him at the Record Plant.

'High Ball Shooter' Recorded at the Record Plant: Jon used the famous organ in Studio A.

'The Gypsy' I like Blackmore's haunting vibes on the guitar, and there's a real Lennon/McCartney vibe to the songs. It's a fans' favourite.

'Soldier Of Fortune' David was in his element here. I like to hear David singing in this register; he has a wonderful tone.

Want to know about money? This is how Purple worked. There were two managers. Bill Reid was the accountant and Richard Bagehot was the lawyer. Every three months Bill would fly out and have a meeting with each individual member, and he would tell us what was going on with our finances. All I know is that all my bills and taxes were paid and I had a credit card. Truly now, all monies were going into an offshore account: we were buying krugerrands at the time and it was all being invested for us. I knew that the royalties were going into an account where they were being handled appropriately, and also we had to put money back into the band. There was a certain amount of trust between them and me, whereas someone like Ian Paice was very much hands on with Bill Reid.

Back then, I wasn't completely foolish with money, but when you're making a lot of money, you just don't think about it. When I wasn't making any money, I was in fear of the next month, but when I was making money, I just thought, "This is going to be fine." If I wanted to buy a car I did: I bought a Jag and a house. You had to go and ask Bill Reid first, though: he used to call me "Boyo". He was always advising us to be cautious, but some nights we'd be in my hotel room and people would be ordering room service and this and that, which all went on my bill, but I never thought twice about it. If I needed money I'd just go to the tour manager and ask for some.

Ritchie never really socialised. It filtered down through the camp that he was a bit annoyed that there was some debauchery going on, but I never got called into the manager's office or anything. In April or May 1974 it was OK, I was just having a dabble. I didn't think I had a problem. The Cal-Jam went great, and there I was running off the stage to do a line when Jon and Ian did their solos. And look, there I am doing a line during Ritchie's solo, too. When people start doing their drugs of choice, for a while it sort of works, but the wheels start coming off and you're the last to know. I remember the gig in Lewisham in south London. I got some coke from a guy I knew: there's a bit of this on film, with me and David, and you can see that I left the interview a few times to do a bump and come back. But if you look carefully – and people will, now I'm saying this – on that video clip I don't look or sound right. I had a twitch, like Jack Douglas the [English] comedian. It's kind of funny now, but at the time it wasn't.

I was allergic to cocaine, in fact, and I had the worst nervous twitch ever. Some people would be scared, and others would laugh, and others would say, "We really need to get you to hospital." I had such an allergic reaction. I never saw anybody else behaving like this on coke. It was God's way of saying, "You shouldn't be doing this." There was something in the drug that did it: speed didn't do it. I'm a very hyper person anyway. Eddie Van Halen once said to me, "I've got to have a drink when I'm playing," and I thought it was the law of rock'n'roll – in a Keith Richards, Bowie, Sly Stone kind of way – that it was the norm to get very stoned.

Afterwards we buggered off – me, David, and Lordy, plus Tony Ashton – to Munich to do Lordy's *Windows* LP. Jon's pieces are completely different: they're classical, and I always enjoyed putting a different hat on. Jon was my friend: I liked him and he was a great companion to hang out with – very funny and witty and a gentleman.

The funny thing was, I met a bird in Munich before I did *Windows*, and she was a professional ice skater. She was a very beautiful woman and I had a small fling with her. Once, Lordy went over to her house and he was looking up over her bed while he was with her and there was a massive Glenn Hughes poster above it.

We did one gig at the Kursaal in Southend and I remember it because I bought a quarter-ounce of coke in a bit of newspaper and put it down my sock. I went back in the toilet about an hour later and it was all dissolved. I wasn't very happy about that, even though cocaine wasn't my higher power yet.

I was now becoming a problem. I was looking at cocaine and thinking, "That's how I want to feel – that makes me complete. Everybody should be on cocaine. In fact, if you're not on cocaine I'm not going to hang out with you. Why would I want to hang out with you when I feel this good and you're just drunk?"

So we're now playing 50 or 60,000 seaters. I remember it was hot in Connecticut on August 24. The second act was a band called Aerosmith, who I'd never heard of at the time, and Elf were opening the show. At soundcheck, their singer Ronnie James Dio comes up to me and he's upset because this band Aerosmith wouldn't allow him much room on the stage. I walked on stage and told Aerosmith's road manager that this wasn't OK.

Ronnie wasn't a drug fiend by any means: he'd just stay up and have a drink with me. We were really tight on that tour. His drummer,

Gary Driscoll – who was murdered in 1987 – came up to my room. I've met the guys from Aerosmith since they've been in recovery: they're great. I really admire people who can come back from the gates of insanity. Their sobriety guru Bob Timmons is one of the guys who helped me get sober, as well as Nikki Sixx and Ozzy.

On August 30 1974, the venue was the Astrodome in Houston, where Trapeze had taken off. Without Houston, I might not have joined Deep Purple, so there were a lot of Glenn Hughes fans in the audience. I got my big turquoise bracelet ripped off my arm when I went down to shake some hands in the audience. There were 40,000 people in the venue that night, and Magnet – our tech – jumped into that sea of people and surfaced two minutes later with my bracelet. Don't ask me how he did it. Another Magnet story was when he came up to my house in Penkridge one day and asked to borrow my Aston Martin: he had to go to London, where he lived. He called me from London and said, "Your car's been stolen." And I went, "Oh shit …" and he said, "I'm gonna call Patsy Collins" – our head of security – and within an hour the car had been returned – and cleaned. Magnet was involved in the Zeppelin camp, of course, and I think Peter Grant, their manager, might have been involved. They put the word out, and the car came straight back.

Here's another story about the making of *Stormbringer* in LA. On August 31 we were all going to LA in the Starship and we were going to record 'High Ball Shooter' and 'The Gypsy', and have some downtime. Coverdale and I were also going to sing 'Hold On' while we were there. The Stones were coming into the Musicland studio and we couldn't finish the album in time: I remember Mick and Charlie came in and they were great. So I got ensconced in my regular suite at the Beverly Wilshire; it was a corner suite upstairs. We had a couple of nights off and my dealer came over with two kinds of blow, one of which was pure cocaine. I bought two lots: a quarter-ounce of the good stuff and a half-ounce of the other kind for guests when they came over, which I'd put in a fruit bowl or something. I remember that Lori Maddox, Jimmy Page's girlfriend, was there. She was insanely beautiful and we wanted to be together, but I didn't want to start anything because she was Jimmy's LA woman.

I was up all night, and then the next day I got a knock on my door and it's Ronnie Wood, Keith Moon, and Mal Evans – the road manager for The Beatles, who was shot by the cops in 1976. Keith came in and he had a Nazi outfit on: the full costume. I'd met him in 1969 in Carlisle and he was fantastic. He wasn't a bad guy: when he got drunk, he was a court jester. He would throw a TV out of the window and all the things you've read about, but he was going through a lot of turmoil, because he was an alcoholic. I have great memories of him. He wasn't a cocaine addict like me.

I took them into the library area of the suite and I put out four massive, foot-long lines of coke. I knew that Woody – who is a very, very nice guy – was a coke guy, and I knew that Keith and Mal were drinkers. We had a race, and I fucking won that race. I was so proud that I actually beat Woody at snorting blow. In fact, Keith couldn't finish his line, so me and Woody finished it for him.

This is the bit where if you're reading this you're probably thinking, "Wait a minute – he's not saying that he's proud of his voice or his bass playing: he's saying that he's proud that he won that competition ..." I was patting myself on the back, and we went off to town. Keith Moon was the craziest motherfucker I ever met. In 1974 he was having fun: it was all tolerable and it was funny. As for Ronnie, I don't think I've ever met a nicer guy in rock music: just a sweet, sweet guy.

I wasn't seeing too much of the other Purple guys at this point. I'd invited Yvonne Dupree, my old girlfriend from Trapeze, to come and hang with me. Vicky and I were very much in love, but this is my book and this is my truth. I was horny as an old goat, but I don't think Yvonne and I made love because I was too high, man. This is where coke started to come into it. I remember being too stoned to fuck. We may not even have attempted to fuck, because I was so stoned.

We went to a massive party at John Mayall's house on Mulholland Drive in LA, and I was pretty loaded. It was where I realised that out of sex and drugs, drugs were now coming first. When you can fuck on cocaine, it's the most amazing thing in the world, but coke was now a daily thing for me and I was in denial that I had a problem, although I wasn't going out of my way to be a jackass. I was very much alone now.

On the third night, Woody brought David Bowie to my room. There were a couple of people in my room so I figured we'd better go up to Bowie's room, because he's a very private person. Angie Bowie was up there too, and he had a few dancers up there. He had seen the Cal-Jam on TV the night before and he was very impressed with my contribution to Purple. He understood my soul and R&B roots, because he was about to cut *Young Americans*. We felt very comfortable together: it was very different hanging with him. He was very guarded and he liked to spend one-on-one time together. We talked all night while Ron Wood flitted in and out – he's a real social butterfly. I ended up spending the whole week with Bowie: I saw three of his shows and Iggy Pop was with us. I remember one night Iggy jumped on stage, and Bowie's security didn't know who he was and knocked him out. It was fucking horrible: he stayed on my couch in the suite when he came back from the hospital. Bowie was really trying to get Iggy off the hard drugs at the time.

A gun was never put to my head to be funky. Ritchie wasn't writing a lot of music at the time, so perhaps he was losing interest. In hindsight, *Stormbringer* wasn't a very Deep Purple-sounding album, although it is a great record. The songs are really good. The title track is classic Purple, all the way through to 'Soldier Of Fortune', which is a Coverdale masterpiece. All I wanted to do was play and move forward: David and I were not clones of Gillan and Glover and we were going to do what we were going to do. It might have sounded more like Mark II if, for example, Blackmore had chosen to produce the album. I didn't put a gun to Jon Lord's head and make him buy a Fender Rhodes piano, and I didn't put a gun to Ian Paice's head and tell him to listen to Al Green records. I was coming into Purple from Trapeze, who were a funk-rock band, and everybody knew this. I came from a place of pure groove, and songs like 'Speed King' – which had been played wonderfully; no disrespect whatsoever to the Mark II line-up – were diametrically opposed to that place.

The whole experience of making the album, hanging with Ron Wood and David Bowie and meeting Stevie Wonder, was still fun. Alice Cooper was there too, and he was drinking but not being crazy. I was the most mental guy there: wearing a long kimono which some fan had given me and underpants underneath. I was carrying my Yamaha acoustic from my room to Bowie's room and the coke was making me want to play. I was completely maniacal and hyper. I'm a hyper person anyway. There were 40 people in my suite and I got a bill for $8,000 because some of the furniture was damaged, which was a lot of money back then – it would be $80,000 now or something stupid. This is where the wheels started coming off for me, when people were ordering bottles of champagne and food on my room service bill. Like anyone who is in their disease, though, I didn't really think about money: I wasn't really there. I don't think I ever slept: I just had a few cat-naps. We recorded those two tracks and the rest of the time we just had fun. We met John Wayne at the Beverly Wilshire: we were walking out to our limos and so was he. He was as nice as pie: we signed his boot for his daughter. He said, "My daughter would just die if she could have your autograph."

Then we flew out to do a German tour. We were massive in Germany. Babs Blackmore was German: she had been with Ritchie since I joined the band, but their marriage was on the rocks by this point. I would never see Ritchie, apart from at soundchecks: he didn't mix with any of us. He had a young French girl with him by the time we flew to San Francisco on the Starship. I'd flown my dealer up to San Francisco and he brought a massive bag of cocaine. His wife was a normal gal who didn't do drugs. The night of November 12, I stayed up all night with him. He was on the Starship with me, which is actually pretty wrong, having a dealer on the plane.

In the hotel in Seattle, we had to hand in all our paraphernalia because we were going across the border to Canada. We weren't searched, though, so we were like "Fuck!" But the dealer arrived and said that he'd managed to get some cocaine.

By now, my playing and singing was getting in the way of me getting high. I remember I got my supplier a room key and he would come in an hour before we had to leave. He'd been given a couple of coke spoons by Jagger and Richards – Keith's being much bigger. He'd pull out a two-ounce vial of coke and say, "Which spoon do you want, Mick or Keith?" I would always take Keith. My breakfast was always a massive line of cocaine. But wasn't that what everyone else did? Wasn't it normal? I thought it was what every successful 23-year-old did. I thought I was handling it pretty well. I'd get up and do a bump, and I was getting very thin, but I thought it was OK. I honestly didn't think it was bad for me.

It got to the point where I would stick a straw in a vial of coke, which could kill you if you didn't know how much was coming up the straw. It was very pure. By now coke was becoming the single most important thing to me – within not much more of a year of taking it. It was more important to me than sustenance, or my girlfriend. I thought it made me look better, it made me feel better and I thought it would make me run everything with it. But show me someone who's made it big on cocaine. You flush away all your money: I look on it as demonic. I remember collecting a gold album for *Burn* and going to the bathroom for a line, and seeing one of the Warner Bros executives doing some coke too. That was normal back then: it isn't the case now.

Although I wasn't paranoid yet and I wasn't seeing any boogeymen, I was starting to question my sanity – which happens when you stay up for three nights and days in a row. So I was being erratic and I was getting irritable, with mood swings. We went to stay in a hotel in Milwaukee and a guy in the room next to us was complaining about the noise we were making, and at six in the morning he knocked on the door – and it was Yul Brynner! I felt so bad for him. I got his autograph, though.

After the last show before Christmas, Vicky went home, but my roadie Magnet and I stayed on a few more days. We were in the elevator going up to my room, and three beautiful girls were in there with us. Suddenly they took off their coats and they were only wearing garter belts underneath: they'd been waiting for me. I invited them up and Magnet took off to his room, so I was left alone with these chicks. I'd never had any kind of group sex before, and it was a little bit intimidating – because there were three pairs of tits, three pussies, and only one dick. But I thought, "What the hell, it'll probably never happen again", and I got into it. While we were doing it, Magnet picked up one of their purses, took it into the bathroom and took a dump in it … she phoned up later and she was furious. Funnily enough, one of those girls sent a picture of the four of us to my house recently: my wife thought it was hilarious.

I can't remember how I found out that Ritchie was leaving. It would have been in January 1975, right after we played a festival at Sunbury in Melbourne, Australia. The management at the time was switching to a new manager called Rob Cooksey, who is a pretty tough guy and doesn't take shit from anybody. I think Ritchie wanted to be in control of his band and to make Bach-influenced classical rock music, which is why he formed Rainbow. Because I was so fucked up, I don't remember many of my feelings at that time. Coke had now taken hold of me, slowly but surely.

I was unsure of what Purple were going to be without Ritchie: I knew that David and I were becoming the main songwriters, and I was also gearing up to do my own album, but I was too fucked up to do that and I didn't have the balls. I was coasting: partying with my house in Beverly Hills and wondering whether I should quit, but all I really wanted to do was snort coke. I was deep into my disease now. Music was secondary to my drugs: it was getting in the way of my fucking partying. To go and play shows was a hardship to me: I was like, "How dare they take me out of my house?" That's the mind of an addict. A fucking *addict*. And some people don't make it. John Bonham didn't make it. Bon Scott didn't make it. Chris Farley didn't make it.

It was obviously in the back of our minds that Ritchie was leaving. His last performance was at the Palais des Sports in Paris in April

1975, and we were recording *Made In Europe* there. The recordings were going great. After the gig, I remember snorting some coke in a stall in the bathroom, and coming out and seeing Ritchie standing there and smiling. I said, "Man, it's been really great playing with you." But I also had the feeling that Ritchie knew I had become addicted. I felt dirty, and that I'd let him down.

I was always in shame, unless I was in the confines of my home or in a hotel. I felt that Class A drugs were something that we really shouldn't be doing, even though it was the norm for film stars and rock stars at the time. But coke made me feel different, even though I had a twitch caused by my allergy to it. It was like the elephant in the room. A true definition of a coke addict is someone who parties alone, and I would plough through it when I was alone, night after night, and eventually I would pass out from exhaustion. That's the way I lived my life. I was flying dealers in from London on that tour to bring me coke.

CHAPTER 5

A NEW ERA

COME TASTE THE BAND

When Ritchie left the band I was ready to call it a day and go back to LA. I was thinking, "How can we replace someone like Ritchie Blackmore? Could Led Zeppelin ever replace Jimmy Page?"

It was about this time that I became friends with David Bowie. We were pals of the same ilk. We loved coke and we found each other. I loved his work and still do, all the way up to the music he's making now. I was also friends with Ron Wood and the guy who carried the Stones' pure pharmaceutical cocaine in the 60s and 70s, Freddie Sessler, who passed away in 1999. I remember he put a huge mound of glittering, thick cocaine on a plate for me once. We were in a kind of cocaine club, Bowie and Woody and I. I'm not being grandiose about it, but this was what it was like to be a rock star. Cocaine was always there, and this is important: I *thought* I was having fun. It was still working for me back then: I thought I was playing professionally. I was showing up on time, although I may have been a little erratic. The wheels didn't come off for me until 1976.

On January 10 1975 Vicky and I had flown to LA, back to the Beverly Wilshire, our home away from home. I was looking for a house, and I made a friend called Phil Daoussis. This guy was a real hippie, but a real sweetheart: very kind, gentle, and lovable.

Phil Daoussis *I met Glenn in 1974 at a party. I was in between jobs: I'd been working in a cabinet shop, but things got slow and there was a layoff. A friend of mine worked in the clothing industry and he'd been asked to go to this party, but he wasn't feeling well so he asked me to go instead. So I went to the Beverly Wilshire hotel, and there were a lot of people there who were well known in the music business. Alice Cooper was there, and I think Ron Wood was there too. I didn't know what to expect, and I didn't even know who Glenn was, because Deep Purple was not the kind of music that I listened to. It was quite illuminating! Glenn and I struck up a friendship and things progressed from there. He was in good shape that night: his problems started manifesting themselves a little further down the line. He had a good sense of humour: I've always enjoyed the British sense of humour and we hit it off. There were some people there who were shady characters: I could see dealers wanting to take advantage of what they saw as a good thing, and I felt a little protective, kind of big brother-ish, about him. I'd never been in that kind of environment before, and I didn't know the nasty little things that go on, so I was getting an education as well.*

Previously I had never paid for the drugs that any of these guys gave me. No-one ever wanted money from me: they either wanted to work with me, or sit with me and watch me sing or write a song. It was all built around my singing or playing. But by this point I was buying it, because what dealers do is get you hooked on the good stuff and then stop giving it to you for free. I was addicted to the five-star stuff and spending a lot of money on it. Phil picked me up from the airport and we went to his place at Hermosa Beach for the night before we went to the hotel. He wasn't an addict: he would go to bed and get up and have breakfast like a normal guy.

Phil Daoussis *The thing with the cocaine was that everybody was doing it, and some people handled it better than others. At first I didn't see a major problem for Glenn, but as the year progressed his desire to use, and what would happen to him when he used, was real disturbing. He was the poster boy for the story of Dr Jekyll and Mr Hyde: he was really a great person, full of vigour and very funny, and then he would take a sniff. Things would be on the up and up for the first 10 or 15 minutes, and then he would start spiralling down. He would get very paranoid. I'm sure he had auditory hallucinations after a while. It would always go down the same path. I understood that it must have been really unpleasant, but he wouldn't stop doing it. I would tell him, "You need to stop and get some sleep. You're not gonna get any higher!" But when you talk to a person at that point, it falls on deaf ears. He didn't get nasty in a violent sense, but everything that manifested itself when he was under the influence was very negative and suspicious.*

After a week I found a house in Beverly Hills, walking distance from Paicey, because the twins, Vicky and Jacky, never wanted to be far from each other. It was a great 60s house with that open, *Austin Powers* look, and we filled it up with furniture. I got a Teac reel-to-reel and a Fender Rhodes so I could record my own material at home.

Phil Daoussis *I can remember times in the house we lived in up in Benedict Canyon near Beverly Hills, and Glenn would have me looking through the kitchen cupboards and the closets in the house, because he swore he'd heard things. It would get that bizarre, and he wouldn't let up until he finally crashed. He'd be fine in the morning – or afternoon, usually. We were living like vampires, which was not really my style; I lived at the beach. It was different in the rock'n'roll world.*

Before I left to go to Australia for the Sunbury Festival gig, I put Phil in charge of my house. He stayed there in his own room and looked after the place.

Phil Daoussis *Glenn basically needed someone to help him and to watch out for him: someone who knew how to get from point A to point B in Los Angeles. He had business meetings and so on, so because I was between jobs I fulfilled that role. You could say I was his personal assistant. I was caught up in things like Glenn was, but I had a little more sense and coke wasn't really my thing as much as it was for him. When I stopped, which is almost 30 years ago, I just stopped. I didn't go to rehab, I just stopped using it and I haven't used it since. I think I'm the exception rather than the rule, though.*

There wasn't much knowledge around about this kind of thing: you heard more about the glamorous side of this particular substance than you did about the negative side that would throw people's lives into turmoil and cause them to lose everything. You started hearing more about that a few years later, but at this point [in the mid 70s] it was the glamorous thing to do if you had money and time on your hands. In retrospect, I always think of cocaine as an expensive way to get very, very nervous. Most people would end up that way, as if they'd drunk a couple of pots of coffee.

On the way to Australia, we all stopped in Hawaii for a few days' holiday. It was Blackmore's idea, funnily enough. I got a call from David Bowie, asking me to fly to New York and sing on *Young Americans*: everybody said OK, but Blackmore said no. He stepped in angrily and said that it wouldn't be a good idea. It was the first time he'd ever put his foot down. It wasn't a big discussion, it was just "No." I went back to my house with my tail between my legs and said, "So be it." I was hurt: I wouldn't say I was pissed off, I was just like "Fuck!"

We stayed at the Honolulu Hilton – and I never left my room, for five days and five nights. I sat there, sweating coke out of my fucking brain, watching everyone drinking mai tais on the beach. I think I went down to the pool maybe once, dressed in my rock star gear. I thought I was cool. Some people save half their lives for a vacation like that. What a debacle.

I was starting to realise that I wasn't being a very good boyfriend to Vicky: she was basically a willing hostage to my drug habits. It wasn't fun for her. I'd go from tears of joy to self-loathing and anger. If you stay up doing cocaine for 72 hours, shit's gonna get different, even if you're the nicest guy in the world. It's all a part of cocaine psychosis, which I wasn't educated about, although Phil had warned me about the paranoia.

Phil Daoussis *Vicky was around, and she was an angel. I thought the world of her, but she basically left because the cocaine abuse got out of control. The real demons would come out in him: you could tell that wasn't him. It was like someone else had come in and taken over. It was eerie. When you started to see this on a daily basis, after a while you were like "Oh God, I know how this is gonna end up." That's why I eventually left. I had some responsibility: he would want the drugs and I could steer him the direction of people who weren't going to rip him off with stuff that had been cut. These people weren't dangerous, gun-toting types, which was happening at that time. Had I known what the outcome was going to be – you know, hindsight never makes a mistake – I would have steered him away from it. But we were all caught up in it. I was there doing it too, but what it did to me and what it did to Glenn were two different things.*

There was only one night when I got mad at him. At one point, a month after we had been living up in this house, Glenn started to get a little suspicious of Vicky. From my point of view it was totally unwarranted, but he wasn't thinking rationally or reasoning. I knew it was the coke, not him: it would never have happened in the daytime, when he hadn't had any coke. Things of that nature pushed me away, and they weren't doing my mental health any good. I used to feel bad for him: I used to think, "What can I do to make this guy be as happy as he is in the morning and the afternoon?" But like I say, we were caught up in it.

We were headlining over AC/DC, and something happened to make them very angry. I don't know what it was. There was a general air of tension, which spilled over into our downtime. We were in Melbourne for a few days before the show and I remember being in a bar with my bodyguards Patsy and Jimmy, playing pool. I'm a reasonable snooker guy, so I'd won a couple of games against this Aussie guy. On the last game, he picked up his cue and walloped me on the back with it – really hard. This was the only time up to this point that I lost my temper and hit somebody: I punched him and gave him a big old bruise on his cheek. I was crazy, although I had two ex-Green Berets with me, but I was very pissed off. Afterwards I felt deep remorse, even though I was really angry with the guy – I was sick to my stomach that I'd injured somebody. I don't feel comfortable inflicting bodily harm on anyone, even though I was the first one to be struck. After the cops came, I apologised to him. By the way, this wasn't coke-fuelled: I couldn't find any coke in Australia. I wasn't missing it too much because I wasn't fully addicted yet.

When I got back, I was getting the finest-quality coke on the planet.

Phil Daoussis *We went through some real shit together: if you could have seen what the nights up at that house were like … it was just madness. We* *would get as much coke as we needed and we would order stuff from a liquor store on Sunset Boulevard that would deliver to our address. We would start ordering up expensive cognac, because Glenn always had a thing for Remy Martin. I always ended up with a nasty headache the next day. We had a pool table up there, and different people from the music industry would show up.*

Bowie and I would talk for hours and hours. He was in New York and he said he wanted to come over and spend some time with me. Lordy and I flew out to do promo dates in NYC and Philadelphia, and Bowie was doing five nights at Radio City. I was a guest every night. He was staying at a hotel close to mine, and he'd have various celebs up in his room – I remember Bianca Jagger being there. It was obvious that David and Angie had an open relationship: there were girls and guys coming and going. I had no idea what the fuck was going on. I really enjoyed hanging out with David: we'd watch movies and talk and have a laugh.

Angie Bowie *This period of my life, being on tour with David, was like being on a roundabout and trying to find the right moment to jump off. Sometimes I was confused about whether I was in LA, or was I in Europe, or was I on the East Coast? I'd been to a couple of Deep Purple gigs, maybe one in LA and one in London, and the reason why it was so easy for me to get along with Glenn was because he reminded me exactly of a guy I went out with in college, who was from Doncaster. They were so similar. Glenn had a cute, pretty face like a baby. I felt like I'd known him all my life. I wish I could have helped him solve the problems that led him to take drugs. When you got Glenn away from the band, he was so much fun. When he was with the band, I think he really felt the stress and the pressure. He was having a real meltdown and he was reaching out to David. They had a blast: a lot of fun.*

There was a connection between Angie and me: she came back to my room once, and I knew that we were going back to my room to fuck. I didn't feel comfortable with that: she was an attractive girl, and bisexual – which interested me – but it felt as if I was taking my mate's girl to the hotel to shag her. But David didn't care: he didn't give a shit. Maybe I'm old-fashioned, but it felt strange to me. Coke does strange things to you sexually, but I'd never thought about shagging my mate's wife.

Angie Bowie *Glenn was very sweet, and very dear: the most soft-spoken man you could find. We were friends with perks, if you like. I'm not going to fuck you for favours. I'm not interested. I'm only going to be with you because I want to be. I was there as a friend: I wasn't trying to become a big love affair in his life.*

Anyway, Angie took the lead role. Talk about somebody taking control. She was a little too boisterous for me: it was a very loud, aggressive, sexual act, and at that point I liked my sex to be more loving. It was a little too much for me. We were out of our fucking minds on coke, although Angie wasn't addicted like Bowie and I were. Afterwards I took a couple of Valiums to go to sleep, and passed out. I remember walking out of my bedroom suite into the living room, stark bollock naked, and there in front of me were Angie and a female friend of the Bowies. I said, "Nice to meet you." Isn't that rock'n'roll? I'm telling you exactly what happened.

Angie Bowie *The last time I saw Glenn was after he'd had an argument with someone that he shared a house with. He came into the room and I asked how he was, and he kinda snarled at me. I said "fuck this" and walked out. I* *had enough problems of my own at the time, so I wasn't feeling particularly patient.*

You won't believe some of the things that happened back then. Once Bowie wanted to take a train, alone, from New York to LA to see me. I said, "Isn't there a security risk?" but he just wanted to be completely anonymous, because he was preparing for his role in *The Man Who Fell To Earth* and wanted to be around LA. It was just at the time when Purple were on tour, and he was so insistent that he had to come and hang out with me that I almost asked the Purple guys if we could move the dates. We couldn't, of course.

He and I were very tight for a while: he was a fan of what I was doing musically. I'd be on the phone to him for an hour or two hours every night. I remember when we stayed at the Georges V hotel in Paris, I had a ridiculous phone bill. He always used to call me "Old Big Head". I never really found out why. He must have thought I was quite arrogant. It's true that I had a lot of rage, and I was very hyper on cocaine. The coke made me lose my trust in myself and God: I was paranoid and I thought that people were out to get me.

Phil Daoussis *David Bowie stayed at the house. When I first met him, Glenn was in England, and he told me that Bowie was coming out here to the coast to do some stuff, and that he'd offered him the house where we lived. So he showed up on a Sunday afternoon, and he seemed like a pretty nice chap. We talked, and then of course the subject of getting some of the white came up. I said I'd make a call and we ended up staying up till about three in the morning. The first night he stayed there was very interesting, because this gal came by the house, a black gal called Claudia. It turned out that she'd been to a high school in the town of Pomona, where I'm from. She was there to see*

Bowie. He had a lot of interesting ideas and he covered a lot of subjects. He was in pretty good shape, and I've seen him where he wasn't. I know he had a real problem with that substance, but he never got bad like Glenn would get.

Bowie was very paranoid too. He kept carving knives under the bed in the room in my house that he was staying in. He told me how spooked he was about the Sharon Tate murders, which had happened near my place. There was a constant party going on at my house, but he would isolate himself in his room. He was miserable, because he thought his career wasn't going the way it wanted to, even though he'd just headlined a row of shows in the US on the *Diamond Dogs* tour. He'd come round at nightfall with a big hat on. And then, of course, there was Angie.

Angie Bowie *One time Glenn took me to a Deep Purple show: I think it was in London or Los Angeles. He was playing away, and then all of a sudden he got up to sing – and as I listened, his voice was like a tightrope that you could walk on in your dreams. As he sang, I stood hidden behind a stack of speakers with the tears flowing from my eyes. I was carried on his voice to a conspicuously beautiful, restful place. That was my clue that his sensitivity required him to be writing and performing only what he wanted to sing about – and not the collective consciousness of a band or group.*

When I was loaded I was known as the guy who would play a guitar or a Fender Rhodes piano. In fact I once ordered one from John Henry's in London and sent it over to Angie's suite at the Hyde Park Hotel. I bought a whole load of coke and I was up playing keyboards in her suite for 24 hours. We'd be singing along to a bunch of freaks – they were crazy fuckers, the Bowie clan.

Looking back, it's horrible, but when someone is crippled by their disease, the only thing they can think about is their own euphoria. Some people get high and see UFOs, some people get sexually weird: I wanted to jam. The sex and stuff didn't come till later. For a good 20 years I just wanted to play keyboards: I actually learned how to play keyboards on cocaine, which is a horrible way to do it.

Back in LA, at 1290 Tower Grove in Beverly Hills, I was ensconced with Vicky. I had a bar and a pool table in there and it was a real party place. We'd occasionally have a bump with the other guys, although David Coverdale – who was married to Julia Coverdale at the time – would always know when to stop and go home. I had a pretty endless supply of coke, and it was the finest I've ever snorted in my life, because at this time a lot of very potent stuff was coming in from South America. It accelerated my addiction, because it was so pure. I never thought about overdosing, I was too busy chasing the euphoria of the first hit. I never ate when I did coke, I just drank some beer. I'd be recording songs on my equipment, or at least I thought I was.

One night in February, Rob Cooksey, Purple's manager, was staying at my house, and I got a call saying that Ritchie's guitar tech Ron Quinton – who was delivering a Fender Rhodes piano to my house – had been killed on the freeway. I'm not sure if he fell asleep at the wheel or not, but it was a very, very bad moment in the annals of Deep Purple. He was coming to my house and I felt really, really bad. We were all devastated. It was a very sobering moment. Ron was wonderful. We all felt completely fucked up by it, and of course the way I dealt with it was to drink and do more coke. There was always enough: I never ran out. It was usual for me to stay up for five or six nights in a row, because I was so high on this very high-quality drug.

I once went down to my dealer's and he told me, "Glenn, you've

CHAPTER 5 *A NEW ERA*

really got to be careful with this blow because it's really, really pure."
We drove back in my brand-new Lincoln Continental – which I had
for a year and only drove once, because I was so loaded – all the way
down the Pacific Coast Highway, and I was so high and I felt great. I
gave Phil the night off, because I had my dogs with me and I felt
protected. I had at least 11 grams with me of the super-pure coke.

My friend Michael, who Yvonne Dupree had introduced me to,
could go toe-to-toe with me. He was the most fearless man I've ever
met. I loved him and I still do. He used to keep a shotgun in his house
and once, when we were at a party at his house, there was one guy who
was completely fucked up. This guy got in Michael's face and Michael
told him to cool it. This guy went down to his car, fetched a gun and
started waving it around. Michael asked him, "What are you going to
do with that gun?" and the guy started getting aggressive. Michael
took the gun off him, went outside, and shot that guy's car up. Then
he calmly wiped his prints off the gun and walked away. I saw it with
my own eyes. It was my first glimpse of *Starsky & Hutch*-style shit and
it was totally surreal. When you're high on cocaine, though, the last
thing you want to hear is gun-shots and police sirens: we never really
spoke about it again.

My idea for Blackmore's replacement was Clem Clempson of
Humble Pie, a Brummie who was a brilliant guitar player. He came
and stayed at my house and we auditioned him and he played great,
but he didn't have the charisma that he needed to stand up against
Blackmore. I took him to Bowie's house, and for some reason Clem
got a bit of a buzz on and got pretty fucking belligerent with David. It
made me very nervous. I got him out of the house and we went back
to mine. I think it must have been the combination of the booze and
the coke.

The next guy we auditioned was Tommy Bolin. I was blown away by him. I walked into the rehearsal room and I saw a guy with green, yellow, red, and purple hair and I walked up to him and said, "Whether you get this gig or not, you're coming back to my house tonight." And lo and behold, we went into the bathroom and I gave him a bump of coke from this big old vial I was carrying. Although Coverdale and I would party, he wasn't into it in an addictive way like I was, so I was pleased that at last I had someone I could party with. I didn't think I had a problem with coke: at the time I thought I could give it up any time I wanted. Tommy was totally charismatic and slightly brazen and super-confident in himself. He got the gig the night of the audition: we told him the next day.

When Tommy joined, we immediately started writing music for an album in June or thereabouts. I came in with some songs for *Come Taste The Band* that would end up on my album *Play Me Out*. They were just too funky to be played by members of Deep Purple, with the possible exception of Tommy.

So we're back at Musicland in Germany to record the album. We're a new band again and we've been reinvigorated by Tommy, because of his childlike qualities and the fact that he wasn't a Blackmore clone. It was a very relaxed session, even though the band were doing their best to keep me away from drugs. It was impossible, though: I'd put my hand down the sofa and come back up with some coke. The recording was a little fragmented: I did the vocal for 'This Time Around' with Martin Birch at two o'clock in the morning. There was no-one else there, which was very unlike me. David and I recorded our vocals separately.

The only time I ever slept was when I passed out at the keyboard. I drank to take the edge off the coke, not for the fine art of tasting the grape. I don't have my pinkie out when I'm drinking: I'm a glugger. I'll pick up a bottle of Chateau Lafite 1964 and glug it. In fact a dealer showed up at my house with one of those, it must have cost a couple of grand at least. He went in the bathroom to take a piss and I drank half of the bottle while he was in there, and when he came back I puked it up on him. I wasn't good with alcohol.

COME TASTE THE BAND

'Comin' Home' The weakest track, and I don't say this because I wasn't on it. To me it was filler. I'd already gone back to the UK to start my rehab, and it didn't deserve to be an opening song. It was disappointing.

'Lady Luck' A nod to classic rock, with a Bad Company vibe. David sang this really well.

'Gettin' Tighter' Tommy and I wrote this at my house in Beverly Hills, late one night. What you see is what you get with this one.

'Dealer' A funny story: I was in the studio with Martin Birch late one night, and David was sleeping. I recorded all the vocals, but David's were used on the final version. I wasn't angry or anything, David and I were very free about who sang what.

'I Need Love' I like this song, it has that Motown groove to the drums. It's very Tommy: it's what he was all about.

'Drifter' A good song. It could have been on a James Gang album, guitar-wise. It was very suited to David.

'Love Child' David sang this one great too.

'This Time Around'/'Owed To G' I heard Jon playing some chords in the studio late at night. I ran in and said "Stop!" Within half an hour I had the lyrics and within an hour we'd recorded the song. It's just Jon and I. It's a very mature lyric for a young boy: I was obviously going through some things when I wrote it. This song doesn't sound like Deep Purple: I want to thank the other members of the band for allowing me to be myself on it. 'Owed To G' was just Tommy, and his ode to Gershwin.

'You Keep On Moving' David and I wrote this song in his flat in 1973, but we never got to play it for Blackmore and so it didn't make it to *Burn*. It shows what a great duo we were, vocally. It still sounds great 35 years later.

From getting off the plane on April 8 from Paris, after the last gig with Ritchie, to when we flew to Musicland in Munich to record *Come Taste The Band* in the summer, I remember it being one long night. I don't think I saw daylight once in that time. I was only interested in the best possible cocaine. I didn't take any shit cocaine, and only four or five people in the whole of America could get it for me – so I would fly these motherfuckers everywhere, to Hawaii, to LA, everywhere.

My relationship with Vicky was going off the rails. You can't have a relationship based on cocaine and staying up three nights in a row. Poor old Vicky, she'd want to go home for some peace and quiet sometimes. Then she'd come back, and I'd be still up, unshaven. She didn't sign up for this. When I first met her in 1971, we'd smoke a couple of joints and I'd drink a brandy and Coke and we'd hold hands. She never wanted to end up with a fucking coke addict like me. I was a different animal now. I was a whirling fucking tornado and a horribly self-righteous, pompous, ego-driven motherfucker. Bill Reid would come over and say, "Glenn dear boy, you can't possibly go on like this!" but no-one else said that kind of thing. I was a bit afraid of him: he was a kind of grandfather figure. He knew where my money was going, and it was horrible.

In early May, there was a defining moment. Bowie had told me that the Manson family were out to get him, and I'd seen the movie *Cracked Actor*. I had half an ounce of coke and it was a very windy night. I had a very open house, high up in the hills, and I heard a voice going "Glenn … Glenn …" at about three o'clock in the morning. There were intercoms everywhere, and I had the one on the drive left on so I could hear who was coming up it. The drive was about 300 or 400 yards long, so I could hear anyone approaching. I didn't know about cocaine psychosis or paranoia – you don't, until you experience it. Suddenly Tosh, my Great Dane, jumped up and ran across the room to what seemed to be a bunch of shadows over by the swimming pool outside the window. In retrospect, it must have been the palm trees casting shadows, but I thought I heard a door slamming behind me in my bedroom. And in that room was a sawn-off shotgun which my friend Michael had left there, plus a Magnum revolver. I thought "I'm gonna get killed!" So I went into the bedroom, got the shotgun and loaded some cartridges. I was just wearing shorts and the coke was in my pocket. I could still hear this voice going "Glenn … Glenn … Glenn …" so I went into the kitchen, found a massive butcher's knife and shoved it down the back of my shorts. Now I was shouting, "Come on out, I'm gonna kill you!" as loud as I could.

Then I did something very bizarre. I decided that I would put the gun down on the pool table, take the knife out and climb onto the roof, escaping the clutches of the intruder who was about to kill me. I'd forgotten that it was now daylight and that the only house visible from mine belonged to an old actor called Fibber McGee. Down the hill a bit was Ryan O'Neal's house. So now I'm on the roof, high as a kite, eyes as big as basketballs, with a six-inch knife, waiting for the sun to rise. That was the defining moment when I crossed the line from back-slapping, wise-cracking, couple-of-lines good times to the twilight zone. Now it was on. After about an hour and a half, I go back in the house. To do what? More coke.

Suddenly I ran out of the front door, across the driveway on Tower Grove into a park area where there was some long grass, because I could have sworn there was somebody in that grass. I waded in there, with my heart racing a mile a minute, saying, "Who are you? Who are you?" I still had the knife – I could have been shot by the police. I didn't realise until two days later that I'd witnessed cocaine paranoia. Phil told me what it was when he came back. This is the point at which the drugs took my life into a whirling vortex of hell. After this drugs weren't enjoyable: I just couldn't fucking stop. Coke is a demonic possession. It comes from the devil – and I was possessed.

There's more shit to come, too. Phil was getting sick of my behaviour: I was breaking plates all over the house. I was angry and exhausted because I never got any sleep: I thought the world was out to get me. My only comfort zone was in front of my Fender Rhodes piano. That's why *Play Me Out* is so bittersweet and pushes the boundaries of my musical abilities. You can hear that I was in a lot of pain when I wrote and recorded it.

Making *Play Me Out* was like "I'll show them!" And also I thought that Ian and Jon forming Paice Ashton Lord was pretty horrid. I thought, "Well, if this is gonna be a music race, I'm gonna win it." I wanted to show them that I was far superior, musically. I won't hide the fact that I was bitterly disappointed that one of them had ended up with my girlfriend. Any man is going to be disappointed in one of his friends going off with his girlfriend, regardless of whether they were hiding it or not. Let's be clear about that: whether they were hiding it from me or not is not my business, it's God's business. I was hurt rather than angry that Jon ended up with Vicky: she could have picked any other mate to be with – why a member of the band?

The night before we went to Musicland I had been up for eight or nine days in a row. I fell asleep on the plane to Germany and then woke up in a pool of toxic sweat. So I went to the bathroom for a line, and then I spent most of the flight upstairs in the first-class lounge, and Ozzy Osbourne was there. We spent most of the flight out of our brains. We had become fast friends earlier in the year because Sabbath had been in town recording an album. Ozzy loved to do blow and he loved to drink. I met Sabbath when they did their first hit single, 'Paranoid', in 1970. I met them all very briefly. I'd meet Geezer and Tony at Purple gigs, but I didn't really sit down with Ozzy until the night before the Cal-Jam in April 1974. There was a very serious side to Ozzy: when he got high he'd ask a lot of questions.

Years later, I remember he thanked me for saving his life, and I can tell you why that was. Ozzy is a street-tough kind of guy, which I'm not: he kept saying, "I gotta find me a gun," and I said, "Ozzy, don't be so fucking stupid." Ozzy went toe-to-toe with me on the coke: we talked all night, although it was all cocaine-babble shit. When we got back to Britain after Cal-Jam I shared a car up to the Midlands with Ozzy, who lived with his wife Thelma about 12 miles from me, and then I slept for two days at my parents' house. They knew something was going on, but we didn't talk about it.

When I arrived in Germany for the *Come Taste The Band* sessions I flew a dealer in from London, who delivered the coke and went out on the town in Munich, but he got the shit beaten out of him. The band and Rob Cooksey had pretty much agreed by now that my drug addiction was the elephant in the room, so I was going to cut down –

not quit, but cut down. I began to detox a little, swimming in the pool at the hotel, drinking some orange juice and attempting to make the album.

I remember one night, Tommy was exhibiting some drug behaviour, and I realised that people were trying to keep me away from his coke. He'd been sent an ounce over from someone in Denver, Colorado, stashed in the middle of a hardback book. They went out, so I got a key from reception to Tommy's room, opened his suitcase and took some coke. Not all of it, just two or three grams. Cocaine addicts are liars, cheats, and thieves. That's what we are: we snort coke and we lie about it. I remember going to my room and I started to get high, but something happened: I felt remorseful after the first couple of lines. I went to our roadie Nicky Bell's room and woke him up: he was with his girlfriend Anneka at the time. I said, "Nicky, I feel bad: I've taken some coke from Tommy." I gave it back to Nicky. How about that for a transformation? It was because it was Tommy's: I loved him to bits. But then I came down an hour later and I was knocking on Nicky's door asking for it back!

On Tommy's birthday, which would have been August 1 1975, when he was turning 24, we went to a bar in Munich and we asked somebody in the club for some coke. So this dealer guy comes in and gives us some lines – but the minute it goes in my nose, I was like "Whoa!" I felt really warm and I ran out of there. Tommy was used to it, of course, but it freaked the shit out of me. They got me into a sauna to sweat it out, and I sat in there for three hours. I never did it again. Tommy got high on it, but I got violently ill. Of course, the guy who gave it to me was beaten up by my road crew. It was heroin.

David Coverdale *For me, the most difficult time was when overt drug use* *entered the band with Tommy coming aboard. We'd been pretty lightweight until that time. I did my share, but not on the level that Glenn and Tommy went for it. It was scary and I had great difficulty dealing with it, but it was obviously something we all had to experience and go through. Thank God, Glenn survived and came through it all. Sadly, Tommy didn't.*

After the album sessions for *Come Taste The Band*, I attempted rehab for the first time. I had to: I was on my fucking knees.

Sheila Hughes *I had a call from Purple's accountant, Bill Reid, who told me what was happening – and I was truly unaware of it. I know there were times I couldn't get Glenn, and there were times when I left the phone off the hook at night because I was so worried about it, but I honestly never knew he was in such a difficult situation. He'd always hidden that from us. We never saw it. Bill told us that Glenn was coming home and he needed to see someone, so I got in touch with our doctor right away and he saw him immediately. He referred him to a specialist and then Glenn went and lived down with Vicky Gibbs. Obviously he was happier to be with her. We visited him a lot, of course, but we weren't responsible for anything at that time. They were keeping him sedated: he'd never climbed walls or done anything like that at that stage. We never saw or knew about it, so we didn't really know how drugs affected him. I always wanted to know, and I still do want to know, what's happening with Glenn – not to interfere, but just to be in the picture. That's all I ever wanted. So I would like to have been in the picture a bit more, yes. He seemed to recover.*

So Mom and Dad have now witnessed the fact that I am hurt. I had to get out of my brain in order to get out of the now: addicts don't want to be in the now, they either want to be in the future or they want to be fucked up. I thought that every rock star, British or American, wealthy and iconic, had to be loaded, and if you weren't loaded I wanted no part of you. If you weren't fucked up around me, you were no friend of mine.

But back in the day, there was no real rehab in England. They pronounced cocaine "co-*caine*" and the rehab at the time was a heavy dose of a Valium-type drug for three weeks so you could come off the coke and detox – only to go back on it three weeks later, of course.

The actual rehab was simply my staying at Vicky's parents' country club while heavily sedated by a psychiatrist, rather than a drug and alcohol counsellor, as would be the case these days. Back in the 70s, we didn't know too much about recovery from Class A drugs, so I slept and ambled around the grounds daily, completely zoned out on sedatives. There was no counselling at all. I was told to apologise to each of the band-members and management. Meanwhile, my disease was waiting for me, outside in the real world. It was calling me, haunting me, and telling me that I was weak and that I didn't have a problem.

That attempt at rehab wasn't successful, in case you're wondering. It never is when you've got a young, wealthy guy who has put his faith in cocaine, especially in the mid 70s when we didn't know that cocaine was addictive. So consequently I didn't clean up.

I came close to losing my job in Deep Purple at that point because of my addiction. Our manager said, "You're so fucked up, we're in jeopardy of losing the tour – you need to clean up." My clean-up gig was The Butterfly Ball, the project put together by Roger Glover, held at the Royal Albert Hall in London on October 16. I had to sing the first song, which was called 'Get Ready', and they said, "If you can get through that gig unscathed, you can have your job back."

I was nervous, and I had no bass, so I walked on stage with my hands in my pockets. It felt awkward, but I had no problem going toe-to-toe with any performer ever. I was also nervous because I was the first performer, but it was no problem for me and after the show I got loaded, of course. Vicky found out and wasn't happy.

Then we were off to New Zealand, and I remember this tour – the "no drugs" tour. I didn't even attempt to find dealers on this run. I wasn't jonesing, I just knew going into this that I was going to be off drugs. I enjoyed eating dinner with the guys, and I liked the camaraderie: it was back to basics, like the old Glenn. Tommy and I used to chase each other round car parks: he'd jump on me and I'd jump on him. It was just boys doing boy stuff. The shows were great, all through New Zealand and Australia: the Melbourne shows were historic, people still talk about them today. I remember meeting an old buddy of mine from Cannock in Perth: Ian Walker, who had moved there with his family. It was six weeks of nirvana and it was a great time: the crew was great, the guys were getting on great. It was the calm before the storm.

CHAPTER 6
DEATH IN THE EAST
TRAGEDY IN JAKARTA – AND THE END OF PURPLE

In November 1975 we started our first tour with Tommy: the Australia/Asia tour, which started off in Honolulu in Hawaii. That was a successful first show, and we went to New Zealand and then had a great run through Australia. We were galvanised as a band by Tommy. So here we were, on our own chartered plane, flying across the bloody world. It was all beautiful.

On the day of the Hawaii gig, I wasn't at soundcheck for some reason and Tommy's girlfriend Karen Ulibarri came to my room. We couldn't keep our hands off each other. It was one of those moments in life where you just don't think. I wasn't thinking, "I want to go and shag my guitar player's girlfriend." I really liked her. She liked me as well. And I don't think she and Tommy were exclusive: he also had a girlfriend that he was seeing in LA. She was extremely seductive, and I have to be honest with you – you could not *not* want to make love to her.

On December 4 and 5, we played in Indonesia. Neil Slaven, my assistant, had been my producer when I was in Trapeze. He was hired by Purple's management on that tour because I'd befriended him again once I was in Purple. He was a very well-bred, well-read English chap.

Neil Slaven *The idea was that I was going to be Glenn's companion and* *keep him away from people who wanted to give him drugs. He and I had worked together in Trapeze and were friends.*

Neil had his feet on the ground and he wasn't a drunk or a drug addict. He was hired to be my assistant and steer me away from people or keep me away from people – sort of a minder, but more than that, a companion to me. He was a respectable sort of bloke – he didn't really get involved in the wild side of being on the road. A really lovely bloke, actually.

Neil Slaven *By the time we'd been through New Zealand and Australia, I'd effectively become a roadie. I had to carry the bass guitars: there must have been some sort of economy going on.*

So we get off the plane at Jakarta in Indonesia. It's a private airstrip because it's a private plane. The promoter's name in Indonesia was Danny Sabri. It was pretty exotic, and we were excited about going there. I think Cooksey had initially booked us in to play a sports arena, something like the LA Forum, that held about 15,000 people.

Neil Slaven *The band had hired this stretch Boeing 707 with 21 tons of stage gear. There was a spare seat in the cockpit, and I was in it for the landing in Jakarta: the pilot couldn't actually see the airport, all he could see was jungle. In the end we found it, and landed with a screeching halt with very little runway to spare.*

When we got off the plane – and I'm not exaggerating when I tell you this – the streets from the airport to downtown Jakarta, most of which was poverty-stricken, contained literally tens of thousands of people welcoming us. Can you imagine it?

Neil Slaven *So we got off the plane into a jeep full of sub-machine-gun-equipped soldiers. There were six limos, one for each of the band and one for Rob Cooksey, tour manager Ossie Hoppe and me, with a jeep full of heavily armed troops in between each. I told Cooksey, "I don't like the feel of this place at all."*

We got to the hotel and we had the night off. The promoter had arranged for us to go to a local nightclub to see an Indonesian cabaret performance – the fire-eating drummers and all that stuff that goes down.

Neil Slaven *The Indonesian fellow who was organising the show had been in LA when the band were rehearsing. He tagged on to Glenn and promised him that on the first night in Jakarta, he would be taken care of, in inverted commas, in the sense of having female company.*

We arrived on the Wednesday and the gigs were going to be on the Thursday and Friday. We'd been invited to a club. So we get out of our limos and go into the club and sit down. The lights went down and this couple came out, dressed very skimpily, and started doing these dance moves which were sexually explicit without being literal. And he was spouting bits of Shakespeare! It was all rather ludicrous. We were thinking, what the fuck is this? After about five minutes one of the roadies shouted, in this lugubrious Black Country accent, "Show us your piss flaps!" They left the stage.

There were about 40 to 45 people travelling, including the crew and everybody, and most importantly we had Patsy Collins and Paddy Callahan. Paddy is the younger brother of Jimmy Callahan, who was my bodyguard before he left to join Mick Jagger. Paddy and Patsy were best friends, both really tough guys from the East End.

I was very carefree with fans. I'd mingle freely: I liked to sign autographs back then, just as I always have done, so Patsy would shadow me wherever I went. If we had a day off I'd go out shopping or whatever, and Patsy would go everywhere with me. After the show every night there would be some kind of shenanigans going on in my room or suite, and Patsy or Paddy would be with me all the time, especially in a place like Indonesia where we'd never been before.

When we got to Indonesia, that one show in a 10,000 to 15,000 seater had turned into not one but two nights in a venue the size of Wembley Stadium. That's 125,000 people per night – a quarter of a million people – so we would have walked away with about a million dollars' worth of receipts for those two nights, and we were happy about that, thinking that we would be getting a large payday.

Now, this is what you need to know. The promoter's security was the army. So we're dealing with men with guns and machetes and shivs and fucking dogs. It's very, very scary, even though we're travelling with two of our own security guards, who were very tense. I remember the soundcheck in the afternoon – there were tens of thousands of people trying to get in. It was scary. I noticed a lot of Doberman pinschers as security dogs. They were on their leashes, but there must have been 200 of them, all chained up. Big bastards. The place we were in was a soccer stadium that should have held about 50,000 – but they'd crammed all these extra people in, so there was a security problem right there. Rob Cooksey was being told that we had to play because there would be a riot if we didn't. Thank God Blackmore wasn't still with us, or there would have been a riot –

because he would have done something really bizarre. For sure, it would have been death and destruction.

So we went on and did our set. We did a shorter set than usual – back in Australia we'd been doing 15, maybe 16-song sets – and I think that first night in Indonesia we did maybe 11 songs. It was because we felt there would be trouble. We were looking out and seeing all those people with the army as the security force. They were trained fucking killers by the looks of it.

The dogs were gnashing their teeth and batons were being raised, but there wasn't really any violence on that first night. We went back to the hotel and back to our rooms and of course, like pretty much every night, if there was a small party it was back in my room. I remember distinctly that it was on the sixth floor. So we go to my room and have a couple of drinks. The promoter had sent two girls to my room – very gorgeous Indonesian girls in their late teens or early twenties. They could have been prostitutes, but I don't know: back then I didn't know who was and who wasn't. I didn't ask for them – I've never really been into hookers – but they were obviously sent up for a reason.

Neil Slaven *This must be 11 o'clock at night by this stage. Glenn and Patsy and these two girls were all sitting on the bed talking. Knowing Glenn, I think it's unlikely anything of a sexual nature had happened. There was banter and badinage and Glenn or someone ordered a tray of booze from room service.*

So in my room there's me, Neil, the two girls, Patsy Collins, and Paddy Callahan. No-one else. Me and Neil were talking to the one bird and the other one was talking to Paddy and Patsy. After about an hour, I see out of the corner of my eye that Paddy and Patsy are having a bit of a barney. This fracas starts happening and I jump in the middle of it. Patsy had hit Paddy.

Neil Slaven *Apparently Patsy had some moral attitudes, and one thing you didn't do was insult women. There had been some banter about sharing the merchandise, and this apparently annoyed him: he came off the bed and punched me on the bridge of my nose and broke my glasses. He also hit Paddy, breaking the skin of his nose. Everybody's immediately sober and saying, "What's all this?" Patsy is saying, "You don't treat people like that: we're in their country." He must have been aware that these women were professionals: I can't believe he didn't know that. Anyway, he stormed out of the room, and the girls went off after him.*

I wasn't privy to the conversation that was going on. But I ran over to the fight – and this is where it gets really spooky. Patsy gets up and leaves the room. He just says something like "I'm going to fuck off" and leaves the room. Paddy says to me, "It's no big deal, let him sleep it off," or words to that effect – it was obvious that there wasn't much resentment there. So about 20 or 30 seconds later I went out into the corridor to look for him. And the weird thing is that the corridor is empty: there's an eerie silence. There was no-one there in the 30 feet of corridor I could see, or around the corner in the corridor going down to the elevator – I went to look round the corner to see if he was there, too. I had a great view; there was definitely nobody there.

So that's when the party came to a halt. One bird stayed with me for a few hours: it wasn't even daylight when she left. I went to bed with this bird and it was normal sex. It wasn't anything crazy. And afterwards she left.

There was a banging on the door at about 6:30 or 7am, just as the sun was coming up. I opened the door and an army of people came in – I had nothing on, so I threw on a pair of jeans and a shirt. They came in and told me what had happened.

Neil Slaven *At 7:30 in the morning, there was this frantic bashing on my door. I was obviously still inebriated. Cooksey and Ossie are at the door saying, "What the hell happened last night? Patsy's dead!"*

Rob Cooksey came in and told me that Patsy Collins had fallen from an elevator shaft that was not used anymore on the sixth floor. And that he'd got up, staggered into the lobby and died. Immediately, even though I was still waking up, I knew that something wasn't right. Patsy wasn't smashed out of his mind when he was in my room, he had had a couple of drinks like we all had, but he was a professional bodyguard and just would not throw himself down an elevator shaft. So immediately I knew what the game was. I thought, "Oh my God."

Neil Slaven *There was a large lift vestibule. There were two or three lifts on one side that had an attendant, and then on the other side there were three or maybe four lifts that were automatic. Now, behind that bank of lifts, if you turned left out of the vestibule down the side of those automatic lifts, there were two doors, both opening one way onto the stairway that was behind the automatic lifts. You pushed into the stairwell, and on your left there was another locked door that had access to the lift shafts. It had a pneumatic closing device at the top.*

Basically, Patsy had fallen down that lift shaft, he had hit some pipes at the mezzanine level and came out of the lift shaft. He then staggered down the steps and out of the hotel and said, "Take me to the hospital," and he lapsed into unconsciousness in the cab.

I was ushered into a van downstairs and sent to jail. We were thrown together in one cell. The police weren't doing anything physical with us, but they were yipping and yapping to us in their language, which was kind of frightening to me. I was very scared. There were no other English speakers there. Neil was extremely scared, to the point where he was about to start crying.

They separated us and gave us all pen and paper to write an account of what had happened the previous night. While we were writing, there was a guard with a fucking gun watching over us. That scared me. I'm British, I'm not used to being around guns.

Neil Slaven *It would have been quite easy for them to have claimed that we had had a fight with Patsy and thrown him down the lift shaft. It certainly looked like that. But it couldn't have happened: Patsy would have destroyed me.*

Me, Paddy, Neil, and Rob were all put in this holding cell, nobody else was in there. We were in handcuffs. They took our personal possessions off us, too.

Neil Slaven *We sat for a long time and then we were summoned one by one into the room of a detective inspector, I assume.*

What happened next completely freaked me out. In front of us was this head detective, heavily decorated with medals across his chest, and he sat there with one hand on the table and the other hand on a gun, which he was spinning on the table. I'd seen enough gangster movies as a kid to realise that we were in trouble. This was one of the scariest moments of my entire life.

Neil Slaven *It was a disconcerting experience because I didn't know what Paddy and Glenn had told them, so I had to tell them an approximation of the truth without being too literal. I didn't wish to say that these were two professional ladies who had been arranged previously. I didn't know what had happened before Paddy and I went into Glenn's room. So all I concentrated on was the fact that there had been a disagreement and Patsy had hit both of us and left the room.*

Then we had to hand our passports in, and of course that was when we started to freak out – because if you hand your passport in, you're fucked.

Neil Slaven *Passports were handed over and we all went back to the hotel, which is when I was told what had happened to Patsy. Jon Lord gave me two Valiums and said, "Take these, because you need to sleep tonight."*

So now it's noon on December 5, and the band are all waking up to be told that Patsy is dead. I'm stuck in the jail with just jeans and a T-shirt on and no communication with the outside world – none, period. After a few hours, dusk is falling and it's time for the second show. Lo and behold, here come two armed guards, who open the cell, and a translator comes in to tell me that they're going to handcuff me and put me in the van. Paddy was still in the jail, but Rob Cooksey came down, and they marched me to a van, put me in the back and took me to the backstage area. My bass was handed to me – and the armed guards watched me while I played the second show!

This is where the shit gets funky. If you look at the setlist for that date you'll see that there are only eight songs played, so you know there were problems. This time, the problems were coming from the army. During song three or four, they let the dogs loose. There was some kind of skirmish going on. I saw people being bitten really badly on the legs and the arms: above the music you could hear the screams of these poor fucking people.

Neil Slaven *I went back to the police station on the Saturday and was told that I might have to remain for another three weeks while the investigations continued. Suddenly, out of the blue, these two girls appeared, saying that Patsy had opened the wrong door and fallen. So, about an hour before the plane was due to take off, these girls suddenly appeared and gave us our Get Out Of Jail Free card.*

We feel that the girls were sent up for a reason, to get one of us out of the room. To cause a problem so that something would happen and Patsy would be out of the room. The authorities clearly thought that Purple might have caused Patsy's death through some action of our own.

Neil Slaven *The implication at the time would appear to be that he was victimised. You see, the band never got paid for those two shows. While we were still in Jakarta – or it may have been after we'd arrived in Japan – the theory that seemed to come from the management was that they [the Indonesians] were going to discredit the band as a means of not paying for the gigs. And then the implication became that after Patsy had stormed out of the room, he had been manhandled and thrown down the lift shaft.*

I was pretty shaken up. Paddy Callahan flew home with Patsy's body. Neil Slaven, Rob Cooksey, and the other guys got on our private plane and Vicky flew out to meet me in Tokyo. The whole thing had caused us a day's delay. I remember going to my hotel suite late at night and Vicky was very angry with me for being late: she hadn't heard what had happened and when I told her about Patsy, she was mortified. She loved him; he'd been a member of the family. We all did, he was Purple's main guy.

The Japanese run was bittersweet. Tommy had fallen asleep on his hand and pinched a nerve, and I think the promoter gave him morphine. It was the first time the Mark IV line-up had been to Japan, and the shows were completely sold out. The Japanese fans back then were insane: we were like The Beatles in Japan. The shows were all very well organised and presented. I remember there was a lot of drinking going on, especially what I call holiday drinks – mai tais and what have you. We stayed at a lot of Hiltons, where they have Trader Vic's, and every night before the show I saw every member of the band in the bar, drinking some sort of cocktail. They were pretty sickly drinks, with grenadine and apple juice and whatever. They're very sugary, and of course every addict loves his sugar. My drink of choice back then was a pina colada.

At the time we were shooting the *Last Concert In Japan* movie and at one point in that film you can see that I'm about to throw up because I was so drunk. It's terrible that this show had to be documented on film. We were awful, and yet we chose to put this out as a live recording. It's absolutely dire. I cringe when I hear or see it. Why did we have to be so greedy that we put this out? David and I really didn't want to do it. Tommy couldn't even fucking play! Why would you want to commit artistic suicide? It's one of the biggest peeves of my career: it should never, ever have been released. I remember watching it and saying, "We can't put this fucking thing out."

We couldn't go back to the UK, because we were tax exiles and we could only go back there for 30 days a year, so we flew to Thailand on December 16 for a small break. The hotel they had in Bangkok for us sucked, so we hired a car and went to the coast, where we got a really nice five-star hotel. It was a really nice four or five days, a winding-down period. I was in pretty good shape.

Back in England, I went to see Mom and Dad and then went down to Vicky's parents' country club in Brewood to get my clothes. We had Christmas over there and my parents brought my Afghan hound, Karma, over in my Aston Martin or my Daimler Double Six. It was great to see Dad driving a nice car like that. I had Mel and Dave and a couple of the roadies from Trapeze come over and spend New Year's Eve with us. I was jonesing for some coke, though, so a friend got in my Aston Martin and drove down to London with some cash I'd given him. He got back with the coke at midnight – and of course I didn't tell Vicky about this. I tried to hide it, but I would start twitching and stuttering and sweating, and we had an argument. I was a whirling tornado on coke – a volcano! – and it was better to get out of my way. I was so self-righteous and self-centred and full of ego and pomposity.

So off I went in the Aston Martin to Mel Galley's house, and me and Mel stayed up all night snorting the coke. My relationship with Trapeze was still family – I still call them "my band" to this day, and I always had in mind that some day I'd go back and do some sort of reunion. This was the second time that Vicky had caught me doing coke since the Butterfly Ball gig, and she decided that it would be better if she didn't come out with me, because she knew she wouldn't get any sleep. I was the elephant in the room: no-one really discussed it. There was no Betty Ford around at the time: I think people just hoped that I'd get over my addiction by myself.

I went back to LA and spent some time with Bowie while he was recording *Station To Station*. I was with him while he was writing lyrics at the console: it was interesting to see him doing his thing. It was a real privilege to watch him recording: seeing him move from *Young Americans* to *Station To Station* was fascinating. I've taken the way he evolved from album to album into my own career: I might have made more money if I'd stayed with one image and one sound, but if there's one thing I learned from Bowie it's that art comes first. I'll take that to the grave.

So we're now rehearsing for a monumental American tour, and we're going to be flying on a private plane. It was the DC9 that Lynyrd Skynyrd died on later that year – the exact same plane. We're flying to Fayetteville in North Carolina from LA, and I remember that it was a pretty exclusive plane. I was at the back with Tommy; we had this private area. I didn't have any drugs on me because I'd decided not to bring any with me on that run. I knew the drugs would be everywhere. It was freezing when we got there.

This tour has never been documented, and I'm going to start documenting it now, because it needs to be stated for people reading this that I loved playing in Mark IV Purple. My disease wanted me not to be present, though, so whenever I could I'd have crew members go off and buy coke – and now I was doing lines before I went on stage. I never used to do that in Mark III: I'd do a line during the drum solo and the keyboard solo. It got to a point where I'd be doing coke every waking hour. Because I'm very hyperactive and highly strung anyway, I could sing on coke to a degree, but it wasn't high quality. I might have gone off the melody or I might have gone off on a tangent: I've heard a million recordings from early 1976, and I was so high that it was awful. I wasn't singing wrong notes or anything, but I wasn't following the melody and I was ad-libbing. I was more riffing it than singing it: I was hearing something different in my head. Drugs make things sound different. I was very unhappy with my performance, although some shows were better than others.

This is how bad it got: even Tommy didn't want to get high with me any more. I was not a guy that you'd want to get high with, because I'd be paranoid. I had a twitch and I would always think that the cops were coming. I was a fucking nightmare. On that tour I was getting high alone: I was finding my own dealers through local crews or security, and I'd be up all night in my room. Nobody wanted to hang with me, nobody wanted to get high with me, and I was alone. I was a complete jackass when I was high and I hated myself, but I couldn't stop. The craving was beyond what anyone could conceive.

Of the US dates, the Radio City show in New York on January 22 1976 is the one that jumps out at me, and I'll tell you why. I'd seen the Zeppelin guys in LA a couple of times and I'd known Bonzo [John Bonham] and Planty [Robert Plant] for ever. I remember checking into the Warwick Hotel and I got a call from Ronnie Wood, who was up there with Freddie Sessler, the Stones' supplier. He said he was over at the Plaza, so I took Jon Lord and Jim Callahan over there and I met them in the lobby. Ron took us up to Mick Jagger's room. I'd met him the year before when we were doing *Stormbringer*, and I had a quarter-ounce of coke with me. The Stones were funny about coke: they only wanted to do their own blow. Eric Clapton was there too. I spent a good 12 hours up there talking with Jagger and Ronnie. All Mick wanted to talk about was Bowie, because he was fascinated with him. Mick offered me the use of his studio to record *Play Me Out*.

By the time we got to the Radio City gig, I'd been up for three nights on blow. I'd had at least half an ounce in about 15 hours and I ran out. I remember going to soundcheck and I couldn't get any blow because the crew had been told not to get me any. Lo and behold, I got a call from John Bonham and he was coming down to the show. This is a real low point for me, and this is the first time people will read about this: I was so angry because I couldn't get any coke that I actually played down the gig. I was on stage for the two hours of the show but I didn't partake in a lot of the singing. I just stood at the back of the stage. It's the only time ever in Purple that I did that. It was awful, and this was the night that TV cameras were there and the press people were there.

Right toward the end of the show, Bonzo walked on stage and he had a gun on him. He walked up to me and pressed something metallic against my back, and the band stopped playing. Then he commandeered the microphone to talk about Zeppelin's new film, *The Song Remains The Same*. He said to me, "You're coming with me after the show, Hughesy." I remember him coming off the stage and berating Tommy, and that's when I saw this fucking gun. I never even got a chance to go and towel off in the dressing room: we'd been planning to go to the Rainbow Bar and Grill, where they were having a party for us. So I get into the back of Bonzo's limo and he's got this gun and he's having a go at me, saying, "What do you think you're doing, befriending my wife?" but never actually accusing me of anything. I think he'd heard a rumour that I had a relationship with his wife Pat, which was untrue. I never had a relationship with her: we were friends. He loved her and she loved him, let's make that clear. I felt awful about it. We got it out of the way, though, and we went to a party afterwards and spent a lot of time in the bathroom doing coke. After that he took me out on the town, all night, all around Manhattan, in these private watering-holes. He was drinking and we did massive amounts of coke. We got to the Plaza at seven o'clock in the morning and went up to his suite, where he passed out in the chair talking to me. When that happened, I legged it.

By the way, John Bonham comes back into this story one more time. At Zeppelin's Los Angeles premiere of *The Song Remains The Same* in autumn 1976, I was invited by Robert and Jimmy and Bonzo. The night before, Bonzo calls me, having got my number from someone, and asks me to meet him at the Rainbow. So I do, and I go up to John and we go to the Beverly Hilton, where Zeppelin are staying. I'm up with Jimmy and Bonzo all night, out of our fucking minds, and the next night at the premiere we go to the after-party and we hang out with Ron Wood.

Shortly afterwards, I'm living in the UK and I get an invite from Robert, this time to the premiere in Birmingham. So I go to the reception, which was held at the Opposite Lock nightclub, and I go to the bar and Bonzo sees me. Suddenly, I can see him crawling along the floor, with people looking at him and parting the ways to let him through. I know exactly what's going to happen here, because I've seen John in all his glory before.

He comes up to me and says the last thing he ever said to me, "So you fancy your chances, do yer?" and punches me straight on the chin, chipping one of my teeth. He knocks me down and beer goes over both of us. I'm asked to leave the premises and that's the last time I saw John. I'm going, "Oh, Jesus ..." I loved John. I thought we'd been through all this in LA. I think the idea of me being in the same room as Pat triggered him to freak.

You may not believe this, but it's true. In September 1980, I was having a nap in the middle of the day, and I remember Karen coming in and saying, "You'll never guess who's dead." And I said this, out of my sleep: "I know who's dead: it's John Bonham." He'd come to me and whispered in my ear that he'd gone to heaven and told God that he was leaving Led Zeppelin and that he was going to form a new band with Glenn Hughes. And then he said to me, "She's a rich girl now." And that's exactly the dream I had. It came to me while I was sleeping.

Back in New York in January 1976, I'd got home to my hotel after this four-day bender and completely crashed. I was woken up at four o'clock by Nicky Bell, so I showered and went down to soundcheck. I felt so bad about trying to sabotage the gig the previous night: I'd been totally immature. So I went on the next night and it was a way better performance: I really went for it. I remember looking over to the left and Robert Plant was watching us, standing next to Karen Ulibarri, and it kind of annoyed me because I really liked her. That night a friend came down to see me with some coke, and Rob Cooksey punched him because he didn't want any drugs near me. Because I didn't get any drugs that night, I went to sleep in my suite, and the next day I realised how good the show could be when I was in shape. I felt almost normal, although of course I wasn't.

So we played Lakeland in central Florida and then went down to Miami on February 6. I asked a dealer to bring a quarter-ounce of coke to the hotel, but he ran off with my money. So I didn't have any drugs. However, I was on some kind of diet pills at the time, because I had gained a few pounds, and they were basically uppers – so I started throwing these down. I was really tripping out. I was on the 24th floor of our hotel and I called the hotel manager and I told him that someone was trying to get in through the window. He said, "That's impossible!" I said, "No, the guy's wearing a yellow hat and a red jumpsuit and he's got glasses on." In the end they gave me a couple of Red Bombers, which is what we used to call these giant sleeping pills, and I slept for a couple of days straight. We had three days off, luckily. Vicky came out and we were together for the rest of the tour. We had a big party in Houston, because that was a big Trapeze stronghold.

So now I was seeing these things and believing them, because I'd been awake for so long. I was having conversations with beings and angels in my room: I was now in full-on cocaine psychosis and I was beginning to fall to pieces.

About this time was when Jon Lord's famous story took place, the one that he always tells about the dealers coming on the plane and threatening to kill me. It was never like that. What happened was that I had a party in my room for about 20 people that night, and my dealer came down. I was going to give him money for the coke the next morning, when the tour manager woke up. I had a couple of hours' sleep and then I got into the last limo to the airport, so he came with me to pick up the cash. Nobody was threatening to hurt me. He came on the plane, I gave him his money and he left the plane. End of story. There were no guns drawn and no-one chasing me down the aisle of the plane – none of that stuff. I think I would have noticed if somebody was threatening to kill me.

At the El Paso show, the writer Geoff Barton was there, and he saw me sitting there in front of a mountain of cocaine. Someone got me half an ounce. I remember doing massive lines of blow before the show, which was becoming normal for me now. We did the show and flew back to LA, still partying on the coke, and played a show – which we recorded for *On The Wings Of A Russian Foxbat* – and it was a great show. It was very live and very raw. It was all becoming very decadent, with lots of people coming out to see me. I was now becoming widely known as a coke addict, like David Crosby was.

The remaining gigs went quickly. All the way through to the gig in

Tempe, Arizona, on February 29, we'd fly in and out on the same day and use LA as a hub. I wasn't living in my house any more: I was based in the Sunset Marquis, until they banned me for making a huge mess in my room with a party one night.

At the time I wasn't realising what this was doing to Vicky: she liked to party, but she didn't sign up for this. I didn't realise how much of a bastard I was becoming. I was becoming an animal. I never laid a hand on Vicky, but there was a lot of abuse from me. Everybody got it: I was mad, but I didn't know what I was mad at. I was paranoid that people were coming to get me, and I got angry that they were coming. I was all, "Why are they coming to get me? I can hear them. Can you hear them? They're here somewhere. In the closet. On the driveway …" All this drove people away, which of course I thought was a plot to get me. For all intents and purposes, I was insane. I was standing on a ledge, looking down into the chasm of hell and no motherfucker wanted to be there with me. Everyone thought I was going to die. My parents were expecting the next phone call to be the news of my death. It was awful.

We played in Salt Lake City, and of course there was no coke there, so I had someone fly in to the next show in Denver. I split an ounce and we had a huge party. The Denver show was the last US show with Tommy, so we flew back to LA, where we arrived at Burbank Airport at about four o'clock in the morning. Ossie Hoppe threw me in the shower at the Sunset Marquis, packed my bag and I barely managed my flight to the UK. Basically, he was getting me the fuck out of Dodge. LA, this beautiful city that I loved, was now a sin city for me where everyone I knew was either a dealer, a vampire, or some other creature of the night. Ossie took shit from no motherfucker, even though I wanted to change my flight and not go to the UK. He threw me onto the plane and I got back to the UK on March 5. I flew alone and landed at Heathrow, where a limo took me to Cannock. I slept for three or four days: what a sight I must have been. I would wake up in a pool of sweat and eat whatever I could find, and then fall asleep for another day.

So we come to March 15 1976, the day that Deep Purple broke up, after a show at the Empire Theatre in Liverpool. I want to talk about the last five shows that Purple did. Now, it's a famous little thing for me, but back in the day I was known for staying awake for up to a week at a time. Seriously, a week. I woke up on March 10 and I didn't sleep until the 15th. I couldn't play very well at that point: the drugs had started to hinder me as a human being. I couldn't breathe right, and by the time I got to Glasgow on March 14 I was starting to see things. Jon Lord had to drag me on, because I physically couldn't take it. Come the Empire gig, I was a complete mess. This was the lowest point for me in Purple – not as an artist, but as a man.

I never went to sleep during that series of gigs: I was physically and mentally drained, and entirely paranoid by then too. I was pretty fucking stoned, man, and I was alone. The band were in a different hotel to me. Even my assistant Nick Bell wasn't with me, which was pretty tragic. I could have fallen asleep; I could have been in the bath. Today you'd never find an artist on their own, they'd have security or whatever. It's a miracle that I made it to those gigs. How I did that, I just don't fucking know.

After Liverpool, due to fatigue and the sex, drugs, and rock'n'roll, there was a lot of tension. Simply because of my drug abuse, and Tommy's, which were at an all-time high. Tommy was also being berated by Ritchie Blackmore fans, and losing the plot a little bit – and Coverdale was tired of it. He wanted away from all that, and I don't blame him, so he pretty much handed in his resignation to the management that night. Unfortunately, nobody told me.

I wasn't shocked when Purple split. I didn't want to continue making the kind of music that Purple were making. I just wanted to record my solo album, *Play Me Out*: I already had an agreement with the Purple Records offshoot Safari that they would release it. Could we have continued as a band with another singer replacing David? Not really. I could have done the vocals myself, of course, but that wasn't what any of us wanted. Lordy and Paicey were going off to do Paice Ashton Lord; Coverdale was off to do his first solo album; and I was looking forward to doing mine. Did my addiction contribute to the demise of Purple? I think it was certainly a part of it, along with Tommy's struggle with another, even worse drug.

When we split up, EMI released a live album called *Made In Europe*.

Tom Morello [Rage Against The Machine] *I was a huge fan of* Made In Europe, *which featured the classic tracks 'Stormbringer', 'You Fool No One', 'Mistreated', and 'Burn'. I completely wore out that record! It was heavy, rocking and just fundamentally awesome. That LP was a huge influence on me as a songwriter and musician, and Glenn's contributions to it are no small part in that. I was very gripped by the great riff-rock by Purple in the Glenn Hughes era: it really shines through on that album. The interplay of Glenn's bass, the keyboards, and Ritchie Blackmore's guitar is pretty stunning – and the crazy dual-lead vocals of Coverdale and Hughes are a hard rock fan's dream come true.*

No-one knew that I'd unsuccessfully tried rehab in 1975. The disease had got me by the short and curlies. I couldn't escape it.

CHAPTER 7

HEARTBREAK

VICKY, LINDA BLAIR ... AND THE RETURN OF TRAPEZE

I've heard a lot of stories about me, some of which are folklore, some of which are true, and some of which are sort of true. This book is my own truth. I want to tell the story of what it's like being an addict.

At this time in early 1976, although I had my own house in Penkridge, maybe five miles from Cannock, I never stayed there because Vicky and Jacky Gibbs' parents' country club was nearby. The twins were modelling in Italy and I went back there after that last gig in Liverpool and basically slept for two days. Vicky had become increasingly tired of my addiction, and the relationship was coming to an end.

Tony Perry *In 1976 there were all sorts of rumours floating around the music business regarding the future of Deep Purple. I don't know whether they actually split up or decided to take a sabbatical; whatever the decision, it meant that Glenn was freed up as a musician, and as a result we had calls from people both in the States and at home for Trapeze to reform as a three-piece. This was a complex situation with the new guys Pete Wright and Rob Kendrick, who were well embedded into the new look four-piece Trapeze. While work in the UK was not plentiful, gigs in the States were fine. The band had shared the bill with The Eagles at a Rolling Stones Festival at the Cotton Bowl in Dallas in July 1975. The opening act had been Montrose.*

Trapeze were working on another record, not with me, but they asked me if I'd guest on a couple of tracks, and this really reignited the brotherhood between Mel Galley, Dave Holland, and me. I had a couple of ideas for songs that I'd written on my Fender Rhodes piano at my house in LA: a song called 'Smile', one called 'It's About Time', and some others. Trapeze were recording at a funky little 16-track studio, Lea Sound in Pelsall, in the West Midlands, and what a great place it was for me to get stoned in. Mel and Dave had been recording over there, so I said, "I'll bring my acoustic and my Les Paul over and write some stuff." At this point – typical addict – I switched from coke to speed, which I'd tried in Paris and I thought was the happiest drug of all because it didn't make me paranoid.

Jacky and Ian Paice were staying at this wonderful hotel called Il Pelicano in Portofino, in Italy. When I first hooked up with the twins, we'd found this hotel and it had become our place. Vicky went over with Jacky and Ian, and I said I'd show up in a few days. But I got there early, because speed makes me work fast. Remember, an addict doesn't have to do it every day: he can do it every other month and he's still an addict. My album, *Play Me Out*, is a very erratic, vocal-filled album that people love, but it was made by a speed freak. I was completely out of my mind.

I'd been up for five days and I flew to Rome, where I had a cab take me the 110 miles to Portofino. I was sweating and ragged and just fucking tightened up. Now, this is the turning-point: the first person I see there is Jon Lord. I said, "Hey, what are you doing here?" and then, right behind him, I saw Vicky. And there's Jacky, and Ian, and the twins' parents and John Coletta, one of Purple's managers.

Now, I remember Lordy saying one morning in 1975, when we were getting loaded, "I really fancy Vicky," or some suggestion of that kind. Being a young man at the start of my addiction, I didn't pay any attention to it. I didn't think anything of it, but it rang in my ears later on. Lo and behold, when I saw Lordy standing there at the hotel, a light went on in my head.

Now, Vicky and I have talked about what happened next. I must have got very brazen, and I must have got uppity, and also I was coming off speed and my feelings were running ragged. I was very angry and the next morning, after Vicky and I had slept in the same room, we had a huge argument. I was completely out of my mind, remember. She then ran out of the hotel room. I was dressed in nothing but my watch, and I ran out of that room after her, with my tennis racket – I'd been playing a lot of tennis lately – around my privates. The story is that she was frightened that I was going to belt her with the racket. Well, I was actually running with a racket over me to stop my bits from falling out. I was not, repeat not, going to hit her, but I think Lordy heard something later to the effect that I was going to injure her. You can't really blame the girl.

I never really asked her what Jon was doing there, I was just angry. She did the right thing by leaving the room. Her father Frank Gibbs, who was a big guy, came in and gave me a bollocking, and it was the right thing, because I was out of line. I was fucked up. So I put my clothes on and someone came running into my room, saying, "She's gone to the airport!" I thought, "What am I gonna do?" So I pack my bags, go to the airport and get on the plane that I think she's on – and she isn't. She's actually still at the hotel.

The fact of the matter is, Vicky was living with an addict, and she may have thought that living with Jon Lord was a better solution. In the long term, it's worked out better for her, of course: they've been married for decades. Looking back all those years ago, they may have started their relationship while she was still with me, but that's their business. I was extremely hurt by the fact that they were officially together a few weeks later. I put two and two together and thought that they must have been together when we were at the hotel. The thought of them making love turned my stomach.

I almost damn near killed myself over this. You want to talk about a coke-fuelled storm coming? When I got off the plane, Willy Fyffe – one of Purple's techs, who became an assistant – met me off the plane. Vicky had been my girlfriend for three years, so I said to Willy, "We've got to go to a dealer." Poor old Willy: he wasn't an addict, he lived with his mother, and here I am buying a quarter-ounce of coke and crying, because cocaine can be a massive depressant, like any drug if you're in the wrong frame of mind. So here I am now, in a complete blizzard of coke: Willy is just listening to me babble in his home. I was hoovering it up. I must have gone into some sort of blackout.

In the summer I continued to work on the album. I hadn't written the lyrics for the songs yet, so I started to write about Vicky. Wow – listen to the album again! If you listen to 'It's About Time', it says "Come back to me," for Christ's sake … and if you listen to 'Destiny' the lyric is so sad. You can actually hear me crying at the beginning of the song. And laughing, too. I wasn't on this planet: I was not a human being any more.

Play Me Out was written and recorded over a ten-day period without any sleep. I never slept once in that time. I took ten days in the studio to do the basic tracks, vocals, and backing vocals. The strings were done later on, when I was in LA. The album was mixed at Island, and I was there for that.

A lot of people regard it as Glenn's genius record. Was Brian Wilson not high when he recorded *Smile*? He was probably loaded.

Were Lennon and McCartney loaded during *Sgt. Pepper*? Yes they were. I was out of it, but vocally there are some superhuman things on *Play Me Out* that could never be done again. The title meant "You'll have to wear this boy out, because I am unstoppable." Tommy hadn't passed away yet and I was in my mid-twenties, with a lion's mane. I was a guy who could do anything: I thought I was unbreakable and invincible. We all thought – Rob Cooksey and Dave Holland and Mel Galley – that *Play Me Out* was going to be a massive thing for me and that I would go on to great solo success after it, but my disease had other plans, you know?

Ian Paice married Jacky Gibbs in the spring – and his mother died during the reception at Oakley House. It was devastating. I felt so bad for Ian. The reception went on: I wasn't loaded on coke that day, but we'd all been pretty much drinking. He must have been completely freaked; I don't know how he got through it. David was talking to me at the reception about making a solo album.

David Coverdale *I remember flying over for Ian Paice's wedding and Glenn coming up to me saying he'd seen the error of his ways, or whatever, and he couldn't wait to start working together again. He had no idea I'd left Purple. Nobody had bothered to tell him. I think it was very difficult for him at that time to realise the Purple party was over.*

David Bowie was playing a series of seven nights at Wembley at the time, and he invited me to come down. He was staying at a place that I'd been to many times before, a place in Maida Vale that movie studios hire out to actors. I hung out with his wife Angie and went to see Iggy Pop, who I call Jimmy. I was out of my mind. I puked on myself, and David gave me a pair of pants which he'd bought from

Harvey Nicholls. If you do a lot of coke, you'll OD on it and throw it up. There was quite a lot of that with me, and it's never attractive.

So David kitted me out in some clothes that he'd got for me. It wasn't great for me at this point. Bowie thought it would be great for me to get back with Trapeze, I'd turned him on to that band and he loved that funky stuff. As it happened, Tony Perry had booked a Trapeze reunion tour for the USA: I'd finished *Play Me Out* but I was fucking around with it in the studio, as you do on speed, until around mid August. I tried to get Tony to cancel the tour because I wanted to micromanage the album some more, but of course Tony didn't listen to me.

Play Me Out was written and recorded on speed. I didn't sleep for about ten days. I saw a nurse walking through the studio with a poodle, and I had a conversation with her, but she wasn't there. I stopped the tape and said, "There's a girl coming in." Speed made my teeth and gums hurt and I couldn't get an erection. When I did drugs, unless I was in the Embassy Club in London or somewhere, I only did drugs in my hotel or in my home. And one thing I never did was pay for a whore. I'm funny about body parts and where they've been. I don't know – I come from that upbringing. I know a lot of successful men, very close friends of mine, who only fuck whores, because you pay them to go away. I can't do it. I did once hire an escort service to bring some girls over at a party, but nothing happened.

The first Trapeze date was August 18 1976 in St Louis, and then we did the 20th and the 21st in Austin. I was very thin and very sick. I cut my hair – in fact, Bowie cut my hair for me, he convinced me that it should be shorter. It was a cool cut, I thought: Tommy used to go on at me to "cut my fuckin' bangs" because he hated them.

Now, this is terrible. Terry Rowley, who was my front-of-house guy and played some keyboards on some of the songs, was the greatest multi-instrumentalist from the Midlands that I'd ever known – he was like Roy Wood. I adored Terry and looked up to him, because he was very talented and witty. So he's on the plane with me and Andy Field, my assistant, and we go from Heathrow to Chicago St Louis, and in my ego – and because I was coming down off the speed – I wanted to get off the plane for a sandwich. We were getting a connection, maybe between Kansas City and St Louis, and I got off the plane and it left without me. On the plane was the master tape of *Play Me Out*. So me and Andy were getting a sandwich in the deli in the airport, and thank God Terry Rowley was on the plane with the tape. He was looking after it, thinking, "Fucking wanker!" because he also had my bag, which didn't have any drugs in it but it might have had some paraphernalia.

So I get to St Louis and the coke demon raises its head. I had a nervous night, waiting for some coke to show up. I also called Tommy Bolin up when I got to St Louis. Suddenly he said, "Hey, I want you to meet somebody!" and handed the phone to an actress called Linda Blair.

Now, I was a huge *Exorcist* fan, and Linda had just started working on *The Exorcist II* with Richard Burton. Since Vicky and I had split up two months before, I hadn't had a relationship with a woman, because I'd been too loaded. Linda was 17 years old at the time and she sounded great. She says, "I'm on the way to New York to shoot the movie. Can I stop off in St Louis on the way and see your show?" So I said yes, and put the phone down.

The next morning, the coke arrives and I get loaded. The next thing I know, Linda is knocking on my hotel room door. She's got a suitcase and a saddle with her: I thought, "Hello, this is interesting." She was, and still is, a massive horsewoman.

After the show, we made love and it was great. Yes, just like that: when you're with a girl and you're on cocaine, pretty much all the inhibitions go out the window.

Linda was a rock chick back then; she'd been dating Rick Springfield. I didn't look at Linda as a major movie star, although back then she was. The next day we flew to Austin for two shows. The first show was on my birthday, and the next day she had to fly to New York to begin filming.

The opening act at those two shows was The Runaways. I ended up shagging the drummer, Sandy West, who was a lesbian. She passed away in 2006, bless her heart. Lita Ford is a really good friend of mine now, but back then she and Sandy wanted to party with me. I actually went off with Lita first and then I went off with Sandy. Wow … it was fucking crazy.

Tony Perry *While the appeal of having Glenn back was obvious, it was also risky as we didn't want to lose any of the momentum that was building up with the four-piece. Meetings were arranged with Glenn, without Glenn, with Deep Purple's management, and with the different members of Trapeze. Eventually, we decided to revert back to the three-piece Trapeze. It was also agreed that the band would be advertised and promoted as "Trapeze – Galley, Hughes, Holland" so that there would be no ambiguities for fans or promoters. A tour was booked in the States through Thames Talent Limited, Deep Purple's New York agency, to run from August 19 through to September 12 1976. The first show was at the Keil Auditorium in St Louis, with the band moving on to Austin for two nights and then to the Electric Ballroom in Atlanta for three shows. During part of the tour, Glenn was accompanied by Linda Blair: I found Linda easy to get along with and we had several discussions regarding Glenn's wellbeing.*

So Linda's now in New York. I called her and said, "I've got four days off, I'm going to leave the band in Austin and come up to see you." There was a reasonably tight budget, but money was no object to me – I'd just fly off and do whatever I wanted. A fan, Lynn Everett, bought me a cowboy hat for my birthday.

Lynn Everett *I first met Glenn in Austin at a club called Mother Earth. He was on tour with Trapeze and playing all over Texas. After the show we had a party at the owner's house – it was a wild one. We had grocery bags full of pot, and I had taken some orange sunshine LSD. Glenn is the most beautiful person in the world when he's normal, whatever that is. He just can't do certain things, because they're poison for him: they make him crazy and paranoid beyond anything I have ever seen. He doesn't get violent, but it can be scary when the ghosts start coming out of the closet, from under the bed and anywhere else his mind can take him.*

I wouldn't travel with the rest of Trapeze: I had to travel in a white limo that we called the Snowbird. I wanted my own car. The coke had taken over and I'd become the fiend of all fiends.

This was a low point for me: acting inappropriately to my friends Mel, Dave, Tony, and Andy Attwood, my long-term friend and tech. My right-hand man, all through my career, was Andy – he would have taken a bullet for me. He drove me, carried me, and wheeled me through all sorts of wild adventures. He always told it like it is: so blatant and frank in his manner. I don't think I ever had such a loyal friend: most people who've met me would have gone through Toothy, as we called him.

Tony Perry *Even in the early days of the tour, it became obvious to all concerned that Glenn had a problem. But having had my discussion with*

Linda I felt that we could control the situation. I explained to both Glenn and Linda that I would not be giving him any cash until the tour was completed and only then would he be paid his due share of any monies. In other words, I was making it quite clear that the band were not going to fund the purchasing of any drugs while the tour was ongoing. Any goods, or food and drink, that he required when staying at a hotel could be charged to the room. Any monies required for drugs were down to him.

This arrangement only worked for a few days. Members of the road crew were informing me that Glenn was threatening to sell his guitar or equipment to raise money or simply to exchange them for drugs. I was being approached and even woken up in the middle of the night by strangers who claimed that I owed them money for substances that they had supplied to Glenn. This happened on several occasions but I stood my ground and informed all of them that if they had supplied anything to Glenn then it was he, and he alone, that they should approach for payment. The situation quickly deteriorated, especially when Linda left us because of work commitments. In fact after we had changed hotels in Atlanta on at least two occasions due to Glenn's unpredictable behaviour, Mel, Dave, and I discussed the possibility of completing the tour without him and pulling in another bass player. As I pointed out, this was an extremely awkward situation as all of the gigs had been advertised using Glenn's name.

We soldiered on. Things went from bad to worse, with Glenn standing on tables in restaurants asking customers if they knew who he was, refusing to board flights unless he was seated in first class – which, incidentally, was always refused – and constantly causing very embarrassing situations where he always became the centre of attention. He demanded his own dressing room, and as the final three gigs were all in Texas I arranged with the promoter for Glenn to have his own limousine, so that he could be driven to and from each concert, resulting in our spending as little time as possible in his company.

The band were seeing me for the first time as Mr Hyde: the textbook story of a guy that they'd known as Dr Jekyll since the late 60s. They'd seen me on speed during the recording of *Play Me Out*, which was OK, but once the coke came back I was a complete disaster. I was short-tempered with them. I locked myself away in my room with Linda Blair. Even Andy Field, my assistant, said, "I can't deal with this any more." I would tell the promoter that I'd need a coke dealer in the next town, and if they said the nearest coke dealer was 150 miles away I'd go there in my limo and pick it up myself. I was so loaded.

Now I'm in New York with Linda, and I go down to the set. There's a scene in *The Exorcist II* when she's at Penn Station with Richard Burton, and this was the set that I was on. I was in the green room and I think, "I gotta meet these fucking people." So I met Richard Burton, and I felt so bad later when I remembered how I'd met a major movie star when I was loaded. I was sweating badly, and talking about anything that came into my mind, knowing full well that I was loaded out of my gourd, and that I shouldn't have gone down there. It wasn't really appropriate.

I was also becoming a pain in the ass about cocaine. I have always been the sharingest motherfucker on coke, but for some reason – due to part of me not wanting to be on the tour, because I wanted to work some more on *Play Me Out* – I became a total asshole. I just wouldn't share my drugs.

The tour went on for a month, and the last gig was Fort Worth. We were filling a lot of places: in Houston, there were 10,000 people there. This is awful: I remember having lines of coke when I came off stage. We'd just sold out this venue and made a lot of money, and I put ten lines out in front of them and I did them all. This is so awful. The way I acted to my friends on the tour was inexcusable, and it took a long time for them to forgive me – and I didn't expect forgiveness at all, by the way.

At the end of it, I remember Tony Perry coming up to me with my passport. He threw it at me and said, "Now fuck off! I never want to see you again. You've fuckin' damn near taken five years off my life!" He was, and still is, a father figure to me, so when he said that, my world came falling down. I didn't even say goodbye to Mel and Dave when I left.

Tony Perry *It got to the point where the situation started to affect my own health. My hands and arms started to shake, and it steadily worsened on a daily basis. When I confronted him with my condition he actually gave me some tablets to relax me. I then found myself taking drugs prescribed for me by the same guy who was causing my problems! You couldn't make it up. Glenn finished up treating everyone involved in Trapeze with total contempt.*

Our final show was in Arlington, Dallas, on September 12 1976. When it was over I took his passport, which I'd kept in my briefcase for the previous four weeks, and threw it at him, telling him to stick it up his [arse]! As you can imagine, following this tour any communication between Glenn and anyone concerned with Trapeze was put on the back burner.

Linda had a home in Beverly Hills, where her mother also lived, and this is where the shit gets really crazy. I was alone in the house and doing cocaine when Linda's mother was in the next bedroom. I was buying ounces at a time; there were piles of it everywhere. I'd be as paranoid as hell, thinking that her mother was going to come in any second and see me snorting coke. I'm thinking to myself, "I'm 25 and there's a girl in there who's 17. I'm gonna get busted here. She's gonna call the cops and I'm gonna go to jail. And there goes my career." One day, her mother came into the bedroom and put her hand on my heart, saying, "Glenn, your heart's beating really fast." I think she knew what was going on, but she didn't pull the rug from under us.

Lynn Everett *The next time I saw Glenn was during the 1976 Trapeze tour. It was Glenn's birthday and so there was a party at the hotel after the show. A memorable happening was when a groupie walked in with nothing but a sheet wrapped around her, and someone stepped on the sheet. It came off and she was stark naked. Glenn and Linda were sitting on a couch and the girl walked over and stood in front of them for a second – and then proceeded to sit on Linda's lap.*

So now I'm thinking, "OK, I've got an album that's come out in Europe, I'm living in America and I still want to play music, what do I do?" So I put together another band. This is mad – I rented another apartment, and I flew band-members in, two guys in from Denver, a keyboard player and a Denver guy living in LA. And I flew a drummer in from Atlanta, Georgia, so there were three guys I had to fly in.

As we were rehearsing, in early February of 1978, I get a call from the producer Jeff Glixman, who'd made his claim to fame with Kansas. Listen to the Kansas song 'Carry On My Wayward Son'. Steve Walsh and Kerry Livgren told me that when they were writing the middle-eight, they said, "What would Trapeze do here?" They were mad Trapeze fans. Glixman had called me up on the back of that huge record.

So here we are, I'm now going to Atlanta into a studio of Jeff's choice: I can't remember the name, but it was a great studio. I didn't have any songs, because when you're on coke you don't really write songs. So it was welcome back to speed. It had worked on *Play Me Out,* so I figured we'd make some songs which were kind of *Play Me Out*-ish on speed. I was addicted to uppers. I had a little moment with Black Beauties too – black bombers from the 60s. All they are is meth in a capsule.

This is going to be horrible, but fuck it. You remember that I'd slept with Tommy's girlfriend Karen Ulibarri in 1975? Well, she and Tommy split up, and three months later she moved into Linda Blair's home and we struck up a relationship. We were very attracted to one another. It was at that time that Karen discussed that we were going to do a moonlight flit and run. I was falling for Karen, even though she was not a drug user at all.

So I left Linda in the middle of the night. I just got up and left, and never said why. Horrible. I wasn't a man – I wasn't big enough to take the response and the consequences. It was like, shall I tell her that I'm leaving with her room-mate? She hasn't really spoken about me on the record, although there have been books that mentioned a disastrous affair which she had on the set – and that was me. I'd like to make amends to her for this.

I knew that if I ran away with Karen I'd have no-one to do drugs with, because this time I'd backed away from the blow a little. So we moved in with Mark and Patty Stein – the ex-Vanilla Fudge keyboard player and singer, an amazing talent – who was in Tommy Bolin's band. They lived in Reseda. We had our own little bedroom and bathroom, and that's where we started our relationship as boyfriend and girlfriend. We told my parents that we were going to move to England to live in my house in Penkridge. At this point I had zero career plans, except to finish *Play Me Out.* It needed horns and strings on it. I was waiting for the big solo career to come along, and we thought it was going to happen.

CHAPTER 8

LOSING MY WAY

TOMMY, KAREN, AND GARY MOORE

On December 4 1976 I got the call that Tommy had died of a drug overdose. My whole world stood still. Karen was told next. Tommy had sent us a postcard the day before he died, saying that he'd see us at Christmas or the New Year in LA.

I don't have any brothers and sisters and Tommy was the first man, apart from Mel Galley, to be my brother. He was a man who you fell in love with and wanted to hug and hold. He knew I was with Karen and he was totally fine with that. He told me to go take care of Karen, knowing that we were fond of each other. Tommy gave me the green light – not in a sexual way, but as a brother – to take care of her, never knowing that in the end I would be taking care of her after his death.

Karen still loved him, you know. Tommy was the love of her life. It was the first proper funeral I'd ever been to and it was a real morbid affair in the middle of the winter in Iowa. You know that Catholics have open caskets? She passed out when she saw him, and I caught her. It was dreadful for the woman.

We flew to Denver the next day to spend Christmas with Karen's family, who I'd met the previous February when they came down to a Purple gig. So there I am, the new boyfriend, in the midst of the very big Latino family that Karen had. She was one of five children. They accepted me as a brother-in-law immediately: we'd realised that we were probably going to get married, and made plans for a wedding for the following July.

I went and got a ring from Karen's father, who was a big jeweller in Colorado, and proposed to Karen, I can't remember where. Her family lived in a suburb of Denver called Lakewood. I remember going up to a dealer's house with Karen once and getting completely loaded. He was also a chef: his signature dessert was a gram of coke on a plate for special celebrity guests. I had to go home to Karen's family, freaked out that they were going to find me out. On Christmas Eve I saved some of this blow, and her father was up late watching TV. In my cocaine psychosis I went out into the kitchen with a line, and I was going to offer it to him, but I knew that if I pulled the coke out he would have shot me. He was kind of crazy, so I'm glad I didn't do it.

There's a gross story I'm going to tell you now. The Ullibarri family had a pet dog named Thor. It was a Doberman in all its glory, about two years old, a great big fucking dog, nice and friendly. So we get back to the Ulibarris' residence at five o'clock in the morning after a coke-fuelled bachelor party. My best man Michael Castellano, who was Frank Sinatra's valet, is staying downstairs in the basement. So he's down there, and I'm going down with him, tip-toeing downstairs, and I go off and put my robe on. It's an antique robe that I'd got from some fan – a priceless thing. So I'm in this robe and I'm sitting on the edge of Castellano's bed, and I'm going in and out of consciousness as I'm coming off the coke. I thought, "I'll just break wind." But I shit myself! And it goes all the way up my back. So here I am, stoned out of my mind, thinking, "Shit, what am I going to do?" So I go in the garden – it's still dark – and I dig a hole, and I bury this fucking robe. I go in the shower and clean myself up, while Castellano is laughing his head off. Then I completely passed out, and I'm awakened by the dog barking loudly. It had fucking gone out, dug the robe up, and brought it in the kitchen, just as everybody – my parents and like ten other people – were having breakfast, and started shaking it about.

All the family were at the wedding, including Mom and Dad. I had make-up on, and the Bowie-cut hair. Looked good! Karen looked amazing, she had a 20-inch waist. She was absolutely stunning. I remember we had the party in the clubhouse at a friend's apartment. Of course, as soon as I'd cut the cake I was off to someone's apartment getting loaded – I never went to the reception. I was fully loaded, out of my mind. The drugs were calling. There was two or three hours of the wedding where I should have been there, but I was in some bathroom hoovering up drugs. Mom and Dad knew what I was doing, because they were privy to my drug addiction.

Oh God, this is awful.

Sheila Hughes *We never went to America until Glenn married Karen. It was the first time we'd ever been abroad. We stayed with her family, who made us very welcome – but then Glenn had one or two crazy times. He told us to go back home: there was going to be no wedding, and so on. We were in a strange country with people we didn't know, but fortunately they were very kind to us.*

Bill Hughes *Glenn's best man at his wedding was a valet of Frank Sinatra's, and we went to see him play in Hollywood. Glenn went out afterwards and met Frank. We didn't know – he never talked about it. I'd have had it blazoned on my back, you know – "I've met Frank Sinatra!" He even gave me one of Sinatra's personal shirts.*

Lynn Everett *Next time I saw Glenn was at his wedding to Karen in Denver.*

The guy whose house we were at left for a few minutes, came back, put a V8 juice can on the table and removed the top. It was filled to the brim with coke. We went to another house and some strippers came over. I remember Glenn being in the hot tub with them most of the night.

I finally come down, shagged out, in the morning, and now we're on our way to LA before we go to the Caribbean on honeymoon. I'd booked it and it was paid for. But my disease said to me in LA, "Fuck you, you ain't going nowhere: we're going to spend another two weeks at the Beverly Hilton." Poor Karen is thinking, "What have I got myself into?"

I used the excuse that we needed to stay in LA to organise Tommy Bolin's benefit at the Roxy in September. The Caribbean coincided with the time that I thought Tommy Bolin's benefit should be done, so I quickly put Tommy's benefit on the front burner in LA, and squashed the honeymoon.

In 1977 I gave up my house in Beverly Hills. After two years, I wanted to come back to England: I just thought it was necessary to come back after Tommy had died. When you're a drug addict, though, your disease follows you. You take it with you. But I thought, "I'll go back to the UK, settle down in the village of Penkridge, miles from anywhere, and just escape it for a while." But you can't do that, because you start calling a dealer from London to come up on the train and you put him in a hotel overnight.

Sheila Hughes *He'd bought a house in Penkridge, the village near to us, and him and Karen went to live there. Then he'd come ranting up to us about what he was going to do, and what he wasn't going to do, and he'd be in his car and he'd worry us sick. Karen would come with him and she'd just sit back* *and let it go off, because she couldn't control him. He was always going to go back to Vicky's, because they were talking about him and making him small and what have you. Every night when this happened, I was begging him to please not get in the car and to please not go down there, and they'd end up sleeping at our house, night after night. Glenn told me at the time that it was caused by the diet pills he was on, which I know he was, but perhaps I was burying my head in the sand a bit. His grandmother was living with us at the time, and she'd go up to bed, fortunately – we didn't want her to see this side of Glenn. This went on for quite a while. We thought a lot of Karen, and we thought they were happy – but of course you can't be happy in a situation like that. There's no chance.*

Play Me Out was finally released in 1977. Geoff Barton did a wonderful review and Pete Makowski did a great review. It was an album that was looked upon by Purple fanatics as "What the hell's this?" It took a long time to understand *Play Me Out* because it was a deep record. I don't know how many copies it's sold, I just know I get royalties every year. It's been re-released four or five times, and it'll be done again, of course – I'll put another couple of bonus tracks on it and we'll do it again. I was very proud of it amid the drug-fuelled haze.

Ozzy Osbourne told me around this time that he wanted to form a band called the Blizzard Of Ozz, with me on bass. And I declined, simply because I wasn't going to be in a band where I couldn't sing. Ozzy wasn't the kind of guy who you could split the vocals with. I loved him and we got along really well, even though I wasn't really playing his kind of music.

By December of 1977, I had changed my mind again about where I wanted to live. I made the decision with Karen that I'd sell the Rolls-Royce I was driving at the time, put my house in England on the market and move. On January 1 1978 we rented a place in Encino in the San Fernando Valley in LA. I came close to making some music with the producer Jeff Glixman, who was a huge Trapeze fan, but it didn't happen – and by the summer of 1978 Karen and I wanted to buy a property in LA, because we'd had enough of renting.

My cocaine psychosis was in full swing by now. Whereas most people got high and then stopped, I just continued to get high. I was paranoid and I was a lot of work for people. People were worried about my health. I used to look around inside the house – in the closet, under the bed. What kind of happiness is that? And I didn't tell myself that these were hallucinations, because to me the Nazis, the cops and the goblins were there. Right there. Under the bed.

I was a terrible husband. Sometimes, before I got in the Jag and left the house, I'd tell Karen I was going to get some milk or something – and I'd be gone for a week, leaving her all alone, because she wasn't working at the time.

I didn't love anybody until I met my second wife Gabi. My disease made it impossible to let anybody love me, because I didn't love myself. I was not a good husband to Karen. All I did was more and more blow, with the occasional bit of speed. All I wanted to do was go up and up and up. Higher and fucking higher, until I'd freeze up.

I didn't go back to England until 1984. I was ashamed, not because my music had failed, but because I was an addict – and everybody knew about my addiction because it was all over the press. All over it. Wild stories about Glenn Hughes fucking naked on the roof, this kind of thing. I wasn't doing any press, I was out of the loop – and I enjoyed it. Press and music was getting in the way of my addiction.

I used to commandeer people's homes: I'd find a grand piano and hold people there so I could play and sing. I'd call it the "Glenn death grip". When I got high I used to play and sing at anybody's house, anywhere – it was awful. I found it very difficult to talk on blow: I could sing anything to you perfectly, note for note, but I couldn't talk. It was bizarre, and it used to freak people out.

I bought a nice house in Northridge, California, and a cat called Pocket. Karen and I were trying to have a baby, but it wasn't happening. I got a call from Dave Holland, who had now joined a band called Judas Priest. I became good friends with Priest, and I once invited them to my home for a barbecue. I didn't realise that Rob Halford was gay until that day, because he brought his then-boyfriend to my house. Everything was cool. I have a lot of gay friends in my life and I cherish my friendship with Rob. Everyone was drinking and using: we were fucking loaded that night. Rob brought me a studded leather G-string! I didn't put it on, though. He also brought me a gay porno magazine, which was frighteningly wicked. I held on to the G-string for quite a few years.

Rob Halford *Glenn and I have had some roaring nights together, I can tell you. We would just get fucking rat-faced together, on everything. Some of us have been there and some of us have figured our addictions out; some of us have made amends and understand it. I love Glenn to death, I think he's got one of the most amazing voices in the business, no doubt. He's got great character and charisma and style.*

On December 8 1980, we saw what had happened to John Lennon on the TV. He was about to go into the studio at the time. He was an ambassador for peace and he didn't feel comfortable with bodyguards. You don't really get bothered by normal people on the streets of New York and Los Angeles: you do by paparazzi, though. So

Lennon was doing his thing, coming back from the studio, and there's this fucking wacko who wants to make a name for himself by shooting the guy who wrote the greatest pro-peace song of all time, 'Imagine'. John Lennon was one of the most amazing songwriters ever, and he was taken far too early. Alarm bells went up around a lot of artists that day: my old friend David Bowie had a security team around him the next moment, because there are people out there. I was threatened by a guy with a gun in El Paso once, and I had death threats in Beverly Hills back in 1975. It's not fun when that shit happens to you. I've had stalkers and I still do have them. They travel, and they show up, and as a result I travel with people who take care of me. I like to meet people and keep myself accessible, but some people are kind of strange. I think every artist has that problem.

The music was always calling me. I want you to know, all through this book, that this maternal, mother-earth soul of mine kept saying, "You've gotta go back to the music." So in 1980 I went off to see Pat Travers play. The opening act was a young band called Def Leppard – I remember that clearly. They were just kids and no-one knew who they were, but I knew they were going to be huge. On stage with Pat Travers was Pat Thrall on guitar, although I didn't know who he was at the time. I saw Pat and I said, "Fucking hell – that's the new Tommy Bolin. That's it! He's the new guy for me." After the gig I said to him, "Someday we have got to play together," because he was James Brown, Hendrix, and Prince rolled into one. He's a genius: my counterpart. And he was a big fan of Trapeze, so he said, "I'd love to do something one day."

Pat Thrall *I first became aware of Glenn when Purple did the Cal-Jam festival in 1974. I saw it on TV, and I noticed that this guy with all the hair*

*and the white suit was singing alongside David Coverdale. So jump forward
a few years and I was playing with Pat Travers, who showed me the* Play Me
Out *album, which I was so impressed with. I thought to myself, "At some point,
I have to do a record with this guy."*

Four or five months later, Pat Thrall left Travers and called me up
immediately, saying he was in San Francisco. I invited him to stay at
my house. He stayed there for a month, and we started to write songs,
which was the beginning of Hughes/Thrall. His personality was so
strong that I said, "We've gotta split this band into two." No disrespect
to the drummer, but the band was about the two of us.

I was also a massive fan of Gary Moore. 'Parisienne Walkways' had
been released and it spoke to me, melodically. If you listen to Gary in
any persona, whether he's recording in the studio or sitting on a
couch, he's so ferocious. He's got great feel, and his choices of notes
are astounding.

So I met Gary Moore in 1980. I might have met him at the
Rainbow with Scott Gorham, because he was on tour with Thin Lizzy
at the time. Anyway, he was a fan of Trapeze and I met him again with
Phil Lynott, so we went back to my house in Beverly Hills and he
drank while Phil and I got loaded. Then I invited Gary and his
girlfriend Lisa over to my house, and he had a couple of drinks and
said, "Y'know, I'm thinking about leaving Lizzy," so I said, "Great!
We'll form a band." And he said, "Actually I'm thinking of leaving
Lizzy tonight." And I said, "But you haven't finished the tour," and he
said, "Yeah, but I'm gonna do a runner. Can I stay at your house?" So
I said, "Er … I'm all for forming a band with you, but what about
Phil?" And he said, "Yeah, I was thinking about not telling Phil and
just staying here."

Now Thin Lizzy were touring America, and they were getting quite big. They'd been in the charts, and all of a sudden Gary leaves! So I get a call after he's been at my house for three days, and it's Phil, who says, "If you're fockin' hidin' him, I'm gonna rip your throat out." Now, if you knew Phil, you knew that Phil was not a guy to be messed with, and as he said those words I could feel my throat twitching. I had the utmost respect for Phil as a man, a musician, and a poet: he was a one-off, and he was really great to me and really kind, and I had to lie to him because I had Gary there – and I wouldn't fuck with Gary either, because he was another fucking hard-case. So I said, "You know, Phil, I haven't seen him."

So Gary and I formed a band under the banner of a Gary Moore solo project, which he wanted to call G-Force. The percussionist from *Play Me Out*, Mark Nauseef, was brought in to play drums: he was Britt Ekland's boyfriend at the time. We signed to Jet Records, Don Arden's label, who also had ELO. So we go out to Don's house, where Sharon Osbourne was living, and Don was going to manage us. But Sharon took over, and she's now organising equipment and daily sheets for us. She works really hard and we spent a lot of time up there. Like her father, Sharon was a no-nonsense businessperson. Pre-Ozzy, she was all about fun. We were buddies, really good friends. I drove her home one time and she had her ankles round my neck while I was driving the car. She was sticking her toes up my nose – she was a wild woman.

We all spent a lot of time at Don's house: Karen and I, Gary and his girlfriend Lisa, and Mark and Britt Ekland. Don was gone most of the time on business, but Sharon was there and we'd hang out, talking about how we were going to save the world. I kept the cocaine to a minimum at this time, because Gary was very against it.

There's going to be two sides to the Gary Moore story here. On the one hand, I admired him because he didn't need drugs. He was the first rock musician I knew who said, "I don't fuckin' need cocaine, it's shit." I thought, "Jesus – he can actually do it with a couple of drinks. Maybe I should try that." Gary didn't tell me not to do it until 1984, when I was properly high around him. He had great skill as a writer and a musician, and working with him was a learning curve for me, because he had a great work ethic and we rehearsed a lot.

I was 29 in August 1980, so Sharon held a party for me at Le Dôme on Sunset Strip, which was one of the famous hangouts that she and Ozzy used back in the late 70s and early 80s. They could see that I was getting a little bit high. Mark never did drugs and Sharon and Gary were anti-drugs. I was overweight and I wasn't taking care of myself, and I wasn't a professional. When I did coke, I did it for days and drank a lot of light beer – cases of it, which gave me a paunch – and because I was so undernourished after that time, when I came out of the coke binge I would crave two things: sugar and fat. I could eat a pound of Dairy Milk chocolate in a sitting, no problem. And I could have fish and chips, and then a curry, and then another bar of chocolate.

That came from the addictive part of me: because I was so sick, I didn't look at myself in a physical way. I didn't think, "I'm gonna go and fuck this chick" because I didn't find myself desirable in any way, spiritually, mentally or physically. When I was in my disease, I basically became obese and undesirable, and I didn't like the fact that I was getting fat, but I couldn't stop binge-eating after the drugs. I'm a completely different person physically these days, but back then they wanted me to switch from beer to wine, or something a little healthier. Sharon was always pushing for that and watching over me with an eagle eye.

I think Sharon and Gary had a conversation about the fact that I was becoming a little bit too much work. It wasn't that I was untalented, or that I wasn't a great singer or bass player, but I wasn't firing on all cylinders. So on my birthday, I wasn't coked up but I was drunk, and somehow I slipped and fell into the cake trolley. I dislocated my shoulder, which really, *really* hurt. I handed in my notice that night, because I was angry that they were laughing at me. Sharon thought it was hilarious, and said, "You've got to see the funny side of this!" but I was pissed off, and I said, "I'm leaving the band."

The next morning I got up and went to find out what time we were rehearsing, and she said, "Well, you left the band. It's over." And Michael Lipman, the attorney, called and confirmed it. I said I didn't mean it, but they said, "It's over – don't come back." Gary was really upset, but we talked about it later and he forgave me.

CHAPTER 9

THE DOWNWARD SPIRAL

HUGHES/THRALL, GARY MOORE (REPRISE), AND CRACK

This just got worse and worse. Judas Priest kept coming into town and each time they were getting bigger and bigger. I remember in August 1981, when Hughes/Thrall were rehearsing, Priest played Long Beach for the first time. I was there, as I always was, because these were my friends, and they were getting more and more popular, and I was getting more and more addicted to coke. Rob and I would hang out after the show and we'd sing and scream at each other for an hour. People would see this and go "hmm!" and a reputation was starting to grow that I'd become a coke fiend.

Of course, I'd had a reputation in Deep Purple, but in the early 80s it got really bad, because I started to go out in public when I was loaded. It had been a secret for quite a while, but my disease had its way with me, and said that we'd take Mr Hyde out in public. I was full of shame. It was almost like the Fuck-It Flag went up; like I said, "Fuck it, this isn't a secret." And I used to drive to these places, so I always used to have to leave my car and get a cab home, because I could never drive. And the fact of the matter was, I now knew that people were talking behind my back. I had this twitch, see, which some people thought was hilarious, and others thought was dangerous, and others thought was sad. I thought it was all of those. I was full of shame and fear about what people would think, but I was so loaded I couldn't stop.

Every time Priest came into town I'd get worse and worse: they'd come round every year and play Long Beach, and they'd stay at the Queen Mary and Rob and I would get completely out of it. I took him to a drug den one night. Each time, they saw a more fucked-up Glenn.

Meanwhile, Hughes/Thrall auditioned over 100 drummers, because we're mental about drummers: Pat and I are horrible together, because we want what we want. We wanted a guy who had some chops, and my whole thing was groove – so we had to find the right guy. Richie Hayward of Little Feat was amazing and he would have got the job, but he'd broken his leg the year before and wasn't up to playing a lot. Frankie Banali, who I loved dearly, got the gig, although he was already in Quiet Riot at the time.

We started doing a lot of rehearsals. Karen would go away and Pat and his girlfriend Garnette would come over. I'd order a week's worth of coke. I never drove anywhere to get drugs, I always had people deliver them. Those two would be holed up in the TV room, and I'd be in my music room – and I wouldn't even see them. People would be coming and going, and I'd be writing all the Hughes/Thrall songs so that Pat could finish them. It was fucking mental.

Pat and I are complete opposites: I'm very spontaneous, and Pat is very, very methodical. While we were recording the album, he'd be in his bedroom doing eight-track demos, going over every last detail. It really infuriated me, because I would want his time. We were a great team together, and like all great partnerships – Jagger and Richards, or whoever – it's going to be the different personalities that make it great. At the end of the day it was amazing, and it would have continued to be amazing if the drugs hadn't got in the way.

We got a deal from Atlantic and started making an album. We also had an offer from a new label called Boulevard Records, a subsidiary of Epic, which we accepted. Everything on that album I recorded was on blow. The recording budget for the album was massive: the final bill at the end of it was fucking huge. It was about $250,000. We got paid a huge amount for that album, but a lot of it went on coke and a lot of it went on studio time. The producer Andy Johns was a six-foot-six English guy, hands like shovels, cowboy hat, sometimes with a gun in a holster – and he would fucking fire it. At the end of the last session, he shot at point-blank range about two feet above my head: it was a .44 magnum, and I can still hear the ringing in my ears. He was a dear friend of mine, although when he drank or got high, he was a maniac. You wouldn't fuck with him, even though I never saw him hit anybody. He was massive. I would fall out with Pat over his methodical slowness, and he would call it getting everything right. And I would call it fucking slow again. Andy would be the mediator.

We went to do some promo in Japan, and we shot a promo clip for 'Muscle And Blood' and 'I Got Your Number'. It was all going great. We did a tour. Coke was everywhere. If you look at the video clip for 'I Got Your Number', you can see me do a little twitch. What's more, Karen was now running a shop that we owned on Melrose Avenue, having studied fashion, so she now had a career and was out of the house a lot – so I was out of my mind.

I started to hang out with a couple of different coke dealers. There was a Mexican guy who was a really big dealer. And there was a friend of some rock'n'roll friends of mine, and he would ship out coke to a couple of guys in Def Leppard. I met him with Lita Ford, when I went to see AC/DC at the Forum in LA. They're one of the greatest rock bands, because they have a unique vibe and sound and I really do like the way they write music. It was pure rock to me: I don't particularly like heavy metal. It was meaningful to me. I met this cat who took me into his limo and gave me a few bumps. He gave me an eight-ball, which is an eighth of an ounce or three-and-a-half grams of coke. Remember, a lot of people give you drugs when you're a celebrity, so he invited me down to his home in Huntingdon Beach. I found out that this cat had come across a kilo of coke somehow, that he'd found through a drug raid or whatever. He was actually a drummer who had come across this kilo, and he'd keep it in storage and go and get some. So I spent most of my time that summer down in Huntingdon Beach with him, while Karen was off working at the store on Melrose. There were a bunch of birds and beach guys hanging out down there.

This is where my infidelity to Karen started. Gary Moore had dated a girl called Marisa Roebuck: a model, 19 or 20 years old, absolutely drop-dead gorgeous. After G-Force broke up, I'm at the Rainbow one night and I run into Marisa. She's alone, although she's with some guy. I'd never cheated on Karen before – but man, as sometimes happens in life, you run into a girl ... so I started to call her, and lo and behold, when Karen went away on one of her trips, I took Marisa out and we started becoming super-friendly. I went to Japan to meet her and that was the start of an affair with her.

When I got back from Tokyo, the Hughes/Thrall tour pretty much started. I flew Marisa out sometimes. She was an extremely intelligent girl, very funny, and absolutely gorgeous to look at. But she was tough: she wouldn't take any bullshit – later in her career she was in the American *Gladiators*, with the stage name Lace. I moved in with her in Hollywood for a couple of weeks, but then we just parted. She was a very independent girl, and we liked each other a lot, although we didn't love each other.

When Marisa basically asked me to leave her apartment – not nastily, I wasn't high or anything – I went back to mine, and Karen's not home and the doors were all locked, so I kicked the door open to the garage and I walked in. I noticed in one of the bathrooms that there was a pair of bloke's shoes, and some fucking underpants. I walk into my bedroom and there's a fucking guy in my bed! My wife was down at the shop on Melrose, doing her thing, and I've got a dozen roses with me for her … and it's Preston fucking Thrall, Pat's brother! He's sleeping it off, because he's drunk. I see him, and I beat the ever-loving shit out of him with the roses. He actually goes out to the garden and starts puking, partly because he was hung over but also because he was freaked out. When I was loaded, I had a massive temper. He was naked, so I threw all his shit out of the window at him and told him to fuck off. When Karen comes home, I'm sleeping in the bed right where he was. Of course, things could never be the same after that, and although we stayed husband and wife, there wasn't a lot of sex happening. You wouldn't, would you?

It was unreasonable, given that I'd been unfaithful too, but when you're an addict you do unreasonable things. I was out of control: I'm not saying that I was the biggest cocaine addict of all time, but I'm saying that I was possessed by this drug. Pat Thrall knew about it, and it wasn't funny to him. He never really discussed this with me. I think he felt uncomfortable about it.

Pat Thrall *There was some tension, definitely, although I hadn't known that anything was going on. I was really angry with my brother – like, "Why would you do this? Of all the women in Los Angeles." As far as I know, though, it was just one night, and he felt really bad about it. The situation was very awkward. On the other hand, Glenn had it coming to him: he'd been cheating with Marisa and Cherie Currie. Marisa even flew to fucking Japan with us! I felt really bad for Karen that she was going through all this.*

One night I was at a dealer's place, and the dealer had a couple of buddies over there, one of whom was a friend of mine from San Francisco. They thought it would be funny to really mess with me, and they staged a thing in the house so it looked like it was being raided. They got their friends to come in. I was in mid-snort at the time and I damn near had a heart attack. To make it worse, he had this Uzi with a silencer, and he walked in the room as I was chopping a big one out, and fired this Uzi. It wasn't fired at me, but it was meant to scare the shit out of me. Now, when you fire a gun with a silencer, the bullets rage through the walls and outside, and that's exactly what happened – they went straight through my jacket on the barstool, through the bar, through the wall and outside. That was enough to make me think, "Hmm – how many lives do I have left now?" I found myself thinking like that a few different times.

Hughes/Thrall did have a second shot at making a record, because CBS wanted us to make a follow-up. Pat and I were not really at loggerheads over the fact that his brother was involved with my wife, but we weren't seeing eye to eye as friends. We were pretty much going in different musical directions: what mine was, I wasn't quite sure. I think I was going back into a more heavy funk, and he was going into a more electronic direction. The crux of the matter was that we were really getting too stoned. We did come up with three or four songs, but the album really wasn't as great as the first one.

Pat Thrall *The label wanted to give us another shot, but trying to get Glenn to rehearse was impossible. He'd stay for half an hour and then head to a club for the rest of the night. I think he was using rehearsal as an excuse to get out of the house, away from his wife. It was terrible. We were both depressed that the first album, which we'd put so much into, had been such a miserable failure.*

The drugs were really taking their toll now. I was bingeing on blow, with a few different dealers around town, and I was gaining weight again. I'd got some diet pills from the doctor, as people do in Beverly Hills, and maybe lost 20lb, but that wasn't quite enough. Of course, when I was in my disease, using drugs and drinking, after that comes the food – most people consume sugar and fat when they come off drugs. Basically I was unhappy, and it was spiralling out of control.

After Hughes/Thrall I started to hang out in Hollywood, at the Troubadour of all places. I remember on many occasions I hung out with Tommy Lee of Mötley Crüe (who once shagged his girlfriend in front of me when I was at his house) and David Lee Roth of Van Halen. He's a funny motherfucker. I'd met Eddie Van Halen when they were supporting Black Sabbath back in 1978: I'd been over to see Ozzy Osbourne in Texas on Thanksgiving and as soon as I arrived Eddie jumped on me – he was a massive Trapeze fan.

There was this piano at the side of the stage, and I'd be there, playing away, and these guys would come up one at a time and have a sing with me, and I think most of the record industry knew about my addiction at this point as well. But I just didn't give a fuck. I was so far into my disease that I couldn't even look myself in the mirror. I just knew something was extremely wrong. After Hughes/Thrall had failed, I went, "Fuck it! I'm just gonna go for it," you know?

Once, I took off on one of my five-day benders while Karen was stuck in my house with my parents, who were visiting. I let them down and I let my wife down. I had a fight with Karen and she went to the front of the house and started throwing out all the gifts that Mom and Dad had brought her. She took it out on them, not me – and Mom and Dad never spoke to her again. Well, they spoke to her, but they never went back to that house again. They didn't go back to LA until the 90s, because it was devastating for them to hear what their daughter-in-law was saying to them. They didn't deserve it. Mom cried all the way back to England. I forgave Karen for that, as you do when you become sober, but it was horrible. Look, I deserved that treatment for going on that bender, but my parents didn't deserve it, and I had to live with that for a while.

I had another affair, this time with Cherie Currie from The Runaways, who was in *The Twilight Zone*. I first met Cherie at a Hughes/Thrall rehearsal at SIR Studios in Hollywood in October 1982: my tech Tommy's wife was Cherie's personal assistant. I'd seen Cherie perform with The Runaways when they played with Trapeze in Austin, Texas, on August 21 1976, my 25th birthday – and when she walked into our rehearsal room, I couldn't wait to take a break and meet her. We were both in relationships with other partners, but they were both coming to an end. Cherie is one of the most beautiful women on the planet, and soon we were deep in conversation. When rehearsal ended, we went out to have dinner and drinks. The attraction was immediate: there was something about Cherie that fascinated me.

Cherie Currie *I met Glenn in the early 80s when he was in Hughes/Thrall. He was a bit heavier then he is now, and he was wearing a pink suit with musical notes on it. He was larger then life, I might say, but in a good way. Glenn took me to one of their shows and he was up there on stage just killing it, with this presence and a voice like I've never heard before – like he was born for it. He was a great-looking guy, but what got me was that he was so kind: not like the rockers I'd met that would act like they were 'all that'. Glenn was all that, but as down to earth as you could get. I was immediately taken by him. We really hit it off, went out for dinner and that was it for me. I really* *fell hard for Glenn. We really had some great times, very passionate and memorable times, but he and I both were on the road to making some major changes in our lives, so unfortunately, the romance didn't last long. It would be two decades before I saw him again and I would often think of him, because those times with Glenn were some of my fondest, even to this day.*

Cherie is the kind of girl who gets what she wants. She's a fucking sexy woman and volatile, in a good way. She's outspoken and she calls it as she sees it. I was back with Karen and it had only been two weeks since the bust-up, but I think we both knew it was over. We were just living in the same house.

Pat and I were rehearsing for two shows – one at the Hollywood Palladium, and the other in San Brandon at the Swing Auditorium. I asked Cherie if she'd like to join me for the second show. We drove up together, and on the way back, I found myself at her apartment in the Valley. Without wishing to embarrass Cherie, let me just say that it was the full-on fireworks, Fourth of July experience – something that had been missing from my life at that point. We started to see each other as much as possible: she was acting at the time and had just filmed *The Twilight Zone*. The year before she'd given an amazing performance as Annie in the movie *Foxes*.

I really cared deeply for Cherie: she was a very brave girl. She told me about two vile men, vicious predators and low-lifes, one of whom had kidnapped, raped, and almost killed her: how she escaped and survived is a miracle. This is documented in her book, *Neon Angel*.

An awful thing happened with Steve Lukather of Toto at this time: he got a taste of the insane Glenn Hughes. It was five o'clock in the morning at his house, and Cherie had gone to bed. She didn't want to see any more of me on drugs. I commandeered one of

Steve's vintage acoustic guitars for about an hour, but he wanted to show me a tune.

Cherie Currie *Whenever Glenn would partake of any kind of substance, all he wanted to do was pick up the guitar and sing. I'd try to talk to him, but he would get this look in his eye and he would just sing. One time we went over to Steve Lukather's house, since Steve and my twin sister were married at the time, and Steve would try to have a conversation with Glenn – but then, out would came the guitar and he would sing instead. He wouldn't converse or answer questions. I remember wanting to have a real heart-to-heart, so I hid the guitar and he didn't like that. But back then, if you didn't do drugs there was something wrong with you. You would hardly ever meet someone that didn't. It was par for the course. We thought that cocaine was non-addictive and that drinking and popping pills were the norm. That's just what we did, until the mid 80s when everyone cleaned up their act.*

Steve tried to get the guitar, but he couldn't get it off me – he just couldn't. It could be the world's finest instrument you've got … but you couldn't get it off me. You would have to surgically remove the bastard. I wouldn't give it up. So he's standing over me, trying to pull this fucking guitar off me – and eventually he got it, and smashed it on the floor. And he says, "Now play the fucking thing!" That was the end of the evening. I've made my amends to Steve since then, and we're still good mates.

The same thing happened, this time with Neal Schon of Journey, when Hughes/Thrall were playing San Francisco. Neal was driving me in his Porsche to the hotel, and the windows were all fogging up with my steam and perspiration, and I've got my left hand in a death-grip on him, and I'm playing this Casio keyboard of mine with my right.

And I don't want to get out of the car, because I haven't finished playing this song, even though we're at the hotel. So he gets a good ration of what it's like to sit next to this guy, who is a complete fucking commandeering fool on coke.

I loved Cherie, but once again I wasn't capable of loving myself. My disease had other plans for me: plans to sabotage my relationships with anyone. I've made my amends to Cherie: we were together at a time when the blow came first. We're great friends today, she is back making music and is an amazing chainsaw sculpture artist.

The drug dealers that I've mentioned were central to the next couple of years. I used to hang out with them at their homes, and they'd come to my home when Karen was away. She went away a lot – probably to escape from me.

Karen and I had a pretty healthy sex life, but my addiction wanted me to have a partner who did drugs – and when I was with Karen, my drug behaviour became erratic. Karen used to visit her family in Lakewood every three months, and that was nirvana for me, because I knew I could invite my mates over and we could go fucking mental. No birds, just coke.

At some point in early 1979, I tried crack. I'd heard about crack in 1975 – freebasing as it was called – from a guy in Newport Beach: he'd done it in front of me and I said, "What the fuck is that?" I'm not a smoker, so I couldn't ingest it and I passed.

One of them had a small apartment in Hollywood, right off of the 101 on Magnolia. He lived there with his wife. This guy pulled out some coke – he had a never-ending supply – and started to cook it up. He cooked it in vials on the stove in water. We stayed up, freebasing, for Friday and Saturday and into Sunday night, when he ran out of powdered cocaine.

For people who don't know, when you cook the cocaine it becomes purer, which is when it becomes a rock and you call it crack because when you shake the vial, the powder mixes with the water and the rock cracks against the side of the vial. So he's only got crack cocaine left. I'd never really done crack properly, so he walked me through what you have to do to get a hit of this shit. You have to hold it in your lungs for 10 seconds and blow it out.

The first time I took a hit and did it right, I was completely hooked. I saw heaven and hell. I saw everything that I needed in life. I saw my history; I saw my future; I saw everything. I felt that this was it; that this was the missing thing. This was the high of all highs. This was what it was all about. This was euphoric nirvana. This was … *my high*. This was the way it was supposed to be from this point on. But what I didn't realise with crack or freebasing is that you never get that high again. The second hit is not like the first hit. People chase that first hit for days on end, spending hundreds and thousands of dollars on this behaviour.

So here I am. It's a Sunday night and I'm getting into it. By Tuesday I'm a full-blown crack addict and I've been awake for five or six days. It was getting serious, you know? I remember going home, and my teeth were covered in the residue of all the stuff I'd been smoking. It came off, but I was hooked on this shit – and when you get *this* monkey on your back, he's a motherfucker!

Karen was really smart with the finances. I've always been really bad with money, and she hated giving me money to pay for drugs, but I had to have it. So she started giving me bits of money for this and that.

Los Angeles was rife with cocaine in the 80s: good cocaine, the real shit. I spent my time in 1983, '84, and early '85 with four particular drug dealers. I would get completely obliterated with them. After the aborted *Hughes/Thrall II*, with the three or four songs that Pat and I had written, CBS offered me an album deal – so I started to make demos. I had no idea where I was going musically, so I hired Dennis MacKay, who did Tommy Bolin's first album, *Teaser*. CBS hired him to produce some demos with me – and man, it was all over the place. The engineer at the session at the Record Plant was Jim Scott, who has worked with the Red Hot Chili Peppers. Last year, he presented me with a copy of that demo; I thought I'd got rid of it. He said, "I've got a copy in the vault." When I heard it, I thought it was shit. It was completely unfocused: you can hear the blow on the tape. Awful. I really wasn't interested in making music at the time: it was getting in the way of my snorting coke and smoking crack.

Listen to me now. I was more lost in this than you can imagine. I've never spoken about this in public. I've never even spoken about it to my brother David Coverdale. My friends took it for granted that I was loaded: they just never knew *how* loaded I was. Guns were being pulled, and shot; knives were being pulled. When you're around freebase cocaine, you'd better put your safety-belt on. One dealer I knew would wear a green beret hat and a Navy Seal uniform and walk the neighbourhood at night thinking that he was being watched. He thought that another drug gang was coming to kill him. He had a series of guns – Uzis, 45s, magazine guns – and he had me, the Limey rock star, dressed in fatigues, crawling along the floor with a 45 in a holster. I'm actually playing cowboys and Indians with this guy, because I'm so loaded. That's what you do. At one point the dealer had fallen asleep and I couldn't wake him up to get more crack, so I bent his thumb back to the point of injury – and he woke up so startled that he pulled out his gun and shot a hole in the ceiling.

I was doing this for about three weeks, with all my knees scratched up from crawling over pebbles and bricks. I'm looking at the guy next to me and he's out of his mind, and he's got an Uzi. We were so close to being busted and being thrown in jail, and yet all the time I'm completely loaded, 24/7. A little voice would say to me, "You're gonna get busted! And then they're gonna throw you out of America, and you won't be able to go to Japan." It was like God, or some form of divine intervention, telling me years before I got sober to stop doing this. All along, this little voice was saying this to me.

My wife, my parents, my lawyer, my doctor – none of them could stop me from smoking this fucking demon shit. I was now locked into it. I had my own crack pipes, my own vials, my own briefcase full of paraphernalia. I'd go from one dealer's house to another, and I'd take their powder and I'd go in the bathroom and smoke it.

I never thought about my health. I'm 165lb now, which is 75kg or 11st 11lb – but back in the dark period from 1985 to '91, I was as good as 210 or 220lb. When you're a big guy and you're not getting any exercise and you're young like I was, crack makes your heart race – and I'm hyper anyway. Crack would give me states of euphoria where I'd take the hit and I could feel my heart going crazy. I really didn't care about snorting coke any more, because I was a complete freebase addict. When you inject, you're high in a hundredth of a second; if you freebase, it takes about four seconds; and if you snort, it takes about a minute. By the way, I want to be quite frank in this book that I've never used a needle in my life and I never will. No thank you very much. I'm sure I would have died if I'd been mainlining.

Gary Moore called me at home at Christmas 1984 and we became friends again. He'd had a couple of solo records after 'Parisienne Walkways': 'Empty Rooms' had been a hit. I loved that song, man. So Gary came through town in 1984 and he was opening for Rush. He stayed at my house for a couple of days: he knew I was an addict, but not a crack addict. He knew that I used to flirt with powdered coke. Every time he was around me, I would put the pipe down for a few days, wash, do my hair, and look like a normal guy. I did that a few times with Gary.

He was a massive Hughes/Thrall fan at this point and he'd completely forgotten about the G-Force incident, so he asked me if I'd like to work with him. His manager Steve Barnett had been my agent in 1971 and '72: he was born in Wolverhampton but now had a cockney accent, which I found weird.

Steve never really liked me, and I never really liked him – he's actually a co-president at Columbia in America now, but I don't give a fuck. I don't think he would have liked me even if I'd been clean and sober: he had a real uppity way with everyone, not just me. He talked to me like shit, and I didn't like it, but I wasn't the Glenn Hughes that I am today – so I let them lay down some ground rules for the project. One of those rules was my promise that I was no longer using drugs.

They were going to pay me a certain amount to sing and play bass on a record, and they were going to give me a flat in Maida Vale in London, which was wonderful. But they said, "You've got to give us something for security, in case you fuck up," so they took my Volvo, a rather nice black one which I'd bought as a second car to my Jaguar XJS. That was all they wanted: they couldn't get the keys to my house, so they took one of my cars.

Gary always said that he wanted to sing like Glenn Hughes. He loved me – or at least, he loved the sober and funny Glenn. We used to laugh a lot. We were really, really good friends at the tail-end of '84 and into '85. The record was called *Run For Cover* and the vocals were split like me and Coverdale, 50-50.

So here I am now in this beautiful old brownstone in Maida Vale, a really luxurious place. We were ensconced there in rehearsals and writing. We were doing the songs from scratch; he had nothing written. Although I was in the room and writing with Gary, I never really got any credit for any of that stuff, primarily because when you worked with Gary – and I think you might have heard other people say this too – he controlled every aspect of everything, from the syncopation of your bass, to what notes you play, to what kind of bass you play, and what you sing. We fell out a few times, because I said, "Gary, why don't you sing it yourself?" He actually played bass on the song 'Run For Cover', because I said, "Why don't you play the fuckin' bass yourself?"

Now, Gary had hired a crackhead and he didn't know it. I want to be honest with you here: I have no reason to pull any punches. This is the truth: I was with Gary for three months, writing and rehearsing. We only got through four songs before I was asked to leave.

Here's what you need to know. Because Gary was such a Hughes/Thrall fanatic, he hired Andy Johns to produce it, flew him in and put him in an apartment, and added Gary Ferguson as a drummer – it might as well be Hughes/Thrall, because you've got everybody but Pat Thrall on this record. Listen to 'Run For Cover': it's a ripoff of 'I Got Your Number'. He wanted to recreate that kind of vibe on the record.

As for drugs, let's just say that I would pick my evenings. When Gary wanted to take a weekend off, I would find myself at the Embassy Club in the West End. My future webmaster David Harrison told me that he saw me there once, and I was covered in puke. I was on speed. I went there a couple of times with Lemmy of Motörhead, who was very sweet to me and could handle his drugs. I couldn't. I found myself in strangers' apartments and high-rise buildings in the West End, both rich people and poor people. This happened whenever we had a few days off.

Then Steve Barnett wanted me to have a physical examination. I never realised that when you do a physical exam you have your blood tested. I told them that there was nothing in my blood except some wine or vodka, but when Barnett got those results I was on the next fucking plane. There was no conversation about it; I was gone.

I'd let Gary down, and I'd let Steve down: as uppity as he was, he was only doing his job. When I hire my guys, my manager Carl gives them the same spiel, because we don't hire people with drug problems. Steve told Gary, "Don't hire Glenn Hughes, because he's gonna fuckin' let you down."

Now, let's talk about the famous Mars bar incident. Gary's managers were asking me to lose weight at the time because they wanted us to do *Top Of The Pops*. We had recut 'Empty Rooms' with me singing it, and it was going to be on TV. I'd got this one tooth that had cracked down the front and I looked like a jack o'lantern, and Barnett told me that I needed to get it fixed – but I was scared shitless of going to the dentist. My teeth are perfect now, but they weren't then. He said, "We need to get your tooth fixed, and you gotta lose some fuckin' weight!" That's why they sent me to the doctor to have a physical.

So, one day Gary and Ferg and Andy dropped me off at my home in Maida Vale, and I jumped out of the car and went into the newsagent on the corner and bought four bars of chocolate. There was never a Mars bar involved here, by the way. I think it was a Cadbury's Flake. Gary ran into the newsagent behind me, laughing "Busted!"

If Steve had known how sick I was, he would never have allowed Gary to work with me, or indeed with Virgin. I think he was down a few thousand pounds on this: he did tell me later. It wasn't good enough for Gary, and he had to let me go. Steve called me a pathological liar. He said, "You are a fucking liar and you are on the next plane home."

Six months later, Gary told *Kerrang!* a story about me breaking his bathroom scales and going to his fridge and eating all the food, and that was really sad to read. I might have taken food from the fridge once or twice, but I want to address this. I did have an issue with chocolate, and I might have had an issue with some food groups – but to talk about me like I was Billy Bunter or something was just inaccurate. I did go down in the middle of the night and have a sandwich sometimes – and I mean a *sandwich*, not a fucking roast beef dinner. He also said that I'd never come back as a solo artist, and that I'd never sell out a toilet in the Marquee. I've proved him wrong. Talking about me because I'd let the team down was one thing, but referring to me as Mr Creosote from *Monty Python* was another. *Kerrang!* printed a picture of Mr Creosote with my name next to it and the caption "Can I have another Mars bar, please?" This really hurt me. It really did.

Gary Moore was not a man to fuck with. He didn't have the scars on his face for nothing. I never wanted to piss him off, because he was very volatile. We had a very love/hate relationship: we loved each other and we rejoiced in each other's friendship, but when that friendship went south, he detested me. He said so many hurtful things, which really upset my parents. But all that is a long time ago. I was devastated when I heard of his death in 2011. RIP, brother.

CHAPTER 10

ROCK BOTTOM

BLACK DAYS WITH BLACK SABBATH

Not long after that I got a call from Tony Iommi, who was about to make a solo album. I was back at our house in Northridge, California, and I went down to Cherokee Studios on Fairfax Avenue in Hollywood, where Tony was working with Jeff Glixman. Geoff Nicholls and Dave Spitz of the 1985 version of Black Sabbath might have been there too.

Tony Iommi *I've known Glenn for a hell of a long time, since he was in Trapeze, because we'd be doing shows around Birmingham and he'd be playing in the area. Glenn's gifted, isn't he? He's always had a great voice and a great talent. He had all the chops. He had everything! I was really pleased when I heard he was joining Purple. We did a show together at the California Jam in 1974 when he'd only just joined them. I watched some of their set, and Glenn stood out. His talent was remarkable. After the show we went up to his room and had one thing and another.*

I walk in the studio and the first thing they play me is 'No Stranger To Love'. That night I sat with Geoff and we started to write some lyrics. We cut the song and the next night we did 'Dangerzone'. Tony really loved it: it all felt really good. The more songs they recorded, the more obvious it was that I was going to sing on this record.

Tony Iommi *I was going to do an album with a lot of different singers on. That was the original plan, and Glenn was one of the first ones to come in. But I heard his voice and I thought, "Nobody's going to do better than this."*

We then moved to Atlanta, because Glixman wanted to get away from LA and get some work done. I remember, it was the day after my 34th birthday, August 22 1985. We start to dig into the album and record songs like 'Heart Like A Wheel', and it started to flow more freely: I now felt like I was a part of it. Tony was engaged to Lita Ford at the time and we were all staying at the same hotel: it was all cool.

Tony Iommi *Glenn wasn't going through such a good period at the time. I wasn't much better, but I'd try and do cocaine away from Glenn so I wouldn't encourage him any more. The drugs never affected his singing, though – he came in and did it effortlessly. Nobody could believe it. He came and sat down in the control room and started singing, and we all went "Bloody hell!"*

Let this be known. Tony and I had done cocaine prior to me joining up with him, but when we were together we never got high. I just think he got high with Lita, or on his own, or whatever. I did the same thing with my people. Even back then, I knew that when I got high I wasn't so much fun to be around, because I couldn't converse with anyone: the twitch would come back. I never really wanted to be around people who I cared for, because I was out of my mind.

Tony Iommi *We went to Atlanta to record, and he really got bad. I'll never forget, I loaned him a tape machine so he could work with and play the tracks in his room, and the next thing I heard he'd sold it! He owed a guy some money and this guy was looking for him – but I wasn't about to tell him where*

Glenn was. We actually threw this guy out because we were trying to keep [dealers] away from Glenn, but it's so hard to deal with that kind of thing. I could understand it to a point, but I wasn't in as deep as he was. When you're in the middle of making an album, it's difficult to see other people's side of it. It really was frustrating. There was an element of the drug thing coming in, and it was difficult. Glenn was having problems – he'd have dealers come in the studio, and I saw red. There were so many hangers-on around, and he's such a lovely person that he just absorbed them. They'd be in his room.

I found this place called Carlos McGhee's in Buckhead, which is the affluent part of Atlanta. It was a Friday night, I remember it well – the last Friday night of August 1985 – and in walks this blonde gal, about five-ten, barefoot. Beautiful. Nineteen years old, although she looked older. We invited her and her friends to sit at our table, and they did. Her name was Christine McCarthy. I bought them some drinks, and we went to an after-hours bar called Saints And Sinners, where there was a lot of dancing happening – even back then, before the ecstasy craze. There were transvestites and the usual after-hours people that you see all over the world in places like this.

Christine was a bright, beautiful girl and I was immediately attracted to her. We ended up going back to the hotel and we hopped into the sack and made love, and it was great. We did everything you could imagine, and it was amazing. She came back the following night and we repeated the process: we went out and did the same stuff. I started to have feelings for Christine, and my marriage to Karen was really in name only.

There's been a lot of hoo-ha about who wrote what on Iommi's record, which was eventually titled *Seventh Star*. Geoff Nicholls wrote some things, but I did the majority of the writing. I made a commitment to Don Arden that I was getting a fee of something like $20,000 while Tony took the publishing, which was what people normally did back then. It wasn't a bad fee, and you never really questioned what Don wanted anyway. You didn't mess with him, and in any case, I just wanted to be part of it, because I was not at my best. I still performed well on the album, and a lot of people think it's great. Even though I looked like shit and I was in my cocaine paranoia, I could still do my thing.

Meanwhile, I fell in love with a girl. Christine was young and beautiful and she had all the attributes that anyone would want. She was amazing in the sack. I really loved this girl. OK, maybe it was because of the drugs I was taking, because it was definitely lustful, but I was falling in love with her. She was a great girl: very giving with her time, and very loving, and extremely sexual. We hung out together and went to movies: she became my lover for the next ten years.

So we go out to LA for a while, and I go to Karen and I tell her that I'm going to leave her. It wasn't a big surprise to her: we were at the tail-end of a ten-year marriage which had been crippled by my addiction. No-one deserves that, least of all Karen, who only ever had a few glasses of wine at the weekend and loathed cocaine, partly because of what happened to Tommy Bolin. She was hip to the fact that this drug is trouble.

We put the house on the market, and it took about six months to get rid of it. I went back to Atlanta then and Christine's father allowed me to stay at his apartment building with her. He had another place across town, where he spent most nights with his girlfriend, so me and Christine had the place to ourselves.

So here I am with Christine, this perfect specimen of a girl who I really loved. I fell deeply in love with her – really, *really* big time, I thought. We had the same vibe together, even though there was 15 years difference in age between us.

You have to understand something. Cocaine was the Holy Grail for me; it was the centre of the universe. It was my lover, my guitar, my microphone, my everything. Cocaine was my god. It was my saviour. It was the key that unlocked the door to anything in life. It was euphoria. It was sex. It was the deepest possible love affair that you could imagine. It was *my cocaine*.

Christmas came, and I was having an argument with Christine while I was up a ladder next to the Christmas tree. There was some verbal going on and I fell off the ladder, straight through the tree and into the fireplace, and I twisted my knee and the cartilage snapped. I heard the pop and I knew what it was: I'd heard about football players doing it. I went to the emergency room in Atlanta and they told me what had happened: I knew I'd have to go back to LA for some surgery. It was around the time of the Grammy Awards in 1986: the night before the show I had the operation on my knee.

In January 1986 I got a call from Don Arden saying that he and Warner Bros had decided that Tony's album should be by Black Sabbath, not Tony solo – which did not make me happy. I wanted Tony to have a solo career, and I also knew that songs like 'No Stranger To Love' weren't Black Sabbath songs.

Tony Iommi *That really did open another can of worms. It was Warners [who wanted it to be a Sabbath album], but it could have been my management at the time, I just don't know. What I heard was they wanted to release it as a Black Sabbath album, because we owed them one.*

Would I have done the project if I'd known it was going to be released under the Black Sabbath name? I had problems fronting Sabbath: it was Tony's thing. Ronnie James Dio was the perfect replacement after Ozzy Osbourne, and that's the end of it. Ian Gillan had a shot at it; Ray Gillen came in after me; and Tony Martin was there too. They're all good singers, but not right for Black Sabbath. I'm a soul singer, and I love working with Tony outside of Black Sabbath – because Sabbath really is Ozzy. So when Don Arden told me that this was going to be a Sabbath album, I thought, "Fuck me!" It was just weird. I never really found out why they did it: I think they thought it would put bums on seats on the forthcoming tour.

So we went out in spring 1986. I did it out of respect for Tony, because he wanted to do it. He never tells you what he wants: he just comes to you and says, "I'm really hoping that you'll do this tour and I'm depending on you to do it." I love Tony Iommi: I love him like a brother to this day, and he was showing me respect too, by asking me to do this. My self-respect was pretty low after the Gary Moore thing. But all along, I knew that the wheels were going to come off.

Now listen. If you are a singer and you are depressed or nervous or high, you cannot deliver vocally, because tension comes from being fucked up. You have to be completely centred on stage. I was uncomfortable, partly because I didn't have a bass, partly because I was overweight, and also because of that male audience that Sabbath have – young, keen, bristling, black leather-jacketed guys. I was in fear of walking out in front of 10,000 or 15,000 of them every night, thinking, "I'm gonna have to sing 'Iron Man', which is such an Ozzy song." It put so much fear into me. Remember, I am Glenn Hughes the soulful singer that can sing the phone book, but here I am going to sing Ozzy's songs. Ozzy is a very monotonal singer and it was not me at all.

One night before the tour, I was still on crutches and Christine was with me at the Sunset Marquis in LA. I had half an ounce of coke, so within half an hour I was stomping around my hotel room doing blow. There was a band staying at the hotel, a group of little boys called New Edition, which Bobby Brown was in. They were in the next suite to me. What they saw in their first introduction to LA was a British rocker in his underpants, hanging off the balcony two storeys up, with a crutch in one hand. I was just arsing about, behaving like an idiot. I always ended up doing goofy stuff like that. I was actually escorted off the property after I smashed some glasses in the room. I went down to the lobby and I had a Frankie Goes To Hollywood T-shirt on. I remember it as clear as a bell. I jumped onto the desk at the front of the hotel and ripped the T-shirt off with a knife – and they called security. I wasn't taken to jail, but I was banned from the Sunset Marquis. I'm friends with the manager there now, but you knew back then that if you got banned from the Sunset Marquis, you'd done something wrong.

So now we're off on tour as Black Sabbath. They put me in the hotel where the crew were staying. Christine's mother, Carol McCarty, comes in from Colorado, so we take her to the Cat And Fiddle on Hollywood Boulevard, where we have a few drinks together with Tony's production manager John Downing. The crew guys are down there, all drinking pints of beer. I don't like beer very much so I was doing some coke.

John Downing had some coke too, and we were all getting pretty boisterous.

Carol McCarty *Glenn was such a pest. Christine would come to see me and all the time she was at my house, he would be calling and calling the whole time, because they only had one car and he had no way to leave their apartment.*

So we go back to my hotel room and I start getting really rowdy. I run out of coke so I go down to John Downing's room and get some more. Then I run out again, so I go back to his room again and get some more. He tells me I should go to bed, but something happened in the elevator where we get into some kind of pushing. He pushes me, I push him, and when I pushed him he took me to my room, closed the door to my room in front of Christine and her mother – and hit me so hard in the face that it knocked me out.

Tony Iommi *I wasn't there, but apparently Glenn saw John Downing in the lift and something happened. I wasn't aware of what it was.*

Christine and her mom left the hotel that night: they'd seen enough of this shit. I slept it off and then woke up the next day alone, with the biggest black eye you've ever seen. I was in a lot of shame. He'd hit me on the nose and my left eye socket, which shattered. Some bone from that socket went down into the back of my nose, and perforated something. Without me knowing, blood was being stored on my vocal cords in my throat. So when I had to rehearse that afternoon, I had to wear dark glasses. I felt some discomfort: it was painful to touch my eye, although I didn't realise that I'd broken a bone. For the next two or three days I was in rehearsal, and then we had the weekend free before we did a pre-production gig on March 14 in Hollywood, where we used to rehearse. A lot of my friends were there – Tommy Lee of Mötley Crüe, his wife Heather Locklear, and others. Although it's a week later, I've still got a huge black eye, so the make-up artist covers it up and it works pretty well.

Tony Iommi *We had a showcase in LA, which I didn't agree with doing, but*

Don Arden thought it was a good idea. I thought, "Oh God …" but he said, "We're gonna do it! I've organised it!" so I was like, "Oh, right." We were at a bit of a low point in our careers, it was a bit awkward, so we ended up doing this bloody showcase with Glenn – and he was so gone at that point. I virtually had to shove him on stage. It was so embarrassing.

I should have known then. My voice was in good shape, and it had been in great shape during rehearsals: I'd been singing like a bird. But I was so tense, and my self-esteem was so low: I felt like I was a piece of shit, so the show wasn't great. I thought of myself as one of the greatest singers out there, but I wasn't able to do my job properly.

Tony Iommi *He had a problem from day one. He wasn't supposed to be singing Black Sabbath songs and he was also doing a lot of coke. It does tighten your vocal cords up. It's very difficult when you get to that point, and then you drink a lot and whatever.*

What concerns me most is how a production manager who'd been on the road for a long time with The Move and other bands could hit the lead singer of a band who were about to go into pre-production for a tour in two weeks. He never apologised to me, and we never really spoke again.

So after that mediocre show, we were off to Cleveland, Ohio, to start the tour. We'd rehearsed five days a week for six weeks, because Tony is a stickler for rehearsals. I remember thinking, "I can do this," even though I knew I was overweight and not looking good. I went off to Atlanta to see Christine for a couple of days before the tour – I'd wanted to bring her on tour with me but it was no birds on the bus, so I couldn't do that.

After the incident at the Sunset Marquis, Don Arden hired a young security guard called Doug Goldstein, who went on to manage Guns N' Roses but was only 20 or 21 years old at the time. He was a bodybuilder who chewed tobacco and he called me "Sir". He was my first real security guard since Patsy Collins and Paddy Callahan. He was perfect: he would have a key to my room and he'd check on me, 24 hours a day. He had a room adjoining mine and I was never out of his sight.

Tony Iommi *I brought a bodyguard in to look after him, 24 hours a day. This guy would end up tying a string from his foot to the door at night so that he could feel the door opening, because Glenn would have people creeping into his room, doing deals. We were concerned not just for the show, but for him as well, because he'd be up all night.*

The only time I escaped was the night when I was out with John Downing at the Cat And Fiddle, when Doug went to see his family: if he had been there it would never have happened. He had his hands full with me. If I wanted to score cocaine, Doug made it impossible – he was incredible. I was still fucked up, though: I still drank.

Tony Iommi *Glenn just disappeared one time and went off to Atlanta, and we had to send the bodyguard to get him! It was just really, really difficult.*

At Cleveland we had W.A.S.P. and Anthrax opening up for us. Don Arden was there, and he said to me after the show, "What the fuck do you look like? You've got fuckin' make-up on, you're fuckin' overweight – you look like a hooker!" It was the first time that Don had ever said anything disrespectful to me, and I was hurt by it. But the thing is, he was right. I looked fucking awful. I also had a beard, which I was trying to hide behind.

Tony Iommi *It wasn't Glenn at all: he was just so gone. It was an awful experience, to be honest. I can understand why he was nervous, though: it was the first time he'd ever sung without a bass. He was just becoming a singer, and it was a terrible waste in a lot of ways, but it just seemed like the way to go at the time, with the way he was. I was tempted to get him to play bass, but I didn't think he was in any condition to do it at the time. Singing was where I saw him, even though he's obviously a great bass player – but if he'd walked out there not wanting to sing, we'd have had no singer and no bass player either!*

The next gig was in Detroit, where we were taping the *King Biscuit Flower Hour*. Of course, my disease wanted to jeopardise anything good in my life. I wasn't on coke but I was a bit intoxicated. Before the show I was singing one of the songs – maybe one of Ronnie's tunes – and I was thinking, "I can't sing this ... I can't hit a middle C, which any average singer could hit." Unknown to me, the blood was building up in my throat and aggravating my vocal cords – and maybe I had some infection as well, because I was on antibiotics. I couldn't sing because my throat was closing up. We started the show with 'Mob Rules', which is really low, and I thought, "I can't even sing this!" It came out like a croak. It was a nightmare.

Tony Iommi *We did some shows, but Glenn was really struggling. As I say, it's understandable to a point, because some of the stuff he was doing was Sabbath stuff, which he wasn't supposed to be doing. He wasn't supposed to be doing 'Black Sabbath' and 'Iron Man' and 'War Pigs' and stuff like that, so* *he really did get thrown in at the deep end. That, combined with being on stage for the first time without a bass, must have been like having your arm cut off. It must have been just awful, and I really didn't appreciate that at the time.*

By the time we hit East Rutherford, New Jersey, which was a famous gig that I know a lot of my friends went to, I was barking like a dog. I've seen the footage and it makes me want to puke. It is fucking abysmal. And in soundcheck they were rehearsing with another singer, Ray Gillen. I'd seen him around but I thought he was in Anthrax's crew. I became friends with him, actually – he was a big Glenn Hughes and Trapeze fan.

After my final gig with Sabbath, in Worcester, Massachusetts, on March 26, I couldn't even speak. Something was wrong with me. I was thinking, "I've been ill before, but I've always had this God-given talent to sing."

Tony Iommi *I got really annoyed about the whole thing, because I wasn't 100 per cent, I was trying to get myself going as well – and when you see something like this happening around you it gets to everybody. Everybody gets concerned, like, "Is he going to be behaving tonight? Is he going to be able to do it?" And everything was on my shoulders at that point, because it was Black Sabbath. People were coming along expecting a show, and it went bad, and that was it. We had to cut it after a certain number of shows. We just couldn't carry on like that.*

I was allowed to go to the after-show party but Tony wasn't there – I was alone with the crew. Eric Singer, the drummer, came up to me and said, "Hey man, I hear you're being replaced by Ray Gillen tomorrow" – and I walked straight out of the party, up to Tony's room and started banging on his door. I did it for 20 minutes but he wouldn't come out.

Tony Iommi *There was no option, to be honest. Everything was on my shoulders and I felt so bad about the whole thing, because Glenn had been a mate for so many years. We couldn't carry on like this, and Glenn wasn't in a state where you could stand and talk to him, although he probably didn't realise that at the time. He was raging and frantic about everything. You couldn't stand there and say, "This is why, Glenn," because he'd freak out, you know. So there wasn't any discussion because there couldn't be any discussion. It was like dealing with a drunk: you can't get through to them, and Glenn was like that. It was the only way we could deal with it, and we had to bring somebody in. Don Arden was going potty about it as well: he was saying, "We've got to bring somebody else in! We've got to replace Glenn!" and I was saying, "How are we going to do that? We're right at the start of a tour." But it had to happen. I had to bring Ray Gillen in and audition him in the afternoons. I always felt bad about it, but there was no other way. Even today I still feel bad about it.*

I banged on everybody's door, but they wouldn't come out. Eventually Doug Goldstein came to my room at four in the morning and said, "Look – they're letting you go. Here's your plane ticket." We went to the hospital before I got on the plane, and that's where they told me that the bone had gone into my nose and ruptured some tissue, which had caused blood to drip onto my vocal cords. They had to go in and scrape some of this shit out. They numbed my throat and cleared the blockage. The doctor told me that I couldn't talk for three months – that I'd have to write notes for people – and that I might never sing again.

Not only was I out of the band, I was also thinking that I might not be able to sing again because of this infection that was damaging my sinuses. Still, I had a sense of relief when Tony let me go: come on, he had no choice. I let him down. They'd sold all the tickets on the tour. And yes, I got beat up, but it all happened because of my addiction. Normal people don't get beaten up in hotels at four in the morning.

Tony Iommi *We arranged for Glenn to go into rehab, but he wouldn't have anything to do with it, and you can't force somebody to do it – you have to let them do it themselves. He just didn't want to do it: he enjoyed what he did, and that was that. He wasn't ready to stop.*

It was quite a while until I saw Glenn again. I always thought, "What a waste of talent." He'd burned so many bridges over the years that he had to rebuild everything. Everybody said, "Oh God, why would you work with him?" It was sad to hear, because I knew what talent he'd got.

This was the lowest point for me: letting my friend Tony Iommi down after being on stage with Deep Purple and being hailed as one of the greatest rock singers of all time, and becoming this blithering mess who couldn't speak, let alone sing. These are the dark years now.

CHAPTER 11

TURNING THE CORNER

ATLANTA AND JUDAS PRIEST

So here I am, back in Atlanta, and I've got no gig. The Deep Purple royalties were the only thing that was keeping me going at this point. I knew that I had a drug problem, but I thought I could control it. Nothing was happening musically.

Basically I wanted to do something, but I didn't know what, and I was too fucked up anyway. I really went for it with the coke this time. I was still getting people wanting to work with me, but I wasn't interested – I just said, "I need to take a break." No-one in particular: new artists in the Texas area who wanted me to be the new singer in their project for RCA or Warners or whatever; but I listened to the music and thought it was OK, not great. After Sabbath I went into a real dark place, and eventually when I sold my home in LA I leased a really great condo in a place called Eastlake, California, and Christine and I moved in together.

At the time coke would cost you $100 per gram if you were buying it on the street, but if you were buying in bulk it would cost you less. So I gave my dealer $10,000 – and I know this is fucking crazy – so that he would buy coke in bulk and sell it back to me at the usual high rate. I was so fucked up that I didn't care. Now I had my own shit, my consumption went up: I'd tell him that I needed a certain amount for the weekend and he'd deduct it from my outstanding balance.

It was euphoric because I was with a girl. I was paranoid, though. This is classic coke stuff. I thought that *they* – cops, Nazis, witch-hunters, boogeymen – were outside the window or under the bed. I could have played for England in the Olympics of looking in closets. That's what it was like the whole time we were together.

My relationship with anybody – even Karen – was run on cocaine, from Vicky at the end of Purple right through to the end of my drug use. Every girl I ever had was a hostage. Friends were hostages too. I only wanted to hang out with people who did vast amounts of blow – mine, yours, whatever. I only wanted to hang out with people who were interested in blow and talked about blow. Music got in the way of my cocaine use. I had a couple of guitars left, and I liked to play and sing a lot when I was loaded, but it would be tangential: I would write 30 seconds of a song and then stop and write 30 seconds of another song, and it was awful. I'd write really miserable songs: none of them got recorded. I'd go home every single night with an eight-ball, which is three-and-a-half grams of coke, and we'd snort it. A normal couple couldn't get through that in a week, and we were doing it every night.

I never got through the ten grand I'd given my dealer, because Christine's mom, Carol, started sniffing around. She'd heard that her daughter was hanging around with this international rock star, and she came to Atlanta. In the mad autumn of 1986, in around September or October, we had Carol's 40th birthday in my house. She was only five years older than me.

In the daytime, I didn't have any business concerns to think about: the royalties came in and Purple deducted taxes at source, so I had no worries. I had two cheques a year from Purple, and they were what I was living off. I never saved anything: any drug addict, whether they're making $100,000 a year or $10 million a year, is going to get through it. I'd pay six months' worth of rent and bills in advance every time I got a cheque, so I wouldn't have to worry about them. Everything else went into my mistress, cocaine.

One night, Christine and I got into an altercation over this really amazing gold chain that she had. I grabbed her chain in my hand and twisted it, and she freaked. It was reparable, but she hit out at me, deservedly so. Her mother heard this altercation and came into the room with her gun. Christine was pretty pissed at me and siding with her mother – even though she usually sided with me against her parents. So they proceed to tie me to a chair with rope!

Carol McCarty *He came to the house where we lived and he was just outrageous. He wanted cocaine and I said "I don't have any." I got a pistol out, pointed it at him, and made him sit in a wooden chair. Christine and I tied him up, just so that he couldn't have access to a telephone. I didn't have any intention of shooting him. He was all tied up, just like you see in the movies.*

I was thinking, "I'm gonna die here!" because when you're around people with guns, you don't know what's going to happen. This went on for hours. Eventually Christine and I made up and she let me go.

All this went on until the spring of 1987. I'd lost the Gary Moore gig, I'd lost the Black Sabbath gig: all was lost for me. For all intents and purposes, my life was over: I thought, "I'm just going to spend the rest of my life as a drug addict, living off Deep Purple royalties, eating bad food and ballooning up to a huge, unhealthy weight." That's what it was like for two years.

There was one night when I was out at a club with Christine, and

Carol came to meet us. I had got so fucked up that I couldn't leave the club: you've heard of people being so coked up that they're frozen? Well, I couldn't move: sometimes I used to joke that when I drove I could only make right turns because I was frozen on my left side. I finally got outside, and I was standing there – and Carol ran over my foot in her car and stopped the car on it.

Once, I hadn't eaten any food for four days, so when I came down off the blow, I wanted to make myself some french fries. I didn't have a chip-fryer: I just put fat in a pan, which is really dangerous. So there I am: I chop up the potatoes and put them in the pan, and then I go into the lounge to watch TV. I fall asleep … and I wake up, and I look at the fucking TV and I see reflected in the screen that there's a fire raging behind me in the kitchen. But I'm so out of it that I put my robe and my socks on, walk into the kitchen and try to take the pan off the heat with my bare hands. Of course, the pan is red hot, so I drop it: I still have the scars on my hand. And then the burning oil runs down onto the floor. The skin is hanging off my hand and I see it bubbling, so I try to run but I slip on the burning grease and knock myself out on the dishwasher cabinet as I go down, dislocating my jaw. That's when the sprinklers come on – right before I hit the fire on the floor.

I'm absolutely serious when I say this: as I lay there on the floor, I heard a voice saying, "Get up. Get up and go outside." Now that was God; He was very clearly telling me to get up. I could clearly see the fire brigade and the ambulance coming. Two fire trucks and a helicopter were coming, plus like 50 cops. The skin was now hanging off: there was a nasty big hole in my foot that you could put your finger in. I was in so much pain. I got Christine on the phone and the next thing I know is that she's there, crying, and they're strapping me onto a gurney. I'm now being taken to a hospital and the pain is excruciating.

They give me a heavy dose of morphine and I watch them cutting the skin from my hand and my leg – and I'm laughing. That was the greatest high I've ever had in my life. I'll never have it again – or at least I hope I never get that sick that I have to have it. Now I know why people who are dying in hospital have morphine: I know what it's for.

They bandage me up, and the next day I have to go to the funeral of Christine's grandfather, who had died a few days before. We drive there: me and Christine and her sister Carisa and Carol and Christine's dad, Lee.

Carol McCarty *My father had just died and I got a call from Glenn saying that he was on fire: I could hear him screaming down the phone. Now, Glenn used to say all kinds of crazy things just to get your attention, but when we went over there we saw him on the porch, with his socks all melted off. I remember the paramedics cutting the skin off his burned feet and hands. We had to rent a minivan in order to take Glenn to my father's funeral in Michigan, so that Christine could take care of him.*

They stuck me in the back in a wheelchair, with a massive amount of painkillers. I don't know what they were, but they were great! They were so good that I went through all of my prescription – a week's worth – in one day. I went to get more in Ohio. I was getting high on the pain pills, although the pain from my burns and my dislocated jaw was intense. It was sad: here we are at a memorial, and it's all about Glenn: Glenn's dislocated jaw; Glenn's in a wheelchair; we've got to go and get Glenn's pain medication. It was all about me, and it sucked.

We leg it back to Atlanta and we stay at Christine's parents for two or three days. I go back into my condo, which has been repaired and renovated. I remember getting another six-month cheque from Purple, so I put down another six months of rent. There were rumblings from the management at Eastlake, who were getting tired of my behaviour, although they never actually asked me to leave. I needed to get a house, though, because in a condo there's always somebody either above or below you. I said I could never live in one of these again, and I haven't. So I rented a home on Mountaintop Drive in Marietta, on top of a hill with a great view. There was a lot of land, and the neighbours weren't too close – I could make noise if I wanted to.

In 1987 Pat Thrall and I recorded a song called 'City Of Crime' for the film *Dragnet*, starring Dan Aykroyd and Tom Hanks. Dan and Tom were rapping on the song, which we did at the Hit Factory in New York. It was great to work with such good guys. Tom and Dan were very, very nice men – and remember, around those guys I'm not going to be getting high. Dan and I would talk about John Belushi, and the impact that he'd had on the world of comedy, and Dan was hip that I was a coke addict. He was concerned for me, as was his brother Pete.

Later in the year we did a video clip, just before the film came out. I went out to LA and I missed the first flight because I was so loaded, which was terrible because these productions cost so much money. All these extras were wearing goat outfits, and of course, I'm the last guy to show up so they put me in goat pants up to my waist. I looked like a fucking idiot! I wasn't loaded when I got on the set, but I was coming down after four days of being awake. I remember being completely paranoid that I was not myself: I had a tooth chipped, which I'd broken in some fracas – I was always getting in a fracas with somebody or other. Typical addict.

It was really bad. Now I was getting into conversations with myself, and I used to hit myself. I used to get really angry and hit myself in the face: it was really bizarre. A lot of people do that in their disease, actually. And I've got to be 220lb at this point. I'm in this video clip knowing that it's going to be a Top Ten hit, and it was: 'City Of Crime' was in there for eight weeks in the spring of 1988. The first day on set was very hard with those two guys. I had to do a lot of close-ups, but I hated the way I looked. I couldn't lose the weight and I couldn't stop the drugs. As soon as the last frame of me was shot, I was on the phone to the dealer.

This whole period was one of the most embarrassing times for me. I stayed near LAX and went to a dealer's house and got completely out of my mind. It was awful – fucking awful.

I went back to Atlanta to Christine in 1987. I had Christmas that year in the condo. She had a brief affair with a guy called Larry, who was one of her neighbours growing up. He was an asshole who had come out of the navy and started to hang around with her. On one of the occasions that I was loaded, she went off with him a couple of times and didn't come home. Later on, she confessed that she'd had an affair with him. It was difficult to accept, but I had to accept it. I had been faithful to her until then, because the only mistress I had was cocaine. And I wasn't particularly in shape to go out and look for anything anyway.

It was fucking horrible for me. I completely and utterly broke down, and she'd never seen me cry like that. I was broken-hearted that she did that to me, because I really loved her – this was my friend and my soulmate. She'd dressed my burns for two months –

sometimes in the middle of the night. She washed my leg and my feet and she saved me from more scarring. She did everything for me, because I couldn't bend down to do it myself. She loved me, I know that, but I was awful: living with a drug addict is not fun. This is an important part of the book.

There was one dealer who would let me stay with him for days and days. He'd leave me alone in his house while he was in his bedroom or bathroom doing something alone, but I knew that at any moment his place was going to be busted big time – I'm talking helicopters. I met some of his clients: heavy motherfuckers. This was a big operation. Guns and fucking knives everywhere! I remember this real redneck came over one night and he was loaded, and I was loaded too and did something funny – like singing or twitching or something – that made him really angry. Guns came out, and he threw a big knife at me; it landed close to my foot. It could have taken it off. It was all fun and laughing, but I thought, "I've got to stay away from this place." A week later, the place was completely busted.

All along, through my drug use, a voice had been saying to me, "Glenn, if you get busted, you're gonna get deported, and there goes your American life, and there goes your career." Just a little voice, always telling me this. The real Glenn Hughes was saying to me "You've got to get away from this shit." That dealer went down for two or three years. It was that close. Awful.

Now, Judas Priest were on the *Turbo* tour and played a show at the Atlanta Omni. It was a big show, maybe 18,000 people – they were at the top of their game. I took a bunch of blow with me and at this point I'm getting pretty grotesque. While the Priest guys were on stage I was getting loaded in their dressing-room. By the time the band came off stage I was completely and utterly high: beyond workable, and completely stoned. I'm banging into things, and I can't walk and I'm paranoid. At this point Glen Tipton says to me, "Glenn, you're going to have to leave." He said it nicely: he said, "We're gonna take you outside and get you some air." This is one of the moments in my life, looking back, where I'm completely full of shame.

So I'm in the parking lot, with about 100 fans who are trying to get backstage, and I remember about an hour later, when I was slightly coming down, that Rob Halford and Glen Tipton and the guys were leaving in a car and pulling up to me and saying, "Man, are you gonna be OK?" And as the car drove away, I experienced a moment of clarity. It was one of the first times that I prayed to get sober, which I'd started to do around this period. I felt like a piece of shit as I sat outside with some friends, puking cocaine on the floor.

KK Downing [Judas Priest] *We didn't ask him to leave personally; I think our tour manager pushed him out of the exit door. But that was par for the course with Glenn. Before the show he was absolutely wonderful, but after the show … it was like a Jekyll and Hyde situation! But he's a lovely guy. What a serious talent he is. All was forgiven and forgotten the very next day.*

This book is letting you know what it's like to live with addiction. A lot of people in the music industry have said to me, "The reason why we're angry with you is because you threw your fucking talent away for so many years." When I finally got sober, my friends Malcolm Dome and Dave Ling, who are well-known British journalists, said, "Are you really gonna stay sober this time? Are we really gonna depend on you?"

In early 1988 I get a call from John Norum, whose band Europe had had a massive hit the previous year with 'The Final Countdown'. That kind of music has never been my cup of tea, but I saw the video clip on MTV and I thought, "Fuck me, that guitar player is like Gary Moore!" He was good. Anyway, John had left the band and wanted to do a solo project. He was playing a gig at the Hammersmith Apollo in London, supporting Ace Frehley, so he flew me over and we met. I was sober that day, and he asked me if I'd like to come to Stockholm, make a record and tour.

So Christine and I made a pact that when we got to Sweden and we were in a new environment, we wouldn't do any coke: we were going to cold-turkey it. This is a crazy story. I'd been up all night the night before doing drugs, as you do, and I remember going to Atlanta airport – and because I'd been on drugs, my body craved sugar and fat and I ate a hot dog. As the plane was taxiing along, I puked up this hot dog. This is horrible. There was a woman next to me and she was looking at me – this wild-eyed guy with red hair and a tooth missing, having to hold my sick in my hands while the plane was taking off, then walk all the way down to the toilet to clean myself up … it was fucking horrible. And I had nothing to change into.

So we get to Stockholm and they'd got a place for me for stay, with a friend of John Norum's. We started to rehearse and it was going great. I was playing bass. He'd booked a bunch of shows for us for August, and I was going to rehearse with him from April. Things were going great until one night when someone casually said that he had some speed, which I'd done on *Play Me Out* and liked, because it didn't make me paranoid and it made me horny. It made me want to play and sing, and I thought it was all good, although I didn't think what it was doing to my heart. So I did a couple of bumps and stayed up all night and had a great time. I wasn't looking to get high, but when you're an addict, you'll find yourself in a situation where you'll get high.

I started hanging out in a restaurant-bar called Geno, where I met a guy whose nickname was The Tomato. He was a great guy: not a dealer or an addict, but because of my conniving way, I figured that I needed to find some speed and a musician that would want to hang out with me. So he found someone down at the docks who had some speed, and I started getting a couple of grams each weekend. Only at the weekend, though. I'd work with John, Monday through Friday, and then Friday through Sunday would be my time where I'd hole up with Christine and start the bad behaviour. But that behaviour started to creep into Monday and Tuesday, and by Thursday I'd be craving for Friday to come along. I became unfocused, and John was sensing it – and he probably found out about it.

I was becoming the old Glenn. The rehearsing was getting in the way of my addiction. I remember I met the tennis player Vitas Gerulaitis, and I went off with him to his apartment in Sweden and got high with him – on coke. I was becoming addicted again. John and I did one national TV appearance in Gothenburg, where we did 'Reach For The Sky'. It was OK. I was overweight, but it was cool anyway.

Christine and I moved into a second apartment across the river in Stockholm, but John's manager Larry Mazur, who also managed the last days of Hughes/Thrall and went on to manage Cinderella and Kiss, came by and said, "Glenn, you're gonna have to go home. You can't tour like this. You can't do anything like this." I was sad. I liked John Norum, and John hated to let me go, but the fact is that you cannot work with a drug addict. It was an impossible scenario. I went back, tail between my legs. John was crying: he was upset. I've made my amends to him since then: he's a good guy.

CHAPTER 12
LITTLE SECRET
MY RELAPSE HELL

S
o now it's June 1988 and I'm starting to get really edgy. I remember one day in September 1988, I had got some drugs from somebody and I was smoking it with some drug friends, all in our underwear. How fucked-up is that? It was hot and humid, and we were all in our underpants, like a bunch of fucking hillbillies. We all went into the bathroom to do our hits. Sometimes I would do a rock that was so big that there was still some left in the pipe – so when a friend of mine put her rock in and took the hit, she had a full seizure in front of us.

While she was on the floor, her friend – who was next up for the crack pipe – walked over her to get to the pipe. Now that is heavy! We carried her over to the bed. She came around and we were all crying. Six hours later we were all back in there again … six hours later! All of us. That's how heavy it was. That was one of the moments when God said to me, "Well? What are we going to do now?"

This behaviour went on until October, when I got my next pay-cheque. We were evicted from that place because of our cats. Pookie had had a litter of eight kittens at the condo, which is basically why we had to move. You can't have cats pissing and shitting in the house, so we had them all outside. The landlady was tired of the cops being called, too, so we were asked to leave within 90 days.

Eventually I met Jerry Trimble, who was the world champion lightweight kickboxer. Google him: he's from Kentucky and he was a local hero – the Ricky Hatton of Atlanta. He's now a movie actor: a very attractive guy who looks like a young Kirk Douglas.

Jerry Trimble, Jr *I've known Glenn since 1987. I met him at a nightclub. We hit it off and became great friends, and I became his personal bodyguard, his personal trainer, and I was watching out for him – I was a bit of everything! It was pretty cool. I didn't know who Glenn was when I first met him, but then, I started listening to his music and researching who he was, and I was like, "My God – this guy is incredible!" His talent and creativity was amazing. There was something inside him: he was on fire inside. The turmoil was intense back then.*

So I meet Jerry and he looks at me and says, "We have to get you in shape." He started paying numerous visits to my home and started trying to get me off drugs. We would go away at weekends.

For some reason, big six-foot-nine rednecks in cowboy hats from Atlanta would want to fight Jerry, knowing that he was the world champion kickboxer, at five or six in the morning. He'd be like, "Here we go again …" and say to them, "You don't want to do this," and then take three of them out in like a second. He hated it: he was remorseful for knocking people out.

Jerry Trimble, Jr *A hard part was all the people that we tried to keep him away from! Dealers … you know, everybody wanted to be his friend, giving him this and giving him that. Slipping things in his pocket! I was a martial artist – the two-time world champion – and although I was only 145 pounds back then, I could handle myself. We knew everybody in the clubs, so we had* *carte blanche. I wouldn't go into a club unless I knew the owners, the managers, the bouncers, everybody – and then we were taken care of. If any confrontation came about, the bouncers would say, "Jerry, do you want to take it outside?" and I'd be like [reluctantly] "Oh man … let's go." It was funny.*

Now, ecstasy was very popular in the South in the 80s and it was really good back then, not like it was over here. It wasn't a Class A drug at the time: it was legal, kind of. Everyone was doing it: sports people, actors, they were all doing it. So I would do it.

Jerry Trimble, Jr *These were people who were giving Glenn drugs and being assholes. It was the 80s: the drug time. Glenn was trying really hard to get straight: I think that's how we hooked up, because he wanted me to train him and take him through exercise programmes, because that's what I did with quite a few guys. He wanted to stay away from the people, but they'd somehow get past me and the next thing you know, I'd say, "Where's Glenn?" and people would say, "Er, Jerry, I saw him walk past the bedroom with a guitar," and I'd be like, "Oh shit!" When Glenn grabbed an instrument, you knew where he was going. He had got a hold of something and he was going to create. It was so weird. He'd start playing a song and you'd think, "This is great!" But then he'd go over that same song over and over again. Then he'd go to another tune. He'd sit there and create a whole song.*

The guy was a ball of creativity, but God, there were so many demons inside him. I'd say, "Glenn, come on dude, it's time to go home," but he was so into it, and he'd say, "Jerry, I just need to play!" I'd say, "I know, but it's five o'clock in the morning and we've got to sleep!" After a while you realised that we weren't going to train the next day. His biggest enemy was himself. Sometimes it was possible to get through it, though, because he'd get sober and we'd train. We did kickboxing; I had him punching and kicking and doing sit-ups and lifting weights. He was into it: he'd do it for a few days, and the next thing you know we'd go out. He'd say, "Jerry, I really want to stay clean tonight," and I'd say, "OK, let's focus on that," but then somebody would be around and they'd want to be his best friend and give him drugs. The guy's a legend: they all wanted to be his friend.

I lived with Glenn for about the last six months or so before I left Atlanta in 1990. I said to him, "I gotta get out of Dodge: this place is driving me nuts!" and I left. Thank God he got it together after that. It was a war: an eternal war.

By Christmas 1988 all my money had gone. Christine and I were so poor. The gas, heating, and phone had all been turned off. For our Christmas dinner we had a little tin of stew each. This was all caused by my addiction.

I'd got divorced from Karen in the fall of 1988. I went to see our cat Pocket before he was put down, and that was the last time I saw Karen Hughes: 22 years ago. We're not friends. I tried to get in touch in 1994, but she doesn't want anything to do with me, because of my behaviour to her and my inability to be a good husband. I'm remorseful about it: I wish I could have been better to her. I've made my amends, but it's not really what she wants to hear.

I moved my stuff out in late February 1989. I was actually weaning myself off the drugs for a while, just doing the occasional bit of ecstasy – the coke was gone. I realised that I was in dire financial trouble until my next cheque came from Purple in March. I had nowhere to go except to my parents' house in England; I was pretty much penniless for the first time in my life. I was too embarrassed to ask my friends for help, so we put all our shit in a storage space in Atlanta and came to England. It was early February. I still had some money in an account in the UK, and I was thinking, "What the hell am I gonna do?" We stayed at Mom's for two months and I was sober at this point.

One day Mom told me, "David Coverdale's just called up, he wants you to come to Lake Tahoe and work on his album." Coverdale and my mom are really good mates and he said to her, "I know Glenn isn't in great shape. I want to get him to a nutritionist and put him on a diet." He just wanted to help me out and pay me a lot of money – $25,000, which is like $75,000 now – just to sing some background vocals. He was very, very good to me.

So David flew me and Christine to Reno, where his band Whitesnake were making the *Slip Of The Tongue* album. We were picked up at the airport by David's assistant, Jimmy Ayres, and we checked into a great suite in a great hotel. David came over and gave me a big hug, looked at me and said, "I'm going to get you sorted out," and I went on a diet. I was completely off the coke: I was clean until that April. So David was getting a clean Glenn, even though I wasn't looking great. I was still drinking beer.

David played me the songs and we started to record. I wasn't in the greatest shape, but David stood by me 100 per cent. Even to this day, I look at David as my brother. We still talk to each other like that David and Glenn from Purple. There's no grandiose pomposity between us, it's a beautiful thing. I owe him so much for what he did for me back then, because the first inkling of my getting clean and sober came from him. He wanted the best for me.

It wasn't easy singing on the album. David had me singing a third above his vocal, which was super, super-high, so I didn't get a lot of vocals done on that record, just three songs. But it set me up so that I could now move back to LA and rent a place. I moved back on July 1. It was a house belonging to Emmett Chapman, the guy who designed the Chapman Stick, in Laurel Canyon. It was up on Yucca Trail. I met Emmet and his wife, having been clean and sober for three months and looking and feeling good because I'd lost 20lb, and took a six-month lease. It was right across from John Mayall's house and it had a fantastic view. I now also had an attorney, who set up the deal with David, so I was now about to make a comeback.

Yeah, right.

The first weekend, I call up my old drug dealer. I just thought, "I can do a bit of coke. I mean, look at me – I've done the Whitesnake album, people love me again." But at the weekends the phone would be off the hook and I'd be out of my mind. I'd be doing ecstasy and crack with an array of heavyweight people – big drug guys from Vegas. I'd hear them talking in my kitchen about some big deal that was going down.

At this point I got a call from Pete Winkelman, one of the early *Kerrang!* guys who was at Warners and is now the owner of the Milton Keynes Dons football club. He's from Wolverhampton and is a big Glenn and Trapeze fan, and he was telling me that I'm one of the best singers in the world. The CEO of Warners wanted to sign me to a solo deal, and so they gave me a big advance and equipped me with a 16-track studio in my home. I was down there a lot, working on music – well, actually just fucking around on drugs.

When Christine was away one weekend, my dealer came to the house and he was out of breath. He had a big bag full of cocaine with him, with five kilos in it. He said, "Can I leave this here?" He told me that he'd set up a place in LA, where a drug deal was about to happen with some other dealers, who came in with guns. There was gunfire and bad shit was happening. I think somebody was killed. Years later I'd look back at that coke as death coke: people died for that stuff.

While these kilos were in my house, I was visited by Las Vegas gangsters, street hustlers, actors, and a former Miss Louisiana – who, sadly, gave blowjobs and had sex with gangsters to get hits on the crack pipe. This party lasted for six months, with 20 people and shit flying everywhere. You could never get through five kilos of coke in a lifetime, and I'd done enough coke in my time to kill most people. Grandiose as it sounds, I should be dead. I'd shovel it up my nose, I don't know how I survived.

People would be coming to my house for six months afterwards just to smoke crack. They'd bring piles of it, knowing that I'd be a great host to them. I was now becoming the guy in the robe at end of *Boogie Nights*. There were always drugs in my house. When I moved out I found bags of it – thousands of dollars of it – and flushed it down the toilet. You'd trip over cocaine in my house, there was so much of it.

CHAPTER 13

A NEW DAWN

SOBRIETY AT LAST

In January 1990, people were getting busted everywhere. One night, someone smoked some crack in my bathroom and then walked out into the bedroom, where she fell and had a massive seizure. I screamed, and apparently the neighbours told the cops that they thought someone in my house was being murdered. I picked her up and put her in the bed, and just as she was awakening, the cop lights were outside my house. I saw three or four cop cars and I heard them all running up the stairs to my door. In my bathroom was a big bag of coke. If they'd come in at that moment, I wouldn't be here now.

I turned the lights out in the bedrooms and on in the hallway, so they couldn't see in the bedrooms – and for some reason they just left. Can you imagine my heart? Three days later we put our stuff in storage and legged it to England.

Pete Winkelman put me in a hotel for a week and we got a six-month lease on a beautiful two-storey house in Kensington. It was a mews house; it was fantastic. Winkelman was a huge fan of this guitar player called Robin George from Wolverhampton, and he wanted him to produce me. Robin had some songs that he wanted me to record. I wasn't clean and sober and firing on all cylinders, but I met with Robin and the songs he had were pretty good. They were pop, not rock, and not really Glenn songs, but they were OK. We started to record them at his house, and we also commandeered Nomis Studios and Ridge Farm, the great studio down in London.

I was coke-free but I wasn't drug-free, because what do you do when you stop doing coke? You go to speed! A friend of mine knew a dealer in the Midlands who would come down every other weekend to London. I loved speed, although it didn't like me.

It didn't take long to do the demos with Robin: about a month. About five or six songs were recorded at Ridge Farm. It was great weather that year. That summer, with the Warners advance, I bought a house in Atlanta without even seeing it. Christine went home to her parents while I was in London recording, and she found a beautiful house: five bedrooms, 5,000 square feet. It was huge and cost a lot of money. I flew back on my birthday and we bid on it, bought it, and moved into it in September. It had a huge basement and a big old garden with its own creek. It was an amazing house – and I said to Christine "I'm never gonna get high in this house. Never!" I remember the truck pulling in from LA with all our stuff on a beautiful day, and we hugged each other. Lo and behold, the next week I was ordering speed, because it was great to shag on.

Something had to change, and it came when I was asked to sing on a song called 'What Time Is Love?' by the KLF, and appeared in the video clip.

Bill Drummond [The KLF] *We were originally supposed to be doing the song with Axl Rose of Guns N' Roses, but he never turned up to the session. I can't remember who the fuck suggested Glenn, but as soon as they did I said, "What, that guy who I saw fronting Trapeze in 1971? Great idea!" When he came in I assumed he'd be jaded and I wondered if he'd take the piss, because we'd worked with people who'd given us all kinds of attitude – but as soon as* *he went into the vocal booth, he was absolutely and utterly stunning. He was so full of energy.*

Jimmy Cauty [The KLF] *Glenn was totally the right man for the job. He was brilliant. We sat around for an hour or so going through some ideas, and he got it immediately – which was great, because the music was a rather odd rock and techno combination. I didn't know that he was about to go through rehab. Funnily enough, I was taking loads of drugs at the time. … He was brilliant and not at all fragile, because the video shoot was an ordeal, with tons of cold water flying everywhere and everyone getting soaked. You can't be fragile in that situation.*

We all knew that 'What Time Is Love?' was going to be Top Five around Europe. Subconsciously there was a voice in my head saying, "Well Glenn, this is it! You're going to be on *Top Of The Pops*," so I checked into Betty Ford in January and came out a month later.

Oh, and by the way – that heart attack I mentioned in the introduction to this book didn't kill me, but it didn't get me sober. When I went into the ER room in the Atlanta hospital, I was hooked up to machines which indicated that the heart attack hadn't been severe. The oxygen simply wasn't flowing freely to my brain. Thank God I had this moment of clarity in order to come to my senses. I knew something was different: I couldn't form a sentence and I could barely speak. A red flag, for sure. I truly believe that God sends us all messages throughout our lives. This one was clear – I had stepped into hell, but my angels were there to guide me back to safety.

I go to England, and the first day I get there, the single enters at Number Five or something, so while my sober brothers and sisters are going to meetings, I'm doing PR for 'What Time Is Love?' I'm basically on a slippery slope, but I didn't use drugs or alcohol. But although I was absolutely clean and sober, with no slips at all, I wasn't working my sobriety. I thought, "I'm not going to that many meetings and surrendering to the fact that I've completely been an idiot."

When you first get sober, the first thing you have to do is give your life completely to it, 100 per cent. Not 99 per cent. I hadn't done that – and I was working on half-measures. In sobriety, half-measures will only lead you back to your drug of choice.

A word about a dear friend of mine. I met Mitchell Binder in the early 90s: he had a dream about designing rock'n'roll jewellery. We would get together once a week for coffee, or just to talk about life. I started touring more, and we lost touch for a while. My second wife Gabi, Chad Smith, Chad's wife Nancy, and I were having dinner in the Pacific Palisades one Sunday evening in late 2005. As we were leaving the restaurant, Mitchell walked in. We hugged, and I asked him how life was; he told me that he had put his dream into action. I'd been seeing adverts all over town, and noticing people with insane-looking rings, necklaces, and bracelets. His company is King Baby – that's Mitchell's world. He has a strong vision, and he's fearless with his art. I admire him immensely. Mitchell is one of my closest friends: we have walked the same path. Anyone who is true to themselves gets my vote. Those who participate in life – the chosen few.

In 1991 my dear friend Andy Field died of cancer. He was the right-hand man of Fish, the original singer of Marillion, and he was the first of us to go. I did a benefit for him over two nights in Cannock, and gave the proceeds to his family. We also did a show with Fish at the Apollo in Hammersmith – and that was the start of the official Trapeze reunion, which took place in 1994.

I'd spent the intervening three years working on my sobriety, getting my health back, and doing the odd bit of music such as the *LA Blues Authority* record in 1992. But I wasn't yet the man I am today, and the next real milestone in my career was the Trapeze reunion. It was fucking great, jamming with Mel again.

Tony Perry *In 1994 I was contacted by Threshold Records, who were planning to release the Trapeze catalogue on CD worldwide. It was agreed that the band would play live again, so a second guitarist was engaged in addition to Mel and rehearsals commenced. Everything went well and the band did a couple of sell-out shows at the Robin 1 venue in Wolverhampton before departing for the States. The atmosphere was good, and all was fine both on and off stage. Unfortunately the tour was poorly organised Stateside, and we were all disappointed with the final outcome. However, what was successful was the working relationship that existed between all of the members of the band, the crew, and the management. It was great to see that Glenn had got himself back into shape, mentally, physically, and emotionally. It was a pleasure to work with him again both on and off stage: what a contrast to the tour of 1976.*

So now Trapeze are doing the reunion tour, in July to August 1994. I invite a friend of mine out to visit me. He comes to my show in Dallas, and he's a bodybuilder. Now, here's the slip that only a few people know about until now.

This is a perfect example for anyone who doesn't understand how sobriety works. This guy, the bodybuilder, comes out and we go to a titty bar. I'm sober and I'm fine and I'm good, and he gives this liquid to this stripper in the back of the limo. It was GHB, which bodybuilders use while they're sleeping to build up their muscles. If you resist it when you take it, you can actually get a buzz off it before you fall asleep, and it makes you horny. It's like ecstasy. But he told me this was an approved drug, like caffeine or nicotine. I thought, "I'll have some of that!" The strippers were really getting off on it, they were getting horny and dishing out blowjobs in the back of the limo. I thought, this is amazing shit. He said, "Don't worry, it's not a real drug," so he put it in some water and I drank it.

The moment it went down my throat, I went, "This is fucking great!" It reminded me of ecstasy, but it was legal. When I had some, the addict in me wanted more and more, and I was with this great chick who had been Miss North Carolina and was now a stripper. GHB gave me these sexual, animalistic, nasty feelings. She was young and gorgeous and I was all over her like a bad suit. We had a great time, but the next morning when I woke up I thought, "Oh God – that was great, but that was wrong." Anything that is that good has got to be illegal.

So that was my first slip. I went back to LA, where I had moved to from Atlanta with Christine in March 1992. Every Monday night I went to a meeting with some industry people. I went home as if nothing had happened, and saw my sober friends and buddies – and I never disclosed this to them. I formed a band, started writing music and touring as a solo artist, and on the surface, everything looked normal.

In November 1994, I went to Amsterdam. Metaphorically speaking, my disease was doing push-ups in the car-park, waiting for me, saying, "You can go to a rave tonight if you like." I met a guy called Burt who ran a bar. It turned out he was a major Glenn fan. So we went to this place called Escape, which was in the middle of the red light district. This club starts at two in the morning and goes on all night. I walk in, and there's 2,000 half-naked men and women, all dancing on ecstasy.

My disease was saying, "You can have one of those disco biscuits." This is a perfect example of a slip: it was saying, "Have one. No-one will ever know." My tour manager didn't know about this. Burt didn't know about my history with coke, he just thought I was a rock star who wanted to get laid and who wanted some ecstasy. So he comes back and about an hour after ingesting this pill, I'm grooving hard. I danced by myself around my hotel room, as one does, and did the other pill, but after five or six hours I'm coming down and I'm thinking, "That was great, and nobody knew about it!" (Except me.)

I went home, and didn't tell anyone. And I didn't feel guilty, because my disease was telling me that I didn't have a problem. Now, I might have felt guilty on a subconscious level, but this thing inside me was saying, "You don't have a problem, because you danced alone and you didn't have a heart attack, and you went and had breakfast the next morning and you were fine!"

So the next time I come back to Amsterdam, I called the guy up and said, "Get me ten pills." So he came down with the pills and I didn't go to sleep for 36 hours. I managed to keep it a secret. I was with him in the club, meeting chicks, dancing, sweating, making promises and making out ... you know the story. But still scrambling under the wire without anybody seeing me.

When I was in treatment at the Betty Ford Center, I was told that newly-recovered people's relationships sometimes end. I had gotten clean and sober. Christine liked the odd glass of wine, and because I would never go to a bar – what's the point? – Chris and her friends would go out at the weekend and I would stay home. It's no fun to be in a bar when you don't partake in adult beverages – at least not for me. It was becoming painfully clear to me that in order for me to grow, I couldn't be around Chris. Something had to give.

I left for a fall tour of Europe. In Stockholm, at a meet-and-greet after the show, I met a beautiful 21-year-old Swedish girl named Åsa Petterson. She looked like an angel: no make-up, a natural beauty. I invited her to come to my show a few days later: she came along with her boyfriend, a great lad. We exchanged details and I dropped them off back in Stockholm and went back to LA.

Things were changing at home. I couldn't stop thinking of Åsa back in Sweden. In December I called to wish her a happy Christmas, and before hanging up the phone, she told me that she was breaking up with her boyfriend. I asked her if she would like to meet me in London in mid February and she said, "Yes." I told Christine that I was going to London to do some promo, but I was really only going to meet Åsa.

I met her at Heathrow. She walked into the arrivals hall, and she was nervous, but so delicate and sweet. We checked into a hotel in Kensington and talked until the early morning, wanting to feel comfortable with one another. It was pure and gentle, and for the first time in sobriety, I had to re-learn how to be intimate with sensitivity.

Mom was rushed into hospital while I was in London, so we jumped on the train to Wolverhampton so that I could be by her side. My parents' health is paramount to me, more than these words can express. Mom came home shortly after, and I had to return to LA. I said goodbye to Åsa, and told her I would call her when I got to the States. By this time we both knew that something was happening – and it didn't matter to either of us that I lived in California and she lived in Stockholm.

So I get back home on the evening of February 21 1995. The next day was Christine's 29th birthday. She was about to jump in the shower, and I asked her the question, "Chris, what would you like for your birthday?" I can still hear her answer to this day. She replied, "I'd like for you to move out." She may have been half jesting, but her words were music to my ears. While she was showering, I called my friend Bill Eskridge and asked him to come over with his pickup truck. By the time Chris was towelling off, I was taking my platinum and gold awards off the walls, tearing down my studio equipment, and loading my musical instruments into Bill's vehicle. We filled two cars with my belongings, loaded up and left the beach house. I placed all my possessions in a secure unit. I went back to the house to collect some clothes and sneakers. Christine's father told me that this lover's tiff would be all over with soon, and that I would be back.

I moved into a hotel in Hermosa Beach. It became my home base for a year. I had a corner suite with a view overlooking the ocean: the sunsets were unreal. I made the *Feel* album in the early spring of 1995 at Gary Ferguson's studio. Pat Thrall came in from NYC, and I had Matt Sorum and Ferg on drums. Matt is an amazing drummer, with enough groove for days, and Ferg had been with me since Hughes/Thrall – a bad-ass heavy funkster.

After I completed *Feel*, I flew to London to meet up with Åsa. I got a month's lease on an apartment in Mayfair, and after that I brought Åsa back to LA, where we lived at the hotel in Hermosa Beach. We would travel back and forth between LA and Stockholm, as I was touring twice a year in Europe, and we eventually leased an apartment in the Ostermalm area of Stockholm – but by this time we weren't communicating with each other very well. She had a group of friends that I didn't know, and I was starting to travel more. In September 1997, she told me she had met a young lad back in Stockholm. This came as no surprise. I was disappointed, but we were definitely growing apart. We flew back to London together, I put her on a plane to Stockholm, and that was it. Åsa came to one of my shows in Stockholm in 2006. She was still gorgeous. I wished her a happy life.

Cut back to the next time I was in Amsterdam. I'd been touring with my band on the back of a new album, *From Now On* ..., which came out in 1994. The tour had gone great, but from time to time I'd encounter what we call a geographical lapse in my sobriety. I was off the road in July of 1995, and I said, "Fuck it! I'm gonna take a weekend in Amsterdam from LA." I flew in and this time I said, "Get me 50 pills!" So we went to Burt's bar. He met me at the airport and I immediately took two of 'em. Right there in the car. We went to his bar, and I was so on fire that I didn't care. I just thought to myself, this is the way it was supposed to be: I love myself, and at least I'm not on cocaine; I'm not going to die tonight. I kid you not, this is not being grandiose: out of 50 pills that weekend, I did a good 40 of them myself. My disease completely took over. It wants me dead. It doesn't want me in a hospital, with tubes coming out of me: it wants me off.

So here's the deal. I was drinking water in the bar. I'd given some pills to some chicks: Burt had his own. This was a Sunday night party, and by Tuesday night at his house, I started to feel really, really ill. Not like vomitous ill: ill like weak, dehydrated, a little bit disorientated – and scared. So I had him ready to call 911 and he watched over me as I drank a lot of water, and I managed to come down and sober up, get some food in me and go, "Whew – that was a close one." It was the classic case of not knowing about ecstasy. I'd switched addictions from coke to ecstasy – because I was thinking, "I can't do coke, because coke will kill me."

By this point I'm lying to my friends and lying to myself. In 1996, I go on vacation to meet Burt, and it's another 50 pills. I start taking them when I'm at the airport, but I had to go back to Wolverhampton to see a Wolves versus Barcelona friendly match, so I only had a certain number of hours in Amsterdam, even though I've got all these pills. My friend Burt liked cocaine, so I bought him a quarter-ounce, because I was loaded with dough and for some reason I felt like spending it. My disease wanted me to be poor: it wanted me to give all my money away. So I bought him some blow, and because the ecstasy wasn't that good, I said, "Just give me a couple of lines, what the hell." So the coke went in me, but it felt wrong. It had been five years since I'd had a line, but I went straight back to the heart attack and the paranoia, the cops knocking, the Nazis coming down the chimney and all that shit. It was horrible. So I pushed away from the table and I said, "You can have that – I don't want any more."

And then the next time I did it was the following week in Dallas, Texas. I was on the way there knowing that my new city of debauchery was going to be Dallas: I'd done Amsterdam, and I'd done the blow, and I called an old friend who I used to drink with when I was in Trapeze. I went to his house, knowing that it would be my safe haven from the world. He knew I'd been sober for a long time, but not about my slips in Amsterdam. My disease was saying to me now, "You know what? You're OK. You haven't done coke for a while." So my friend calls an old dealer friend, and the guy delivers us half an ounce of coke, because I never deal in small quantities. And it was fucking, *fucking* really good, pure stuff. After gram number two, I freaked out. I started to hyperventilate and my heart was racing, and I took a gulp of vodka to calm me down – but it just made me worse.

I was known for flushing massive amounts of coke down the toilet, to stop me doing any more, and that day I must have thrown four grams down there before he said, "Wait a minute!" and grabbed some to take to his girlfriend's for safe keeping. So now the other guy was talking: my sobriety. That's Glenn going "Wake up – you're gonna die!" So we decided that we would spend the rest of my time in Dallas drug and alcohol-free. That lasted about two days, until my 45th birthday, where I said, "Fuck it! It's a one-off, let's go get an ounce of coke and a hundred hits of ecstasy." For the next four or five days, it was like Jekyll and Hyde.

You know, I took the ounce of coke and then went back to the dealer and said, "I want another one. Because that one was crap!" So he sold me another ounce and we did that: that's two ounces of coke between me, my friend Lynn, and some stripper girls, in a week. I found some titty-bar managers who loved Trapeze and they sorted me out with a lot of birds.

Lynn Everett *We went to a strip club and some of the girls came over with the manager of the club after it closed. We did ecstasy and everything else at our disposal, and had a nice little orgy that lasted into the next afternoon. I had a girl that looked like Elle MacPherson sitting on my face: Glenn was in the other room with two more.*

I'd do a line of coke, and then some ecstasy, and then another line of coke, and then some more ecstasy. Lynn woke me up one morning and I was covered in hundreds of $100 bills: I'd obviously fallen asleep counting my money. I spent $20,000 on blow and strippers in that five days. Table dancers, the lot. It was the only time in my 25 years of drug use that I had a euphoric time, where the disease was going, "You did it! You had a great time! You didn't have a heart attack! You got laid!"

Lynn Everett *One night, we were going out to see the band Live, which a friend of mine was promoting. We were getting ready and Glenn was running late as usual. I heard this crash in the bathroom: he had fallen off the toilet into the bathtub. I just laughed and told him to quit goofing around because we were late and would miss the show. On the way back, Glenn fell asleep with his feet sticking up in the air in the back of the cab.*

That was August 21 1996, that debauchery, but it was great. Well, my disease was telling me it was great, know what I'm saying? When I went back to LA it took me a damn good week to recover and get my sleep back. After that I didn't do drugs for a year. Nothing.

Lynn Everett *It was usually when we got home and things had settled down that Mr Hyde made his appearance – usually right when I was ready to call it a night and get some rest for the next day. Mr Hyde wasn't ready to go to bed, because the ghosts were in the closet, under the bed, in the oven, in the bathroom, looking in the window when the blinds are closed … I would have to search the entire house every five minutes for hours, and then Glenn would go into his room and shut the door and I would have to sit at the door to watch for the creatures. He would call out to me every 15 minutes to make sure I was there and on watch.*

Let's be very clear here. I used six times in the three-year period from 1994 to 1997. Between 1991 and 1997 I was completely OK, except for a small number of slips. Now, in 1996 I had the great pleasure of working with Tony Iommi again.

Tony Iommi *I was talking to our management and I heard that Glenn was off all the drugs. I thought, "That could be really interesting," and so it was* *organised that we'd get together. Glenn was great. I was so pleased to see that he was starting to get himself together, but as I say, it was difficult for him because he had to prove himself to everybody. He'd said to people so many times before that he was fine, but then he was out of it again. So I was a bit wary of that.*

The album was called *The DEP Sessions* and was really great, but it didn't come out until 2000.

Tony Iommi *The recording went well. Glenn was really into it and sang great. He played on it as well, of course. You could talk to him on the level, as opposed to someone who you don't know if it's going in one ear and out the other. He was really up for doing something, and he sang so well. He'd lost a lot of weight and he was losing more all the time and he'd had his hair cut short – I was thinking, "Bloody hell, who's this?"*

The following year, who should I meet but Gary Moore? We'd fallen out in May or June 1985, and I ran into him in 1997 in a restaurant called the Spy Bar in Stockholm. It was 1am and I was about to go home. Some guy ran up to me and said, "Hey! Gary's in the bar!" and I said, "Great – if you like, you can let him know I'm here." So Gary comes in, looks around and doesn't recognise me, even though I'm standing right next to him – because of course I've lost like 50lb, maybe 70lb. I grabbed him and said, "What's going on?" and he started to get really emotional. I made my amends to him as a sober man.

I said, "I really want to make amends for being a complete letdown to you and your manager and Virgin: it was one of the lowest points of my life and I really hope you can forgive me. I want to apologise from the bottom of my heart." After that it was cool: he was sad, and then glad, and then mad, as you do. He said, "I'll play on your record if you like." I walked away feeling a lot better.

So, do you want to hear how I finally got rid of the drugs for good?

It went like this. I was on tour with my band in 1997 and I was dating a Swedish girl. I had St Patrick's Day coming up and I was going to spend the whole week in Dallas. A whole week in Dallas, yeah! I got a room at the Marriott Courtyard Hotel in Dallas – a suite, a really massive one with three bedrooms – because I knew what was going to happen. I acquired a stereo and a portable TV, plus a video player to watch pornos. It was like a club in there.

This is where it starts to get weird. I started to have trouble breathing, so my friend Pete got someone to bring some sleeping pills around to calm me down – which is dangerous when you've been doing coke. I thought I needed to sleep, and I remember falling asleep in my food – which I'd never done before. Every rock star should do it once. But I knew that I'd had enough, so I went into my room, shut the door, put earplugs in and went to sleep.

I went back to LA and I thought, "I can't do this any more." I thought, "I've done it six times in three years and nobody knows about it." So I went home in that summer to LA, where I'd bought a house after I'd finished with Christine. I wasn't really dating anybody, I just hung out with my friends. One day I was with my cats in my bedroom, just looking through my suitcase, throwing some stuff away, and inside one of my socks there's some fucking ecstasy which I'd stashed there and didn't even know it. I was the king of stashing shit and not knowing where I'd hidden it – a typical addict.

So there I am: it's 11 o'clock at night, and I'm looking at this ecstasy and I'm thinking, "Well, it's not cocaine ... I'm alone ... ." I drew the blinds and took this ecstasy and I felt OK. Then I did another hit, and called a girlfriend of mine, a very well-put-together girl who didn't have a clue about me doing drugs. I called her at five in the morning and said, "Come over! Wear something nice under a raincoat or something." So she comes over and she sees me sweating, with a completely tortured face. It was completely Jekyll and Hyde: I might as well have had a top hat and a cape. That's what it was like. I completely changed from being a normal, nice guy into this kind of freaky, animalistic motherfucker. She'd only been there an hour when I said to her, "You've got to call an ambulance. I'm going to have a heart attack."

Within a minute and a half, we could hear the sirens. The cops came in. This is a true story. I prayed, "Lord, please don't let me die tonight. Please, I beg you." I was terrified: thinking that I was about to die loaded, not sober like I was supposed to. I wanted to meet God sober. They get me in the ambulance and hook me up to these things, and we're racing to the hospital, and I'm thrashing around, freaking out, thinking that I was going to die.

So I say to the guy that's driving the ambulance, "You don't understand. I'm not like those other addicts that you have in the back of your ambulance." He told me "Shut the fuck up, you loser drug-addict piece-of-shit cocksucker. I'm gonna come back there and beat the shit out of you!" A light went on in my head. Bing! And from that moment on, I've been completely clean and sober.

It's not my business what people think of me: my business is how I conduct myself. I know that any drug that affects me from the neck up will send me into a state that is not right, and that I might die from it. In fact, I will die from it.

We could have got through this book without anybody ever

knowing about those six episodes between 1994 and 1997, but I wouldn't be happy. My drugs of choice – cocaine, crack, ecstasy, and speed – are poison to me. My mother, doctors, lawyers, physicians, they all tried to get me off drugs – but that ambulance driver was the one that did it. Was it God talking through him? I don't know, but he was the one that got me sober.

The funny thing is that when they checked me out in the examination room, they said "There's nothing wrong with you." I stayed in there for two days of surveillance; it cost a fortune. When I got out, the old Glenn Hughes would have said, "Let's do some more drugs." But at that point, I was done. Completely finished. I told my disease to fuck off.

People will ask why I didn't speak about this before. Well, it needed to be spoken about in the right context and on the right platform. If people read this book thoroughly and read about what happened to me in the ambulance, and they still don't get it, then they just won't get it. On the path I went down from 1974 to 1991, I missed out on a lot of things. I missed out on growing spiritually for 17 years. There was no growth in me. I was completely spiritually bankrupt. I snorted a million dollars' worth of cocaine, and that was stupid – I could have probably made another $100 million by not doing it. When I came back from the heart attack, I had zero in the spiritual account – nothing. I came back from being a grossly overweight, freaked-out, unhealthy drug user to what I am today.

Sheila Hughes *I trusted him completely. I knew when he finally did it that he wouldn't go back.*

CHAPTER 14

REBUILDING THE MACHINE
LIFE REBORN

In 1996, I was looking for a new hairdresser. A friend had suggested a girl who worked at a salon on Melrose Avenue in Hollywood, so I went to get my hair cut, and met Cindy Levinson. She was full of life, and had this infectious laugh: we got along really well. She told me she was married to an English musician and left it at that. Six weeks later I was back again, and I asked her the name of my fellow Brit. His name was Lol Tolhurst, Robert Smith's boyhood friend: they formed The Cure together. I remembered how much I'd loved this band in the late 80s. They were totally unique: you immediately knew it was them when one of their songs was played on the radio.

I was invited by Cindy to dinner at their house and we made an instant connection. I was single at the time, and probably needed to be, as I'd been in a couple of disastrous relationships with Swedish girls. Every Sunday for four years, Cindy, Lol, and I would have lunch at the Old King's Head pub on Santa Monica Boulevard. Then we would go shopping on Third Street Promenade, where I tried to fill the hole in my life by buying clothes. I never wore most of them: I eventually gave them to the Salvation Army. Cindy and Lol were really kind and loving to me: they were there for me through this difficult time in the mid 90s.

At Christmas 1999, I was visiting my parents at their home in

Cannock. I hadn't been in a relationship for a couple of years, and Dad said, "Son, do you want to keep getting your arse kicked by dating young Swedish birds, or do you want to find a woman with a career who lives in the same area code, who you can relate to and grow together with?" This really sank in with me.

Tony Perry *As the months, and indeed years, went by, it became apparent that Glenn had started to face up to his problems and showed great courage in meeting them head on. He slowly regained his old personality and eventually both Mel and Dave joined him in certain recording projects. We once again became comfortable in each other's company.*

When I was in my disease, the last thing I was thinking about was hitting on chicks. I wasn't in great shape; I didn't find myself that desirable. When you're in your disease, the first thing you think about is your drug. Sex on drugs and sex not on drugs are completely different things. I want you to know that when people are high on drugs, especially addicts, their sexual behaviour is nothing like it would be if they're weren't in their disease. It's very animalistic. It's very euphoric, and when you come it's a great climax, but that's never going to be enough to make me go back and use drugs again. I'd been completely out of my brains, but I was never the kind of guy who would get loaded with his friends for three or four days and then go into a bar and expect to pick up a chick. That was never going to happen. I was also never going to be with the kind of chicks that hang out at coke parties, even in my fucked-up state. I had some sort of morals, and the fact is that I never found any of those birds to be attractive. I got loaded and I may have thought about sex, but it never really happened.

It was three months after my conversation with Dad, on March 10 2001, that I had my fateful first date with Gabi Dotson.

Gabi Hughes *Glenn and I got set up on a blind date by his drummer Gary Ferguson. I'd known Ferg for maybe five or six years. The company I was working for at the time did music production for TV commercials, and one of our clients was having a big party and Ferg was there. He was asking me backstage who I was dating, and I said, "No-one right now: when you get to be in your thirties it's hard to meet someone to date, because everyone's married already." He said, "Well, I have a single friend, he's a singer – the best singer out there. Do you want to meet him?" I said, "Sure!" He said, "He was in Deep Purple," and I said, "Don't tell me anything about him, because I don't want to judge him before I meet him."*

I knew vaguely who Deep Purple were, so I had a visual in my mind that some guy was going to knock at my door. He'd probably have a receding hairline and long hair, and look like he hadn't accepted that he didn't look like a young man any more. I had 'bad rocker dude' images in my head, but no real idea of who Glenn was. But I knew he'd be OK if he was a friend of Ferg's, and that it wouldn't be a big deal: it would be fun just to meet up.

So we met up at a place in Venice, California, called 72 Market Street: Dudley Moore was one of the owners. Glenn had a really nice pin-stripe suit on and nice hair and I thought, "Oh, he's not what I expected." He was pretty tanned, and he confessed to me that he'd been to a tanning salon. I said, "Oh, that's really bad for you: you really shouldn't do that."

I didn't know that he didn't drink, and of course all I wanted to do when we got there was sit at the bar, because I had just come from a whirlwind trip to New York, where I'd been sitting down at dinners with clients. I didn't want to sit at another table in a restaurant, I just wanted to go to the bar and get a drink and talk. So I made him sit at the bar and drink water, which he can't stand: he wanted a Diet Coke, ha ha! And then he had to order his dinner and eat it at the bar. He was very funny – and I knew that when I got up to go to the ladies, he was looking at my ass.

When the date was over, I didn't know exactly what to think, but I did think, "I kind of like him: I hope he asks me out again, because I'd like to get to know him better." I wasn't looking to get married or anything: I was just looking to go on a date once in a while. I wasn't shopping for a husband, know what I mean? I always thought I'd be a single career woman with two cats, and that I'd do whatever I wanted to do.

It actually happened pretty quickly, though: within a month I thought I'd better ask him what he wanted to do in terms of dating, so I said, "I have to ask you a question, and by the way the answer will have absolutely no negative effect on me. I just want to know what you're thinking. Should we date each other exclusively? I have no problem with either answer, I just want to know so that we're both on the same page." If he'd told me that he wanted to date other women, I would have dealt with that. But he said no, that he was looking for a committed relationship and that he'd be fine with dating just one person and that could be me. Once we had that conversation, it allowed us to open up so that there wouldn't be any game-playing like you have when you're young.

Things moved at a quick pace after that. One day we'd had some people over and I was putting some things in the dishwasher and he said, "You know, I'd really like you to move in with me," and I said, "This is nothing personal: I would say this to any man, but I'm never going to just live with a guy. That's like playing house and there's no benefit in it for me. You don't have to take anything seriously. Why would I do that? I'm going to live in my own place or I'm going to be married, but I'm not going to play house." And he said, "I totally get it. Why don't we get married?" and I thought, "Maybe that is the next step in my life," and said, "Sure!" Two weeks later I had a ring on my finger.

Without any disrespect to any of the other ladies from my past, I knew from the first date with Gabi that I was conversing with and learning from a highly intelligent woman, who is without doubt the funniest female on the planet. I say again, there are no mistakes in God's world: we were supposed to meet at this time, because I was able to hear and see more clearly what I couldn't have perceived just a few years earlier.

She is the backbone of our family, and she encourages me to fulfil all of my heart's desires, as I do her. We spend a lot of time together in the garden, with our hands in the soil, planting seeds, and watching our garden blossom and bloom. Our dogs are our family: anyone who has dogs will understand this. I'm a very lucky man to have survived my trials and tribulations, and then to finally meet my twin soul was the icing on the cake. We're both rather eccentric, but if you know us and have seen us together, you'll get the picture of a life so divine.

Now let's look back at November 23 1997, when I thought I was dying of a heart attack and that ambulance driver changed my life with his words. I'd been through the addiction programme before, and I had worked the 12 steps with my previous sponsors, one of whom was a musician and the other a lawyer. In my first meeting, I identified as a newcomer in the 90 seconds that they give you, and I talked about my previous three years of relapses. Then I noticed that this guy Andy, a Vietnam veteran, said just one thing: "I drank to oblivion." When he said the word "oblivion" I took the word "drank" and put "used" instead. *I used to oblivion.*

It's crazy to think that I'd been so near to sobriety, and yet so far, just a few months before. On August 31 1997, for example, I was at a dinner party in Beverly Hills and I was at a bar ordering some drinks.

I was sober this evening, like I always was when I was in LA. It suddenly came on the screen on CNN that there had been a massive accident in Paris, and that Princess Diana had been killed. I stood there for 20 minutes. I remember I'd never really drunk tea or coffee before that evening, but that night everybody ordered huge cappucinos and I knew that I wanted to stay up to watch what was going on back in England. I didn't want to use cocaine or speed, so I drank two or three of these massive coffees and I was wired out of my mind. I was up all night watching the TV, because I couldn't sleep. I remember everything about it: it was very sad. Diana had her problems, but we all fancied her, didn't we?

What I hadn't really looked at in my inventory in the 90s was that I had always taken the same amount of drugs while expecting different results. The same thing happened every time I ingested cocaine, ecstasy, or speed: as soon as it entered my bloodstream, I was off to the races in my own little world, and it was not a pretty place. I wouldn't want to go there alone. There's a bad neighbourhood in my head, and when Andy said he drank to oblivion, I realised that here was somebody who had 20 years of sobriety and was a soldier in the programme. He spoke really tough, and I said to myself, "I have to ask him to sponsor me." I went up to him and said, "My name is Glenn: I have one day sober. Can we talk over lunch?"

I opened my heart to Andy and asked him if he'd sponsor me, because I really wanted to work this out. He said, "Are you willing to go to any length?" I said, "I'm willing to take any direction you give me." A sponsor works you through the steps, and the steps work you. I needed to do this thoroughly and be rigorously honest, because I hadn't been honest: I'd left chinks in the armour. I was a secret for those three years of relapses. Now I wasn't a secret any more: now I could tell someone on a one-on-one level, and the only person who could understand me was a fellow alcoholic addict. I needed to be walked through the process by someone who understood it.

Andy is known for being a very tough but loving sponsor: we would read daily, go to a noon meeting at Hermosa Beach five days a week and have lunch and talk about what I'd done and heard that day. Just simple things like getting out of bed, doing some meditation, making your bed, cleaning your teeth, and having a shower: it's a routine that works for me and I've been doing it ever since. Reading books on spiritual guidance is really important for me too. I call my sponsor every day, and I recommend that for anyone who suffers from my disease.

So it's coming up to Christmas 1997, and we're thoroughly working the steps. Andy is spending more time at my house than he is at his own: he comes over to write and read with me. He told me that I would write brilliant music and be the greatest singer in the world if I went through the steps, and I laughed at him when he said this because I thought I'd peaked as a writer, with Purple and my solo albums such as *Feel*. He said, "Just trust me on this." So I told Andy that for the whole of 1998 I would stay in LA and I wouldn't travel.

I do not have any time for people who are not loving and nurturing. I have no time for people who are dark and morbid and not growing. I believe that the life we are given is just a breath of what is to come. I'm a firm believer in the hereafter and I want to clean house before I leave. One thing I don't want is to have an inventory of lies and deceits: in fact, I asked my sponsor if I should talk about my six 90s relapses in this book, and he said, "You must, because you may be saving someone's life."

In January 1998, my friend Marc Bonilla had put together some shows with Keith Emerson. I'd met Keith at the Cal-Jam in 1974, and we put together a band with Bob Burch from Elton John, Joe Travers on drums, and Ed Roth on keys. It was a great little combo, and I got to sing a track from *Tarkus*, ELP's great album, in my own way. Now, Keith is a great man: I've met musicians who were great at what they do, but they were jackasses, and Keith's not like that. We became very close. If you look at photos of us, you can see how relaxed and calm I was. I was really working the steps and feeling good.

We played in Holland and I became friends with a guy called Carl Vanempten, a doctor whom I told about my relapses. Every time I go to play in the Low Countries now, I stay with him and his lovely family. Just as I used to plan my geographical relapses, I plan stays with nurturing people the same way. Remember, I'm always in recovery, and I take it seriously. My disease is still doing push-ups outside the damn window. I know men and women with 25 years of sobriety who could walk into a pub right now and start drinking. This disease is cunning, baffling, and powerful.

Later in the year I moved into a property in Palos Verdes, an area where I still live: it's a peninsula that overlooks the ocean and I always wanted to live there. Lo and behold, as my sponsor said, if you want it, you can get it. It's a place where you go if you want to have some peace and quiet. I don't even know the neighbours, it's that quiet.

On August 21 1998 – my 47th birthday – I was in Denver again, playing with a different band. I'd had a major relapse just the year before, but this was the first time in years that I'd had a sober birthday: for the first time in a long time I could call Mom and say, "It's my birthday and I'm sober." It's a big deal. Now I was off to play the Monsters Of Rock festival in Sao Paolo with Dream Theater, Manowar, and Slayer: kind of a mish-mash of bands. No disrespect, but not the kind of music that meant a lot to me. I had a really old-school, funky rock band and the only one that had any soul, but it was great: we got to play to 30,000 people and it was fantastic.

In September I brought my guitar player J.J. Marsh over to spend six weeks of solid writing before recording my next album, *The Way It Is*, like I always did back in the day. We recorded it in October. I'm regimented in everything in my life now: I'll say which day I'm going into the studio and I'll say which day I'm going to hand the record in to the company. To this day I'm still like that. I wanted to get the song 'The Way It Is' off my chest: I needed to state that I wanted to move forward in my life. People didn't realise, but I was talking about my disease. Nobody knew that I was talking about my recovery here. It's a great album: a classic, fresh piece of music. This was my private comeback album.

As the millennium approached, I realised that I had to work harder on keeping myself well. I'd been clean and sober for a few years, but I knew that I needed to work on myself as a person, so I took some time off to be alone. I doubled up on meetings and I worked harder with my sponsor. I started having meetings in my house, because what keeps every addict or alcoholic in faith rather than fear is action, and I have to be in action.

I can talk about how great my life is but if I'm not acting on it, it means nothing. I know a great artist who told me he was going to make a great album in 2000 but he still hasn't made it. While people are smoking and drinking coffees all over America, I'm actually doing things and remaining active – not for money, but because I have to sustain my soul. God takes care of me that way. I'm the problem, and also I'm the solution. I call it "slowbriety": one step at a time. I'm not working the steps now, they're working me: they're embedded in my brain. It's a simple programme for complicated people: intellectual people try to out-think it, and they end up on a bar stool somewhere.

I was now almost three years sober and I was starting to reap the rewards of sobriety. I wanted to show to myself that I was back. In July 2000 my friend Bill Eskridge had said that I needed to do a Christmas album, and I thought, "I can't do this in a rock way." There are rock artists who have butchered the Christmas songs, but I didn't want to do it that way: I did them in a soul, R&B, jazz voice. I loved my album, which we called *A Soulful Christmas*. On November 25 2000 Gabi and I got married: Bill passed away from cancer in December. He was a fantastic guy. I miss him still.

Around this time, I met Paul Rodgers at a festival that we were playing together. In the 70s he was the epitome for me of the onstage rock presence, and we became friends. He was a really great guy for whom I have a tremendous amount of respect. It's great when you meet a rock star who is a decent person: I have zero tolerance or time for people with tremendous egos who give off this aura of "don't talk to me." We're all God's children and we all come from the same place. Paul was a sober man and we were walking the same path: for obvious reasons, I admire anyone who can struggle with their demons and come out the other side.

In 2001 I took part in a tour which I won't name: it was truly awful. I wanted to do it because my friend Joe Lynn Turner was involved with it. It was a corporate event, and I thought, "It'll be OK, I'll make some money and I'll be with my friends." Now, I'm a stickler for rehearsal and pre-production, and I always want to know who plays what part and who's harmonising where. But I didn't realise that I was getting involved with people who didn't rehearse and didn't really care what it sounded like. In my world, you don't get on stage with anybody without knowing what's going on. The first show in Hawaii happened before any rehearsal. I had charted my parts, but basically I went in cold. I'm not blaming the other singers: it's whoever was in charge of the band. They kept chopping and changing and it was a shambles. Then again, if life was perfect we'd be screwed.

An interesting note: I went to Amsterdam in June. You remember Burt, who had got me all that ecstasy? I met him at those gigs, and he was genuinely happy to see that I was sober. You attract what you seek. I don't hang out with fucked-up people any more because I'm not looking to get high.

Gabi Hughes *I've been to a lot of Glenn's shows, and I've learned how difficult life is on the road. There's nothing glamorous about it. You arrive, you throw your shit into the hotel, and you go soundcheck. You may or may not eat, and then you go to the show. You're out of the building anywhere between midnight and three in the morning, when you scramble to your room to get some sleep so you can wake up and start all over again. And by the way, you only get a few hours of sleep because you're driving everywhere: if you don't get up early enough to make it to breakfast, you starve until you get to your next place. You really do get to the point where you wake up and you forget what city you're in – and then you get so far into the groove of that lifestyle that when you get home, your real life almost doesn't seem real. But I go along when it works for everyone: no-one in the band wants to have the* Spinal Tap *wife there to get in the way.*

That summer I'd been writing the first Hughes Turner Project album with Joe Lynn Turner, and I wrote the song for Joe's voice and his genre, which is pop-rock. If you like 80s rock singing, Joe's the man: he's got a great voice. I'm a 70s singer, and I did write a couple of songs for myself too, but the album was pretty much geared toward the Japanese market and Joe's voice. I remember on September 11 we were due to start pre-production on the album at my house, and Joe was on his way to the airport in New Jersey. He was having his breakfast at home and he could actually see the Twin Towers burning. I got a call from him, and of course the TV was on, and I watched the second plane hit the second tower live: it was about 6.20am in Los Angeles, I believe. Obviously HTP was put on hold for a few days, but then he came over a week later and we sat down together and worked out the lyrics to *HTP I* and recorded it in October. I have a lot of respect for Joe, even if the genre that he comes from is not my own.

In 2002 I played in South America. My God – I'm glad I never toured there in the 80s because I never would have made it out alive. I remember telling my band that I wouldn't be going to after-show parties with anybody, I'd be going back to my room – and I was the only guy in that entire 14-man entourage who was completely sober. I set myself aside from that. Some of them said, "Don't worry about us, we haven't done coke in years" and then the next morning, when I went down to breakfast, they were still in the bar from the night before, carrying on.

I knew that was going to be a test for me, but I surrendered to the fact that drugs and alcohol had completely and utterly kicked my ass and I accepted that a line of coke or a drink would lead to paranoia, psychosis, and death. I didn't want to play Russian roulette any more, and I realised that I didn't have to do it any more.

Cherie Currie *I happened to be at the NAMM show in 2003. I heard Glenn was playing there so I ran over to his gig to see him. I hadn't seen or spoken to him in 20 years. There was this gorgeous guy on stage with an* *amazing voice, but I was looking for a heavier guy. I was asking people in the crowd when Glenn was going on, and they pointed to this very svelte, beautiful man up there – and then I recognised his face. I couldn't believe it … I was amazed. I ran to the stage and mouthed "Glenn?" He looked at me, smiled and said "Big difference, huh?"*

Let's be clear about this. There are three different kinds of drug users. There are weekend warriors who work hard all week and have a few cocktails and a few lines on Saturdays, and then you've got the heavy drinkers who are borderline alcoholic and may have lost their job – and then you've got the people like myself, for whom one is never enough. I don't advise anybody to start doing Class A drugs, because there's a good chance you won't be able to stop, but I never condemn the guys who could do one line or one drink. I just didn't want to mix with them. I did see cocaine use in South America, and I did see excessive drinking and some strange behaviour – but I'm just glad to report that it wasn't me. I've never once had the urge to do it since I got clean and sober.

Gabi Hughes *I didn't know a lot about sobriety before I met Glenn; I'm sure I drank way too much when I met him. It definitely cut me back, which is a good thing. He taught me a lot about that: I understand where he gets a lot of his character traits from. If I drink more than a couple of glasses of wine with dinner, I wake up with a raging headache. And I've never done any drugs. I have no desire to do them, so he doesn't have to worry about that. Women can often get what they need from their girlfriends, anyway: we talk and we get stuff out, whereas guys internalise a lot. Glenn doesn't internalise because he has learned not to, and also the programme teaches that you shouldn't do that.*

Skip to 2004, by which time I wanted to make music that was completely fulfilling and natural to me. This was *Soul Mover*, the solo album for which I'm best known. I'd done *Songs In The Key Of Rock* the previous year, and it had been a good album, but as I was writing *Soul Mover* I realised that I had gone back to my roots without any preconceived notions of what a record company would want from me or what some guy in Japan wants to hear.

When I listen back to the songs, I hear a man who has got his life back in order and has no business worrying about what other people think of him. The songs are fresh, they groove like a motherfucker and they tell you exactly where my mind was at. I didn't just want to be as good as I'd been before: I wanted to get better. You can hear that with this album. After this album I wasn't going to do anything I didn't really feel 100 per cent.

Let me also tell you about my dear friend and brother Chad Smith, the drummer in The Red Hot Chili Peppers. He played on this record and he gave it that giant groove thing that he gives to the Peppers' records – it wouldn't have been the same without him. I love that guy: I call him the big galoot. I'm honoured to be godfather to his son Cole.

For me, this album stands up best because my voice is at its peak. It's been said by many people that Glenn Hughes is forgiven once he starts singing. Dave Ling, Malcolm Dome, Gary Moore, and other people have said it over the years. It wasn't like I used to think it was OK to get stoned because I could sing better than anybody else, though. I'm a survivor – we all know that I could have died five or six times, for Christ's sake. Because I didn't, I got to make albums like this one, which really marked my creative rebirth and the beginning of the path that I'm still on today.

When I write music, it makes me a better man. I walk with a stride in my step: I look at the sun and the flowers differently. I'm lucky to have my songwriting and to be able to sing my songs in front of people – songs like 'Soul Mover', which I've done on my own because I didn't have a $2 million promotional budget to push them into the charts. I became famous through word of mouth, and I'm going to go out the same way. People have been coming to see my shows for years and years and now they bring their children, because I have a special gift: my voice. When you see people crying with emotion in the audience, you know you've done a good thing.

Everybody has opinions about what I should do: I can do rock, funk, soul, jazz, and blues, and mix all those things up and that's me. I'd done the *Feel* album in 1995, which was funky and sassy, but I wanted to make a record that had more groove to it this time. With songs like 'Dark Star' and 'Orion', I was making a statement: I didn't know *Soul Mover* was going to be a hit for me, and now everybody wants to hear it. I recorded it in the summer of 2004, in the heat of the San Fernando valley, and we did all the basic tracks in two days. I remember making it very vividly: I knew that it was going to be one of my favourite solo albums. It was great to write, great to play, and great to sing: it was very natural to me. There were elements in there that were reminiscent of Trapeze: there was less Hammond organ and more of the major seventh chords and minor ninth chords that are all over my music. These are not chords that people usually play in rock: I really wanted to pull out all the stops. 2004 was a great year for me, creatively. Europe is my main market now, just like Japan used to be, and it was starting to pay off now that I played in Europe every year or two.

The two albums that I did with Joe Lynn Turner – and this is no disrespect to him whatsoever – reminded me of the music that I didn't want to do any more. I wrote some great songs for those records, and they were very melodic, in-the-box 80s-style material, but it wasn't fulfilling me. I'll say this till I die: I've got to write, play, and sing music that completely fulfils me. This album did that.

I was also doing Tony Iommi's self-titled solo record at this time. We started to work on it at the same time as *Soul Mover*. Tony had rented a studio in Birmingham, and first of all we sat down and figured out who was going to play drums on the album. A couple of guys came down. Chad couldn't do it, and we thought of Taylor Hawkins from Foo Fighters, but in the end Kenny Aronoff did it – and let me tell you, man, he was amazing. He laid down a huge groove for us, and he was the perfect drummer for that record. Then we got the songs sorted out, and arranged for Bob Marlette to produce it. Tony gave me free rein to work on the melodies and the basic structure of the songs on guitar, probably because we've known each other for so long and because we've been through so much together. You've got to know Tony to work with him like that. With him it goes deep: he's family to me.

I didn't want to make a Black Sabbath-sounding record with Tony, because I'm not a Sabbath-style singer, so we wrote songs with a lot more swagger and groove, and they turned out to be among the heaviest Tony had ever made. I felt very comfortable with the hard rock side, but I was also very happy with my solo direction: I was happy to wear different hats.

So here I am in 2004. I'd done a great solo album and I was making a record with the greatest hard-rock guitarist of all time. Chad wanted to do a cover song with me at about this time, and I realised that you have to cover artists who don't sound like you: I couldn't do a Stevie Wonder cover, for example, although he's been a huge influence on me. So we covered The Moody Blues' 'Nights In White Satin', because it's a classic song and they gave me my first break, as you know. We rehearsed the song once and recorded it live. John Frusciante played guitar on it, beautifully and very much in his own way. It appeared on the soundtrack of the Jamie Foxx film *Stealth*, and on my next record, *Music For The Divine*. That album, and the one that followed it, *First Underground Nuclear Kitchen*, continued to bear witness to my new life before the arrival of Black Country Communion, the band I was always meant to be in.

Gabi Hughes *I'm completely committed to Glenn's career. I'm prepared to put his interests first, and I'm OK with that. I'm a lot less emotionally needy than Glenn is, and I've always been attracted to an artistic type of personality. I understand what some people would call his eccentricities. I have my own stuff that is weird too: I'm a pack rat, and I live in the past and I just want to watch old episodes of cop shows and* Charlie's Angels. *I'm not always there with you, but I get Glenn's whole persona and I'm supportive of it. I mean, Glenn can't get a job at a bank. I don't want him to, either: I'm not one of those wives who wants him to drop everything for me because I'm having a moment. I'm not even sure that Glenn understands what I do at my work, and I'm OK with that as well. I just need him to remember my birthday and Christmas.*

Actually, on one of our wedding anniversaries he made arrangements to go out to dinner with Chad! I said, "Look, it's OK" – so he left a brown bag on the counter for me that had some lube and a purple dildo in it and he went out for dinner with Chad. I thought that was hilarious.

CHAPTER 15

WE'RE JUST THE BAND

BLACK COUNTRY COMMUNION

The year 2010 was a pivotal one for me … to say the least. When I was asked by Tony Iommi to sing at Heaven And Hell's tribute show to my friend, the late Ronnie James Dio, at the High Voltage festival in 2010, there was only ever going to be one answer, and of course it was yes. I was there to honour Ronnie and celebrate his songs. I think he would have wanted me to do this, and I think if the tables were turned, he would have done it for me.

You have to remember, he and Wendy Dio were practically living in the same house with me and Karen when he wrote songs like 'Neon Knights' and 'Children Of The Sea'. When Ronnie left Rainbow in 1979, he moved to LA and called me up and asked me to help him find a place in Northridge, where I lived. We went everywhere together, the Hugheses and the Dios, until 1982 or thereabouts. He wasn't a drugs guy, he just liked a little bit of pot, and he had a very British sense of humour: he was the only American I've known who was like that.

He was the kindest, most gentle guy you'd ever meet. When I was really at my worst point with drugs, he'd come and take me aside, and put his arm around me – almost like a father – and he'd say, "We've got to sort this out." A lot of people laughed at me, but Ronnie never did. He was concerned about me, and I cried on his shoulder a few times.

This was also the year in which my new band, Black Country Communion, made its debut impact. I first met the great guitarist Joe Bonamassa at the 2007 NAMM show in Anaheim, because I knew his drummer. He was backstage in a bar and he was shy – a very unassuming guy. We said that we enjoyed each other's music, and a few days later we jammed together. A few months later Joe and I were both playing on an album by a Russian band called Pushking, and we ended up having lunch and going to his studio.

Over the next six months, we met three times to jam. He asked what kind of music we should play, and I suggested that we play stripped-down rock. The key moment came when we played together at a Guitar Center event at the House Of Blues in LA, and Kevin Shirley, the well-known producer – who I've known forever – was there.

Kevin Shirley *I first met Glenn back in 2000 when I was working with a now defunct band called Tidewater Grain, and he came and sang some vocals on one of their tracks. He stayed at my place and we hung out for a few days. I saw him some years later when Joe Bonamassa invited Glenn down to this Guitar Center event and I went along. When I saw the two of them playing together, it was the first time that I'd seen music that really sounded like classic rock. As much as people reference classic rock influences from bands like Zeppelin and Purple, nothing ever really sounds like them, and seeing Glenn and Joe play was a lightning bolt for me.*

After the show Kevin came running over, panting, and saying "We've got to form a band! Why don't I call Jason Bonham and Derek Sherinian from Dream Theater?" Joe and I both said, "Er ... OK!" – and 24 hours later, it was done.

Kevin Shirley *The obvious thing for me was to get Jason in the band, and I also wanted a Jon Lord-style partner for Joe, so I asked Derek Sherinian. And their music is what has made them successful now. They take direction really well and the second album is a little tougher than the first: it's BCC finding their feet. It's more legitimately the sound of the live band than the first one, which sounded a bit like Free-meets-Zeppelin-meets-Purple. This one is more like BCC playing together in a room. They're a great band and they're very pleasurable to work with. They're like a brotherhood.*

As I write this, we're two albums into what promises to be one hell of a career, God willing. We were the Number One act on Planet Rock radio a while back – and we're going to have a great few years.

Joe Bonamassa *Glenn owns the stage, and he is a bona fide rock star. Sometimes "rock star" has the wrong connotations, but it describes him perfectly. Off stage he's funny, humble, and even shy, but you put him on stage and plug in his bass and all of a sudden he's running around. It's awesome. Black Country Communion is the little supergroup that could, know what I mean? The underhyped overachievers!*

Call it mumbo-jumbo, call it fate, whatever you want, but I believe in karma. Everything comes together in God's plan, whatever you want to call him, her or it. A lot of my friends are dead, maimed, or in mental institutions, or they've lost their craft and they're flipping burgers. This group of guys came together at the right time.

Julian Lennon *The first time I saw Glenn and his band take the stage, it reminded me of the great bands from the old days, like Cream, except that they had a soul and funk element which I think very few of those groups have. It* *gave me a completely new understanding of those kinds of music. Black Country Communion absolutely floored me. His voice! My God! I was blown away.*

I'm supposed to be working with Joe; I'm supposed to be working with Bonham's lad. I've never written so much music as I am now. I write 365 days a year. There's a lot of laughs in this band and there's a lot of belief. We're in the moment and we love the music. I've been preparing for this moment for a long time.

Kevin Shirley *Glenn's just remarkable. He's a multilayered singer: he can sing many different things. He has the Stevie Wonder soul thing and he can do the scream too: when he does 'Burn' it just blows my mind. My favourite is his controlled 'rock' voice. The other thing is his bass playing, which is often overshadowed by his genius voice: it's nothing short of brilliant.*

I want to look back for a moment at my career as a songwriter. I guess I must have been 16 when I started writing poetry and adding music as I went along. I'm not sure what age John and Paul, and Mick and Keith, started writing, but looking back you could say that I was right on schedule. I was fascinated by the ocean, so I set about writing a piece that I called 'Seafull'. It was haunting, from the lead guitar line to the way that I expressed myself vocally: it was the first time I sang without fear. I'd written 'Nancy Grey' and 'The Giant's Dead' in 1969, the year before, but 'Seafull' was a watershed moment. At the same time I wrote my first big rock track, 'Medusa'. The lead guitar line – played on acoustic over F major seventh and E minor chords – has become part of my DNA. Those two chords still appear in my songs today.

'Medusa' was a massive song for us in the USA, especially in Texas.

This song and Mel's 'Black Cloud' were all over the radio in 1971, on every radio station from Memphis to Houston. This was my real beginning as a songwriter. I'm convinced that living and touring in the USA in 1971 and '72 lit the fuse for the next round of songs – which were recorded for *You Are The Music... We're Just The Band*.

'Way Back To The Bone' and 'Will Our Love End' were written about Yvonne Dupree, my statuesque LA girlfriend. The former was my ode to her as I watched her dance at the Whisky A Go Go in LA – the sexual tension was insane as she turned heads with her bumping and grinding. The latter was the tale of how it ended. 'Coast To Coast' was written in the aftermath, a song about leaving the UK and touring the States – a boy becoming a man.

Play Me Out is a very painful album for me. It's all about my break-up with Vicky and how she shacked up with Lordy. I was close to death on that album; I didn't sleep for two weeks straight. Although it's a drug album, it stands as a real turning point for me. I needed to write selfishly and record this album to deal with my self-denial and to grieve the loss of Victoria to my sometime mentor.

I really enjoyed writing in Hughes/Thrall. Pat and I had great chemistry: who knows what could have been? But writing with Tony Iommi for Black Sabbath's *Seventh Star* album was a combination of pleasure and pain. I had just met Christine, and I wrote 'Heart Like A Wheel' for her, while 'In Memory' was written about Tony's mother. Working with Tony in later years on the *Fused* album was a lot easier. We really turn up the heat, me and our Tone – we could write a song every day, 365 days a year. Our songs 'Grace' and 'I Go Insane' say it all about our partnership.

I was told early in sobriety that I would go on to write deeper songs. What the drugs did was strip me of my pride and take away my passion – the ability to write freely. I've recorded many solo albums over the years. The *Soul Mover* album was my return to rock. When I hear 'Don't Let Me Bleed', 'Blue Jade', 'I Don't Want To Live That Way Again', 'Addiction', 'Satellite', 'This Is How I Feel,' 'Imperfection', and 'The Way It Is', I feel that I have done something with my life.

For me, songwriting is the second greatest gift I have been given after my sobriety. It allows me to be free. Nowadays I normally start writing in the evening. Gabi is usually around. Something always happens late at night – it just comes. I record into a dictaphone that I keep next to my bed. In the morning I wake up and listen to see if it all makes sense: if so, I go into my studio and get to work.

As for Black Country Communion, words fail me. The first time I sang "I'm going back to the Black Country" and the fans sang the chorus back at me, at Wolverhampton Civic Hall at Christmas 2010, I felt the earth move. I knew from that moment that everything had been elegantly navigated and I could finally forgive myself.

A word on my loved ones. I've lost four dear friends in the two years before this book was completed: Mel Galley, Mike Watson, Andy Attwood, and Ronnie James Dio. In January 2008 I got a call from Tony Perry to tell me that Mel had not been diagnosed yet, but that he had a lump in his throat which they thought could be cancer. I knew about oesophageal cancer because my friend Mike Watson had been through it – he eventually died of it in 2010 – so I knew that Mel would be in trouble. When I called him the next day, I could hear it in his voice: his throat was becoming closed off. Poor Mel: he was given a terminal diagnosis.

I decided that I would stay in Cannock as much as possible. I saw him five times before he passed away: and each time I saw him he was surrounded by love from his wife Annette, his son Mark, Tony Perry,

Andy Attwood, and myself. He didn't want to see anybody else. Andy played dominoes with Mel right until the end. I talked a lot with Mel about spiritual matters: we talked about fear, and I comforted him and held his hand. He got thinner every time I saw him: he was like a skeleton at the end; he didn't even look like Mel. I put my arms around him and it was like hugging paper, he was so tiny. He died in July. I loved him. He was like a brother to me. Without Mel Galley there wouldn't be a Glenn Hughes. It was great to be of service to him, and to hold his hand and tell him that I would do anything for him and for Annette as long as I am alive.

I spoke at his funeral and I was doing OK until I had to speak about his comeback shows, which were supposed to be in May 2008 in Cannock: he'd sold them out. I miss him so much. I think of my youth and how Mel and I sold out those shows in Texas in 1972: we were having a riot. Me, Mel, and Dave, and a lot of work from Tony Perry: we were just three guys from the Midlands, and we did it ourselves. We had the world by the balls, so much so that it attracted the attention of John Bonham and The Moody Blues and Stevie Marriott and Stephen Stills. Andy Attwood told me that Bonzo had told one interviewer that Trapeze were the best three-piece in the world.

A quick word about our dogs, who are all our children. There's Lily, who we got in New York City in 2001. Wolfie I found in a pet shop in Hermosa Beach in 2002. Mac is an Orange Belton English Setter we rescued in 2007. He was shot in Oklahoma and found in a field, minus a front leg, before we heard about his plight and rescued him. And there's Daphne, who we rescued in South Central LA in 2009, when I heard she was going to be homeless.

And my dear parents? I try to spend as much time with Mom and Dad as humanly possible. To be of service on a daily basis in sobriety is paramount to me. My folks can't travel these days, as Mom has a heart condition. This saddens me deeply.

Sheila Hughes *He blames himself for my heart condition, but that's life. I would never blame him for anything, because these things happen, whatever else happens in your life.*

Dad has always said that they should have moved to a place in the sun earlier in their lives. I always made a fuss over them when they visited me in LA: they loved to dine at the places that Sinatra and the Rat Pack used to frequent, like the Cock & Bull on Sunset Strip or Trader Vic's at the Beverly Hilton.

Cherie Currie *I got to see Glenn last year in New York, and he and his wife Gabi and I had a bite. It was just so lovely. She is delightful, and it's just terrific to see him so happy, so in the present. I'm thrilled to be able to witness him at his best – and he is truly at his best now. It gives me hope for myself and anyone else in this business who has a dream that we can come back better then ever. Our past was a gift to me, really. Seeing Glenn sing, especially now, is like a spiritual experience to me. He is the true Glenn Hughes: the real deal, amazing, exceptional. He and I will always have that spiritual connection. We did from the start. Glenn is a beautiful human being and I just love him. I always have, I always will … and I am so proud to call him my friend.*

Carl Swann *Glenn was opening for UFO in Europe in 2000, and I was good friends with Glenn's manager at the time, who also managed UFO and Michael Schenker. I went along to help out and lend a hand with the merchandise, and you know what it's like – when you integrate into these organisations, you find your feet and it becomes apparent to people that you* *can get things done. I grew up as a big fan of the Mark III and Mark IV Purple, and Glenn was always one of the intriguing characters, because he dropped off the radar. He was an enigma, like a potential Nick Drake, so it was a real thrill to meet him. We'd stop and have a chat because we were the only two Brits on that tour. A couple of years later I became his manager. I don't want to sound pretentious, but it's almost as if it was destined to happen.*

Tony Perry *I have experienced many situations with Glenn, some good and some bad, but I have never doubted his ability as an artiste. However, what is more important is the fact that he has faced his demons, won through, and finished up being a really great guy.*

Jerry Trimble, Jr *Glenn would definitely have died if he hadn't cleaned up. He was meant to move on to bigger and better things, which he has done. He's still the same loving person: he's always been caring and the nicest, best friend. He's still that, but now he's so disciplined and focused and driven, whereas before you'd see little spurts of that drive and focus but it would soon disappear and he'd go on a rampage; it wouldn't be Glenn any more, it would be the tyrant inside. Believe me, he was still a great guy; I could see it in him and that was why we hooked up. There was a great side to him: the exact opposite of a bully, and the bullies were the ones I couldn't tolerate. Back in the day he was overly nice; I think he's a little bit more reserved now. He's still the Glenn Hughes that I knew back then, but he's really got his shit together now.*

John Varvatos *I met Glenn through Chad Smith. I told Chad that I really loved Glenn's new CD, which he'd played on, and he told me that Glenn would be so excited to hear that. The next day I got a call from Glenn and we had a nice chat, so he came by my design studio when he was in New York. It was such an honour: I'd been a fan for so many years. I grew up with Glenn's* *music, from when he was in Trapeze – I'd seen them play in Detroit when I was in high school – and then in Purple. I remember reading about him and Tommy Bolin, when they were out of control together. After that I followed him all the way through Hughes/Thrall and his solo career too.*

I have all his music and I'm a huge fan. It's very special that he likes my work. He looks amazing: the way he moves on stage. He's definitely at a very special point in his career now, whereas most people are fading at this point. He's very thankful to be where he is today, which is an endearing quality about him. I had a picture of him at the Cal-Jam in 1974, when he had the white suit on, and I had that picture blown up on my wall in college. There was something about it, and it was really the way I got into fashion. I'd worked in a clothing store when I was growing up, playing my way through school, and I'd buy clothes so that I'd be able to look like Glenn Hughes, Robert Plant, Jimmy Page, and guys like that. That's my connection with it. I think Glenn and I look at what we do in the same way: somehow there's an underlying connection. Music and fashion have always been intertwined, all the way back to rock'n'roll and Elvis.

Tom Morello [Rage Against The Machine] *I met Glenn at a benefit concert at the Roxy, at which we both performed. I wasn't expecting to see him there, and spent a lot of time gushing praise about my love for his work in Deep Purple. We hung out afterwards at the Rainbow and he was just a great guy: smart, erudite, generous with his time and eager to answer my fan-like questions about any phase of his career.*

Phil Daoussis *I was so happy to see Glenn clean and sober. I knew he couldn't go on the way he was. The only way there's going to be a happy ending with drugs is if you get sober – otherwise you'll be dead or in jail. I know he's doing fine.*

EPILOGUE

I couldn't imagine my life without the ability to write and perform music. It's become very clear to me that, in the grand scheme of things, I've been one of the lucky ones to have been freely given a gift. I am continually humbled by this. I couldn't breathe if this passion did not exist.

My disease tells me that I don't have a disease – it lies. It wants my last breath. My disease did the unthinkable: it took away my love of writing. But I wouldn't change a thing. My life is my life. I don't have secrets any more: it's the secrets that will kill me. I could have quietly gone on living, burying my dark chalice of denial and vile conduct inside me. To be rigorously honest and accountable is the message I hope to carry.

Tony Iommi *Glenn's got a great attitude and I'm so pleased for him. You've got to take your hat off to him – he's pulled through it all. Any other bloke would be dead by now.*

Bill Hughes *I'm very proud of Glenn – not just because of his music, but because he's a really good man.*

David Coverdale *Quite simply, Glenn has grown up. We were mature as musicians in the old days, but not really as people. Our success enabled us to be as immature as we wanted to be during that time. But our life experience* *and our spirituality has helped our growth. He's a pleasure to know. The music business is indescribably disloyal and unsupportive when the glory days are seemingly over – and that rubs off on a lot of players, too – but Glenn and I have remained friends and been mutually supportive from day one. We're both still pushing the boundaries and still going for notes that only dogs can hear. I delight in his success. Glenn is my sweet soul brother and always will be. I am honoured to know him and to have worked with him, and I wish him continued growth and every success in every avenue he pursues.*

I needed to be brutally honest about my geographical and periodic relapses, as I believe that it has helped quench the thirst of the other Glenn. These relapses have played their part in my eventual surrender and recovery – let's say I was rendered surrendered.

For me all the promises happen when I breathe God in and let fear out: I believe the truer one is to oneself, the more gratifying the result. The one thing I have done is to grow spiritually. I have listened, read, and learned, in order to allow God's graces to be shown to me, in his time, not mine – after all, he is quite busy.

The wife of a good friend of mine said in the 70s that I would have the last word, and come from behind in the final furlong and win the race – but all you need to know is that I'm breathing on my own, on the right side of the grass, in the tropical sunlight, with an open mind.

I've had an epiphany: this may be a new beginning.

With love,

Glenn Hughes
Los Angeles, 2011

DISCOGRAPHY

SOLO

Play Me Out (1977)
L.A. Blues Authority Volume II: Glenn Hughes – Blues (1992)
From Now On … (1994)
Burning Japan Live (1994)
Feel (1995)
Play Me Out (1995) – special-edition reissue containing four bonus tracks: 'Getting Near To You', 'Fools Condition', 'Take Me With You', and 'She Knows'
Addiction (1996)
Greatest Hits: The Voice Of Rock (1996)
'Talk About It' (CD single, 1997) – includes previously unreleased tracks 'Kiss Of Fire (live)', 'Coast To Coast (acoustic)', and 'You Keep On Moving (acoustic)'
The God Of Voice: Best Of Glenn Hughes (compilation, 1998)
The Way It Is (1999)
Return Of Crystal Karma (2000)
From The Archives Volume I: Incense & Peaches (2000) – demos and unreleased tracks, released on Glenn's private label, Pink Cloud Records
A Soulful Christmas (2000) – an album of Christmas songs, released on Pink Cloud
Building The Machine (2001)
Different Stages: The Best Of Glenn Hughes (compilation, 2002)
Songs In The Key Of Rock (2003)
Soulfully Live In The City Of Angels (CD and DVD, 2004)
Soul Mover (2005)
Freak Flag Flyin' (2005) – recorded live in the UK in 2003, released on Pink Cloud
Music For The Divine (2006)

This Time Around: An Anthology 1969–2007 (2007)

Live In Australia (CD and DVD, 2007) – acoustic set featuring guest
  appearance by Jimmy Barnes on 'Gettin' Tighter'

First Underground Nuclear Kitchen (2008)

Glenn Hughes Alive Drive (USB drive, 2009) – music and video tracks, web
  streams, and exclusive content

Official Bootleg: Live In Wolverhampton: Full Band Show (iTunes download,
  2009) – eight tracks recorded live at the Robin, June 6 2009

*Official Bootleg: Live In Wolverhampton – You Are The Music: An Evening Of
  Trapeze* (iTunes download, 2009) – 11 tracks recorded live at the Robin,
  June 7 2009

Live in Wolverhampton (CD and DVD, 2011) – audio and video from both
  nights at the Robin

The Scenes From The Life Of A Rock Star (EP, 2011) – 400 copies pressed on
  ten-inch black vinyl, followed by 100 copies pressed on ten-inch white
  vinyl and packaged with a signed screen-print

BANDS

Finders Keepers, 'Sadie, The Cleaning Lady' (single, 1968)

Trapeze, *Trapeze* (1969)

Trapeze, *Medusa* (1971)

Trapeze, *You Are The Music … We're Just The Band* (1972)

Trapeze Featuring Glenn Hughes, *The Final Swing* (compilation, 1974)

Trapeze, *Trapeze* (1975)

Trapeze, *Way Back To The Bone* (compilation, 1986)

Trapeze, *High Flyers: The Best Of Trapeze* (compilation, 1995)

Trapeze, *Live: Way Back To The Bone* (1998)

Trapeze, *Welcome To The Real World: Live 1992* (1998)

Deep Purple, *Burn* (1974)

Deep Purple, *Live In London* (1974)

Deep Purple, *Stormbringer* (1974)

Deep Purple, *Made In Europe* (1975)

Deep Purple, *Come Taste The Band* (1975)

Deep Purple, *Last Concert In Japan* (1976)

Deep Purple, *The Deep Purple Singles A's & B's* (1993)

Deep Purple, *On The Wings Of A Russian Foxbat: Live In California 1976* (1995)

Deep Purple, *California Jamming: Live 1974* (1996)

Deep Purple, *Mk III: The Final Concerts* (1996)
Deep Purple, *Days May Come And Days May Go: The 1975 California Rehearsals, Volume 1* (2000)
Deep Purple, *1420 Beachwood Drive: The California Rehearsals, Volume 2* (2000)
Deep Purple, *This Time Around: Live In Japan 1975* (2001)
Deep Purple, *California Jam* (2003)
Deep Purple, *Perks & Tit* (2003)
Deep Purple, *Just Might Take Your Life* (2003)
Deep Purple, *Live In Paris 1975* (2004)
Deep Purple, *Burn: Remastered 30th Anniversary Edition* (2004)
Deep Purple, *Stormbringer: Remastered 35th Anniversary Edition* (2009)
Hughes/Thrall, *Hughes/Thrall* (1982)
Hughes Thrall, *Hughes/Thrall* (2007) – remastered edition with bonus tracks
Black Sabbath, *Seventh Star* (1986)
Hughes Turner Project, *HTP* (2002)
Hughes Turner Project, *Live In Tokyo* (2002)
Hughes Turner Project, *II* (2003)
Tony Iommi, *The 1996 DEP Sessions* (2004) – official release of infamous bootlegged sessions
Tony Iommi, *Fused* (2005)
Black Country Communion, *Black Country* (2010)
Black Country Communion, *2* (2011)

SESSIONS

Roger Glover & Guests, *The Butterfly Ball And The Grasshopper's Feast* (1974) – lead vocals on 'Get Ready'
Jon Lord, *Windows* (1974) – backing vocals, bass, and guitar
Tommy Bolin, *Teaser* (1975) – co-lead vocals on 'Dreamer'
Various Artists, *The Wizard's Convention* (1976) – lead vocals on two tracks
Pat Travers, *Makin' Magic* (1977) – backing vocals on 'Stevie'
4 On The Floor, *4 On The Floor* (1979) – lead vocals on all tracks
Climax Blues Band, *Lucky For Some* (1981) – backing vocals on 'Shake It Lucy'
Night Ranger, *Midnight Madness* (1983) – backing vocals (uncredited)
Heaven, *Where Angels Fear To Tread* (1983) – backing vocals on two tracks
Phenomena, *Phenomena* (1985) – lead vocals on most tracks
Gary Moore, *Run For Cover* (1985) – lead vocals on four tracks, bass on five

Various Artists, *Dragnet: Music From The Motion Picture Soundtrack* (1987) – lead vocals on the chorus of 'City Of Crime'

Phenomena II, *Dream Runner* (1987) – lead vocals on three tracks

Whitesnake, *Slip Of The Tongue* (1989) – backing vocals

XYZ, *XYZ* (1989) – "inspiration" and backing vocals

Notorious, *Notorious* (1990) – backing vocals

Various Artists, *Music From And Inspired By The Film Highlander II: The Quickening* (1990) – lead vocals on 'Haunted'

LA Blues Authority, *LA Blues Authority* (1991) – lead vocals on 'Messin' With The Kid'

The KLF, 'America: What Time Is Love?' (single, 1992) – lead vocals in the chorus

Lynch Mob, *Lynch Mob* (1992) – backing vocals

John Norum, *Face The Truth* (1992) – lead vocals on several tracks

Geoffrey Downes/The New Dance Orchestra, *Vox Humana* (1993) – lead vocals on 'Video Killed The Radio Star'

Sister Whiskey, *Liquor And Poker* (1993) – backing vocals

Marc Bonilla, American Matador (1993) – lead vocals on 'A Whiter Shade Of Pale'

George Lynch, *Sacred Groove* (1993) – lead vocals on two tracks

Stevie Salas, *Stevie Salas Presents: The Electric Pow Wow* (1993) – lead vocals on 'I Was Made To Love Her'

Mötley Crüe, *Mötley Crüe* (1994) – backing vocals on 'Misunderstood'

Manfred Ehlert's Amen, *Manfred Ehlert's Amen* (1994) – lead vocals on three tracks

Various Artists, *Smoke On The Water: A Tribute* (1994) – lead vocals on 'Stormbringer'

LA Blues Authority Volume V, *Cream Of The Crop: A Tribute* (1994) – lead vocals on 'Born Under A Bad Sign'

Hank Davison & Friends, *Real Live* (1995) – lead vocals on 'Highway Star' and 'The Liar'

Brazen Abbot, *Live And Learn* (1995) – lead vocals on three tracks

Wet Paint, *Shhh..!* (1995) – co-lead vocals on one track and backing vocals on others

Richie Kotzen, *Wave Of Emotion* (1996) – backing vocals on 'Stoned'

Liesegang, *No Strings Attached* (1996) – lead vocals on three tracks

Asia, *Archiva 1* (1996) – uncredited backing vocals on 'Tears'

Various Artists, *To Cry You A Song: A Collection Of Tull Tales* (1996) – lead vocals on 'To Cry You A Song'

Various Artists, *Dragon Attack: A Tribute To Queen* (1996) – lead vocals on 'Get Down Make Love'

Amen, *Aguilar* (1996) – lead vocals on one track

Glenn Hughes/Geoff Downes, *The Work Tapes* (1998) – lead vocals

Glenn Hughes, Johnnie Bolin & Friends, *Tommy Bolin: 1997 Tribute* (1998) – lead vocals

Stuart Smith, *Heaven And Earth* (1998) – lead vocals on 'See That My Grave Is Kept Clean'

Various Artists, *Humanary Stew: A Tribute To Alice Cooper* (1999) – lead vocals on 'Only Women Bleed'

Various Artists, *Encores, Legends & Paradox: A Tribute To The Music Of ELP* (1999) – lead vocals on 'Knife Edge'

The Bobaloos, *The Bobaloos* (1999) – lead vocals on six tracks and backing vocals on one other

Niacin, *Deep* (1999) – lead vocals on 'Things Ain't Like they Used To Be'

Erik Norlander, *Into The Sunset* (2000) – lead vocals on 'Rome Is Burning'

Tidewater Grain, *Here On The Outside* (2000) – backing vocals

Voodoo Hill, *Voodoo Hill* (2000) – lead vocals

Craig Erickson Project, *Shine* (2000) – lead vocals on 'Wild Dogs'

Nikolo Kotzev, *Nostradamus* (2001) – lead vocals on several tracks

Max Magagni, *Twister* (2001) – bass and lead vocals on 'Can You Get It Up'

Various Artists, *Stone Cold Queen: A Tribute* (2001) – lead vocals on 'Killer Queen'

Various Artists, *Another Hair Of The Dog: A Tribute To Nazareth* (2001) – lead vocals on 'Piece Of My Heart'

Various Artists, *Let The Tribute Do The Talking: A Tribute To Aerosmith* (2001) – lead vocals on 'Kings And Queens'

Ape Quartet, *Please Where Do We Live?* (2001) – lead vocals on 'It's Gonna Break'

The Voices Of Classic Rock, *Voices For America* (2001) – lead vocals on 'America The Beautiful'

Ellis, *EIII* (2002) – co-lead vocals on 'Growing Wise'

Ryo Okumoto, *Coming Through* (2002) – lead vocals on 'Highway Roller'

Various Artists, *Pigs And Pyramids: An All Star Lineup Performing The Songs Of Pink Floyd* (2002) – lead vocals on 'Young Lust'

Jeff Scott Soto, *Prism* (2002) – lead vocals on 'I Want To Take You Higher'
The Alchemist, *Songs From The Westside* (2002) – lead vocals on six tracks
Aina, *Days Of Rising Doom* (2003) – lead vocals on several tracks
Chris Catena, *Freak Out!* (2003) – vocals on several tracks
Voodoo Hill, *Wild Seed Of Mother Earth* (2004) – lead vocals
Various Artists, *Sabbath Crosses: Tributo A Black Sabbath* (2004) – co-lead
   vocals on 'No Stranger To Love'
Vargas Blues Band, *Love, Union, Peace* (2005) – lead vocals on 'Sad Eyes'
Monkey Business, *Kiss Me On My Ego* (2005) – lead vocals on 'Weekend
   Warrior' and 'Silence'
Michael Men Project, *Made In Moscow* (2005) – lead vocals
Various Artists, *Stealth: Official Motion Picture Soundtrack* (2005) – lead vocals
   on 'Nights In White Satin', recorded with Chad Smith and John
   Frusciante
Rata Blanca, *A Vivo en Teatro Gran Rex* (DVD, 2005) – appears on
   'Stormbringer', 'Mistreated', 'You Keep On Moving', and 'Burn'
Moonstone Project, *Time To Take A Stand* (2006) – lead vocals on 'Rose In
   Hell' and 'Where Do You Hide'
Phenomena, *Psychofantasy* (2006) – lead vocals on several tracks
The Lizards, *Against All Odds* (2006) – lead vocals
Quiet Riot, *Rehab* (2006) – bass and vocals on 'Evil Woman'
Ken Hensley, *Blood On The Highway* (2007) – lead vocals on 'What You
   Gonna Do' and 'The Last Dance'
Frankie Banali & Friends, *24/7/365: The Tribute To Led Zeppelin* (2007) – lead
   vocals on 'Four Sticks'
Robin George/Glenn Hughes, *Sweet Revenge* (2008) – recorded in 1989
Moonstone Project, *Hidden In Time* (2008, reissue of 2006's *Time To Take A
   Stand*) – piano and lead vocals on 'Where Do You Hide Your Blues'
Keith Emerson/Glenn Hughes/Marc Bonilla, *Boys Club: Live From California*
   (2008) – lead vocals, recorded in 1998
Monkey Business, *Twilight Of Jesters?* (2009) – lead vocals on 'Gumball' and
   'History Of Pathos'
Various Artists, *Childline Rocks 2009* (2009) – lead vocals on 'You Keep On
   Moving', 'Mistreaded', and 'Soul Mover', chorus vocals on 'Smoke On
   The Water'
Various Artists, *Abbey Road: A Tribute To The Beatles* (2009) – lead vocals on
   'Let It Be'

Moonstone Project, *Rebel On The Run* (2009) – lead vocals on 'Closer Than You Think'

Various Artists, *An All-Star Salute To Christmas* (2009) – lead vocals on 'O' Holy Night'

One Soul Thrust, *1st* (2010) – co-lead vocals on 'Go Home And Melt'

Kens Dojo, *Reincarnation* (2010) – lead vocals on four tracks

Mike Porcaro, *Brotherly Love* (2011) – lead vocals on six tracks, recorded live in Koblenz, Germany, 2002

Pushking, *The World as We Love It* (2011) – lead vocals on four tracks: 'Why Don't You?', 'Private Own', 'Tonight', and 'Kukarracha'

Joe Bonamassa, *Dust Bowl* (2011) – lead vocals on 'Heartbreaker'

Various Artists, *SIN-atra* (2011) – lead vocals on 'I've Got You Under My Skin'

OTHER CREDITS

Don Dokken, *Up From The Ashes* (1990) – co-wrote 'When Love Finds A Fool'

Phantom Blue, *Built To Perform* (1993) – co-wrote 'Time To Run'

Snakes In Paradise, 'Love Got Wings' (single, 1993) – co-wrote 'Play With Fire'

Snakes In Paradise, *Snakes In Paradise* (1994) – co-wrote 'The Night Goes On'

Dave Nerge's Bulldog, *The Return Of Mr Nasty* (1994) – co-wrote 'If You Don't Want Me To'

Ellis, *EIII* (2002) – co-wrote 'Happy To Be Cool'

Michael Men Project, *Made In Moscow* (2005) – co-wrote four tracks: 'Arianna', 'Let The Fire Rage', 'On Your Marks', and 'The Alchemist'

Quiet Riot, *Rehab* (2006) – co-wrote three tracks: 'Blind Faith', 'Old Habits Die Hard', and 'In Harms Way'

Moonstone Project, *Rebel On The Run* (2009) – wrote 'Closer Than You Think'

Many thanks to David Harrison.

INDEX

Words *in italics* indicate album titles unless otherwise stated. Words 'in quotes' indicate song titles. Page numbers in **bold** indicate illustrations.

ACKNOWLEDGEMENTS

My family: Gabi, Mom and Dad, and my 'kids' – the dogs Lily, Wolfie, Mac, and Daphne, and cats Princess and Hugh: you are all the loves of my life.

Carl Swann, my manager and confidante: cometh the hour, cometh the man.

Stevie Wonder, David Coverdale, Tony Iommi, Geezer Butler, Bill Ward, John Bonham, Chad Smith, Michael Castellano, John Varvatos, Lars Ulrich, Bill Drummond and Jimmy Cauty of the KLF, Tom Morello, and Angie Bowie: thank you for the love and your art.

ACKNOWLEDGEMENTS

Cameron Crowe, Neal Preston, Eddie Trunk, Bob Coburn, Trudy and Bob Harris, David 'Kid' Jensen: thank you for your love and support amid swashbuckling memories.

Dave Ling, Malcolm Dome, Sian Llewellyn, Scott Rowley, and the staff of *Classic Rock* magazine, Ross Halfin, Pete Makowski, Chris Charlesworth, Fin Costello, Carl Dunn, Robert Knight, Gene Kirkland, John Ogden, Debbie Bennett, and Lark Williams: thanks for all the media coverage and making me look good (and bad!).

Tony Perry, Johnny Jones, Terry Rowley, Morris Price, Jack Orbin, Michael Dunham, Noel Monk, Alan Clee, Jed Clampit, Dave Whitehouse, Frank Merricks, and Linda Blair (my sweet little devil): you are the music, we are Trapeze – young and hungry rock'n'roll heroes.

David Bowie, Jimmy Page, Robert Plant, Sharon and Ozzy Osbourne, Ronnie Wood, Bonnie Raitt, Paul Rodgers, Terry Reid, Chris Robinson, Steve Marriott, Iggy Pop, John Frusciante, Dave Navarro, Eddie Van Halen, Steve Lukather, Kenny Aronoff, Matt Sorum, Billy Morrison, Frankie Banali, Slash, Keith Emerson, Leslie West, Julian Lennon, Duff McKagan, Steve Stevens, Billy Gibbons, Rick Canny, Billy Duffy, Perry Farrell, Lemmy, Cherie Currie, Paul Stanley, Gregg Allman, Brooke Taylor, Rob Fraboni, Nicky Horne, Don Jamieson, Jim Florentine, Herbie Hancock, Tal Wilkenfeld, Judas Priest, Mötley Crüe … and the Moody Blues for taking Trapeze on tour in the USA. You are the eccentric, the spiritual, the wild and the beautiful. Mario, Tony, Michael, and all the Staff at the Rainbow Bar and Grill in Hollywood – yes, it's true what happened in the booths (and under them).

Frank Sinatra – thanks for the pink shirt! – and Michael Castellano.

My school friends: you know who you are – from John Wood to Walhouse, to Blake School for Boys to Calving Hill, you have all touched my life, especially our football teams – we were the dog's bollocks!

My schoolteachers Derek Yates (art) and Miss Gooch (music): you are my unsung heroes. Your encouragement was paramount. Dave Farrington (RIP) for the guitar lessons. My school band, The Hooker Lees: Stephen Dangerfield, Pete Hanysz, Stuart Smith, and Roger Gardner.

Margaret Williams Colley, my first girlfriend – beautiful inside and out to this very day.
Drew Thompson, Ken Ciancimino, Jenn McCabe, Deepak Rao, Kevin Shirley, Pat Thrall, Andy Johns, Jim Scott, Michael Scott, Marc Bonilla, Fabrizio Grossi, Pat Travers, Serafino (Frontiers), Joe Lynn Turner, Jerry Trimble, Ami and Micky Dolenz, Dr Carl Vanempten, Par Holmgren, George 'Chip' Walters, Brian Thomen, Manfred Ehlert, Bill Nash, Sterling Ball, Derek Brooks, Dudley Gimpel, Jim D'Addario, Wendy Dio, Bebe Buell, Pete Dovenius, Lol Tolhurst, Cindy Levinson: I'm honoured to have you as my friends.

Nancy Mack Smith and my godson Cole; Michelle Ciancimino and my god-daughter Leah.

Mitchell Binder and King Baby, Bruno and Kyara Mascolo and all at Toni & Guy, Joyce Varvatos, and Sickboy Doug: you have my love and respect.

My band and road crew, my booking agent Neil O'Brien, my agent Pete Sangah, my promoters worldwide, my webmaster David Harrison, and Shirean Harrison: thanks so much for the hard work and keeping the GH brand in good stead.

My Black Country brothers: Joe Bonamassa, Jason Bonham, and Derek Sherinian, as well as Roy Weisman, Phil Carson, and Jonas Herbsman.

Special thanks to Chuck and Wilma Dotson, Carole and John Latham, Annette Galley, Ian Lees, Alan and Mary Murray, Ralph Baker, James Ware (attorney), Arlo Chan, Kristin Davenport, Dave Rat (RHCP), Andy Grow and friends of Bill W, Karen Allen, Jon Finnegan, Carolyn Longstaff, Louise Kovacs, Paddy and Jim Callahan (security), and my assistant and dear friend Mike Moore.

Matt Higham (Foruli Publications) and Matthew Hamilton (Aitken Alexander): my amigos – your enthusiasm speaks volumes. Designer Andy Vella for the extreme vibe. All at Jawbone Press.

Joel McIver: it took four years. Your friendship and dedication have made me a better man.

Gary Ferguson, for introducing me to Gab – a girl that actually lived in LA.

And the boogeyman – thanks for making many appearances. Now fuck off!

Friends lost along the way:

Tommy Bolin of Deep Purple	Bob Timmins, sobriety guru
John Bonham of Led Zeppelin	Andrew Field, personal assistant
Keith Moon of The Who	Guy Mascolo, Toni & Guy
Phil Lynott of Thin Lizzy	Ron Quinton, Deep Purple crew
Ronnie James Dio	Patsy Collins, Deep Purple security
Steve Marriott of the Small Faces and Humble Pie	Maurice Jones, booking agent
Mark Putterford, journalist	Gary Moore, rock and blues titan
Mel Galley of Trapeze	Mike Watson, the bravest man I ever knew
Kevin Dubrow of Quiet Riot	Tony Edwards, Deep Purple manager
Chris Farley, actor	Andrew Attwood, my oldest friend

And to all my fans, new and old: you have given me all that I needed to grow. You are the music.

To my higher power, for what you have given me, for what you have taken away, and for what you have left me with.

PICTURE CREDITS

The pictures used in this book came from the following sources, and we are grateful for their help. Every effort has been made to contact copyright holders. If you feel there has been a mistaken attribution, please contact the publisher. **Jacket** Fin Costello/Getty Images (front); Christie Goodwin (back); **2** Julian Lennon; **6** Glenn Hughes (3); **7** Fin Costello (live); Dieter Zill (peacock); **8** Carl Dunn; **9** Fin Costello/Getty Images (Starship); Glenn Hughes (limo); **10–12** Glenn Hughes (4); **13** Fin Costello/Getty Images; **14** Glenn Hughes (Gabi); Christie Goodwin (BCC); **15** Christie Goodwin (BCC); John Varvatos; **16** Christie Goodwin.

MILLION DOLLAR
BASH: BOB DYLAN,
THE BAND, AND THE
BASEMENT TAPES
by Sid Griffin

ISBN 978-1-906002-05-3

BOWIE IN BERLIN:
A NEW CAREER IN A
NEW TOWN
by Thomas Jerome
Seabrook

ISBN 978-1-906002-08-

BILL BRUFORD THE
AUTOBIOGRAPHY:
YES, KING CRIMSON,
EARTHWORKS, AND
MORE
by Bill Bruford

ISBN 978-1-906002-23-7

TO LIVE IS TO DIE:
THE LIFE AND DEATH
OF METALLICA'S
CLIFF BURTON
by Joel McIver

ISBN 978-1-906002-24-

THE IMPOSSIBLE
DREAM: THE STORY
OF SCOTT WALKER
AND THE WALKER
BROTHERS
by Anthony Reynolds

ISBN 978-1-906002-25-1

JACK BRUCE:
COMPOSING
HIMSELF: THE
AUTHORISED
BIOGRAPHY
by Harry Shapiro

ISBN 978-1-906002-26-

FOREVER CHANGES:
ARTHUR LEE AND THE
BOOK OF LOVE
by John Einarson

ISBN 978-1-906002-31-2

RETURN OF THE
KING: ELVIS PRESLEY'S
GREAT COMEBACK
by Gillian G. Gaar

ISBN 978-1-906002-28-

A WIZARD, A TRUE
STAR: TODD
RUNDGREN IN THE
STUDIO
by Paul Myers

ISBN 978-1-906002-33-6

SHELTER FROM THE
STORM: BOB DYLAN'S
ROLLING THUNDER
YEARS
by Sid Griffin

ISBN 978-1-906002-27-5

SEASONS THEY
CHANGE: THE STORY
OF ACID AND
PSYCHEDELIC FOLK
by Jeanette Leech

ISBN 978-1-906002-32-9

WON'T GET FOOLED
AGAIN: THE WHO
FROM LIFEHOUSE TO
QUADROPHENIA
by Richie Unterberger

ISBN 978-1-906002-35-0

THE
RESURRECTION OF
JOHNNY CASH:
HURT, REDEMPTION,
AND AMERICAN
RECORDINGS
by Graeme Thomson

ISBN 978-1-906002-36-7

CRAZY TRAIN: THE
HIGH LIFE AND
TRAGIC DEATH OF
RANDY RHOADS
by Joel McIver

ISBN 978-1-906002-37-4

THE 10 RULES OF
ROCK AND ROLL:
COLLECTED MUSIC
WRITINGS 2005-11
by Robert Forster

ISBN 978-1-906002-91-6

JUST CAN'T GET
ENOUGH: THE
MAKING OF DEPECHE
MODE
by Simon Spence

ISBN 978-1-906002-56-5